The World Heritage

Since the main mission of the World Heritage is to pass on our legacy to future generations, we dedicate this book to our children Elizabeth, Florence, Juliette and Olivier.

Patrick
Philippe

*O*ur ancestors left us a spectacular legacy
and Mother Nature has given us sites of
indescribable beauty. To fully understand and
appreciate this, we have to slow down, take
a step back and tune out the daily barrage
of media sensationalism. Our world is much
more beautiful and richer than we think!

Patrick Bonneville

*O*ver these past five years, I have travelled the world visiting UNESCO's World Heritage sites - both natural and cultural landmarks - and documenting them by means of panography, i.e. 360-degree images. So far, I have had the opportunity to cover one fifth of all listed sites, although the list gets longer every year.

The way I look at it, if this list is as representative of humanity as it is meant to be, my visits should allow me to understand something about this complex species of ours, which remains an enigma to me. That's what it's all about. The List of the World Heritage is both a breathtaking demonstration and an extraordinary inspiration. It tells us what humans have been capable of - for better or for worse - given the natural surroundings n which they have evolved since the beginning of time. It also gives us the incentive to contribute to make mankind ...kinder or more humane.

One fifth is not much : it took me five years and left me with thousand of questions running around inside my head. But I keep on going on this extraordinary journey, onfident that the answers are there, somewhere in these sites. Still, the further I go, the darker the obscurity of this enigmatic stuff mankind is made of, with part of the answers almost obvious, and the rest, unfathomable. I feel lost like never before. I mull over this idea of humanity, as I roam around the globe, with mixed feelings. ruth be told, here today, at this very moment, I have never felt happier, more laid-back, with a high degree of consciousness, yet contemplative, confident and cheerful.

During my visits to these sites, I feel as if I were a media on my own whose function is to pass on what it absorbs along the way. The air, the temperature, the space, the time are palpable in these monuments and in these natural areas.

Nothing can condense or express this better than the light captured along the journey. This is what I hope you will experience reading this book : light. It is the light which has inspired hundreds of images and quotations and which, hopefully, will quench your thirst for the invisible which the visible exudes.

This book is meant for sharing in the contemplation and meditation. May it contribute to making human beings more humane.

Tito Dupret
Author of www.world-heritage-tour.org
World Heritage sites in panography - 360 degree imaging
Funded by the J.M. Kaplan Fund

It is fitting that the idea of creating an international movement dedicated to protecting world heritage emerged after World War I. Indeed, wars are one of the greatest threats to our heritage, with senseless destruction and "collateral damage" often eradicating irreplaceable marks from our past or devastating our most valuable natural sites.

The first event that aroused particular international concern about our collective heritage was the decision to build the Aswan High Dam in Egypt, which would have flooded the valley containing the Abu Simbel temples, a treasure of ancient Egyptian civilization. In 1959, after an appeal from the governments of Egypt and Sudan, UNESCO launched an international safeguarding campaign. Archaeological research was accelerated in the areas to be flooded. Above all, the Abu Simbel and Philae temples were dismantled, moved to dry land, and then reassembled.

The idea of combining conservation of cultural sites with that of natural areas originated in the United States of America. In 1965, a White House conference in Washington, D.C., called for a "World Heritage Trust" that would stimulate international cooperation to protect "the world's superb natural and scenic areas and historic sites for the present and future of the entire world citizenry". In 1968, the International Union for Conservation of Nature (IUCN) developed similar proposals for its members. These proposals were presented to the 1972 United Nations Conference on Human Environment in Stockholm.

Eventually, a single text was agreed upon by all parties involved. The Convention Concerning the Protection of World Cultural and Natural Heritage was adopted by the General Conference of UNESCO on November 16, 1972.

UNESCO's World Heritage mission is to:

• Encourage countries to sign the World Heritage Convention and ensure the protection of their natural and cultural heritage
• Encourage Member States to nominate sites within their national territory for inclusion on the World Heritage List
• Encourage Member States to establish management plans and set up reporting systems on the state of conservation of their World Heritage sites
• Help Member States safeguard World Heritage properties by providing technical assistance and professional training
• Provide emergency assistance for World Heritage sites in immediate danger
• Support Member States' public-awareness-building activities for World Heritage conservation
• Encourage participation of local populations in the preservation of their cultural and natural heritage
• Encourage international cooperation in the conservation of our cultural and natural heritage

The overarching benefit of ratifying the World Heritage Convention is that of belonging to an international community of appreciation and concern for universally significant properties that embody a world of outstanding examples of cultural diversity and natural wealth.

By joining together to protect and cherish the world's natural and cultural heritage, Member States express a shared commitment to preserving our legacy for future generations.

The prestige that comes from being a Member State and having sites inscribed on the World Heritage List often serves as a catalyst to raising awareness for heritage preservation.

As for us, the peoples of the world, we have the responsibility to protect and conserve these sites, our collective heritage, for the future generations. This heritage belongs to all of us, Egyptians, Greeks, Russians, Asians, Arabs, Americans, Africans, people from the North, South, East and West. It is our duty to learn our heritage and to share it with our offspring.

In this century, the world seems to get smaller, with fewer boundaries and great tensions still arising from our differences. Now more than ever, we must open our arms to the world, to our siblings from different cultures and origins. Their heritage is our heritage, and our heritage is theirs.

Copyright © 2006 Bonneville Connection

Text based on the official descriptions of the World Heritage Centre. The publisher does not guarantee the information contained in the descriptions or quotes.
All rights reserved. No part of this publication may be reproduced or transmitted in any form or by any means, electronic or mechanical, including photocopy, recording, or any information storage and retrieval system, without permission in writing from the publisher.

Editorial Director and Chief Editor Patrick Bonneville
Art Director and Art Editor Philippe Hemono
Consultant Editor Alain Forget
Research Patrick Bonneville
Design Philippe Hemono
Photo Cover Walter Bibikow/ gettyimages
Map Editor Philippe Hemono
Production Consultants Yvon Sauvageau
Carole Maheux

Photos: See Photo credits, page 462
Many thanks to all our collaborators from all over the world

Request for permission to make copies of any part of the work should be mailed to the following address:

Permissions Department
Bonneville Connection
2020 rue Noble
Saint-Hubert, Quebec
J3Y 5K2
Canada

www.worldheritageboutique.com

Legal Deposit – Bibliothèque et Archives nationales du Québec, 2006
Legal Deposit – Library and Archives Canada, 2006   ISBN 0-9781807-0-4
First Edition

Created and designed by Bonneville Connection & PH Production

Printed by Caractéra, Une Société de Solisco Québec, Canada

www.caractera.com

Table of contents

Americas

The New World. A continent fought over by older nations, now divided into three geographical sections: North, Central and South. A continent with rich and diverse ancestral cultures, such as the Aztecs and Incas. A continent where architecture bears the marks of Europe's colonial forces, blended with native knowledge and influence. But above all, a continent that holds extraordinary natural treasures, with diverse ecological systems such as vast mountain ranges, great plains, expansive deserts, lush forests and long, clear rivers.

The Spanish, English, French, Dutch and Portuguese all came to understand the tremendous potential hidden in these natural resources. From north to south, explorers were amazed by the scenery and wilderness before them. Some remote regions still remain relatively untouched, while others, perhaps too many, are sadly overexploited.

Today, an important challenge for all three of the Americas is to preserve nature's priceless heritage. Over the last decades, many countries have established large national parks where flora and fauna can thrive, but industrial pressures still threaten many regions.

Canada

Historic District of Québec   (1)

The only fortified and walled city north of Mexico, Quebec City was founded by the French explorer Champlain in the early 17th century. A few decades later, after defeating the French in Plaines d'Abraham park, the British built a substantial citadel atop Cap Diamant. The city has preserved its historic character with numerous buildings in Old Québec. It is also home to one of the world's most magnificent hotels, the Château Frontenac.

> *"I have no reply to make to your general other than from the mouths of my cannon and muskets."*
>
> *Frontenac, Governor of New France, responding to Sir William Phips, Governor of Massachusetts, demanding the surrender of Quebec, October 16, 1696*

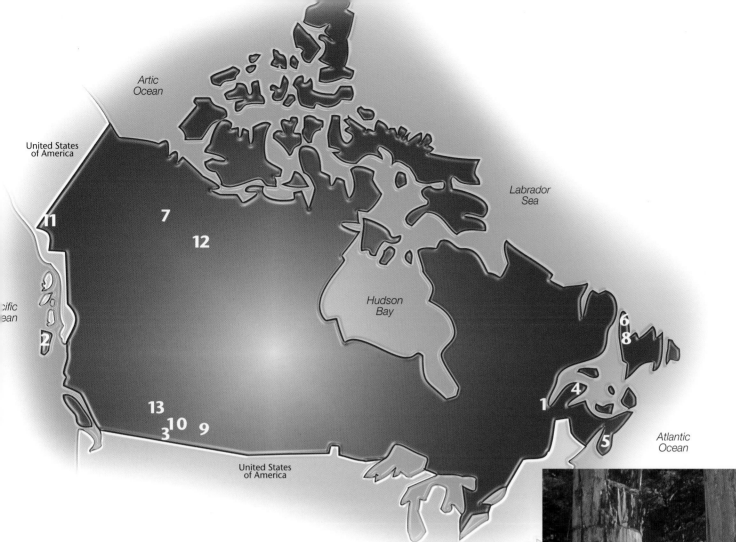

Artic Ocean

United States of America

Labrador Sea

7

12

11

Hudson Bay

Pacific Ocean

6
8

13

3 10 9

1

4

5

Atlantic Ocean

United States of America

SGaang Gwaii - Anthony Island   (2)

On a small island off the west coast of British Columbia, SGaang Gwaii are remains of houses and poles illustrating the Haida people's artistic way of life. The Haida tribe was the first to inhabit the Haida Gwaii archipelago, now called the Queen Charlotte Islands. This nation has always thrived on the wealth of both the sea and the forest. They were and still are masters in the art of building canoes.

> *"Our culture, our heritage is the child of respect and intimacy with the land and sea. Like the forests, the roots of our people are intertwined such that the greatest troubles cannot overcome us."*
>
> *Extract of the Haida constitution*

Waterton Glacier International Peace Park   (3)
(Site shared with the United States of America)

Waterton Glacier Park became the world's first International Peace Park, celebrating the longstanding friendship between the United States and Canada. Straddling the border between these two countries, the park is exceptionally rich in plant and mammal species, as well as prairie, forest, alpine and glacial features.

11

Miguasha National Park   (4)

The park is located in the Gaspé Peninsula in eastern Quebec. In 1842, fossil beds of fish were discovered there. These fossils represent the "Age of Fishes", dating from 370 million years ago. Miguasha is the most outstanding fossil site in the world for illustrating this period.

Old Town Lunenburg   (5)

A small town in the province Nova Scotia (eastern Canada), Lunenburg is the best surviving example of a planned British colonial settlement in North America. Established in 1753, it has retained its original layout and overall appearance, based on a rectangular grid pattern drawn up in the home country. The inhabitants have managed to safeguard the city's identity throughout the centuries by preserving the wooden architecture of the houses, some of which date back to the 18th century.

"A whimsical taste has introduced the custom of painting the exterior white, red, pink and even green, which, on approaching from a distance, raised up before my imagination the original of the little Dutch toys I remember as a child..."

Captain Moorsom,
describing Lunenburg in the 1820s

L'Anse aux Meadows National Historic Site   (6)

L'Anse aux Meadows marks the site of the first known European settlement in North America. Located at the tip of the Great Northern Peninsula of the island of Newfoundland, this site boasts the remains of an 11th-century Viking settlement. These early visitors made their homes in sod huts and, for a brief period of time, lived together in a fertile new land.

"We met with ice crystal spires ascending into the sky from the mouth of an aqua sea."

Leif Ericson,
first Viking expedition
to North America

Nahanni National Park (7)

In the Northern Territories of Canada, this national park is home to one of the most spectacular wild rivers in North America, the South Nahanni River. This is also the place to admire Virginia Falls, twice the height of Niagara Falls, cutting for kilometres through 1,000-metre-deep canyons (3,280 feet) then bending through a tortuous constriction called Hell's Gate. The wilderness here is intact, with no roads, only wolves, grizzlies, caribou and mountain goats, which don't need to worry about their greatest predator: Man.

Gros Morne National Park (8)

Gros Morne sits on the west coast of the island of Newfoundland. This park is rare example of the process of continental drift, where deep ocean crusts and the rocks of the earth's mantle lie exposed. The region offers spectacular scenery, including coastal lowland, alpine plateaus, fjords, glacial valleys, cliffs, waterfalls and many pristine lakes.

Dinosaur Provincial Park (9)

About two hours east of Calgary, this park contains important fossil discoveries from the "Age of Reptiles", including 35 species of dinosaur dating back some 75 million years. More than 300 first-quality dinosaur skeletons have been pulled from a 27-kilometre stretch (17 miles). The region is also known for its spectacular hoodoos, pinnacles, coulees and buttes.

"I was climbing up a steep face about 400 feet high. I stuck my head around a point and there was this skull leering at me, sticking right out of the ground. It gave me a fright."

Joseph Tyrrell,
discoverer of the first Albertosaurus,
1884

Head-Smashed-In Buffalo Jump (10)

This is where the American bison (buffalo) have provided food, hides for clothing and shelter, sinew, bones for tools, and dung for fires, to the Aboriginal peoples of the North American Great Plains. The principal means of killing large numbers of bison was the buffalo jump, where herds were stampeded over cliffs. A vast quantity of buffalo skeletons can still be found in this park.

Kluane/Wrangell-St. Elias/Glacier Bay/Tatshenshini-Alsek (11)
(Site shared with the United States of America)

This tremendous reserve, on the border between the United States and Canada (Alaska, Yukon and British Columbia), covers 97,000 square kilometres (23,969,222 acres). The region contains a spectacular complex of glaciers and high peaks, which are home to many northern species such as grizzly and caribou. This park also boasts the largest non-polar ice field in the world.

"We found a compact sheet of ice as far as the eye could distinguish."

Captain George Vancouver, 1794

Wood Buffalo National Park (12)

This is Canada's largest park, covering 44,807 square kilometres (11,072,050 acres) of boreal forest, plains and some of the vastest undisturbed grass and sedge meadow left in North America. It is home to the largest population of wild bison, also known as buffalo, North America's biggest land animal. The park also contains the world's largest delta, located at the mouth of the Peace and Arthabasca rivers.

Canadian Rocky Mountain Parks (13)

One of the greatest Canadian parks, spreading over two provinces (British Columbia and Alberta), the Canadian Rockies are a paradise for skiers and hikers, offering some of the most breathtaking scenery on earth. The parks are home to spectacular mountain peaks, glaciers, waterfalls, canyons and limestone caves.

"Wonder, reverence, the feeling that one is nearer the mystery of things – that is what one feels in places of such sublime beauty."

*J.B. Harkin,
Canada's first Commissioner of National Parks, about the Rockies*

United States of America

Grand Canyon National Park (1)

Over thousands of years in northern Arizona, the Colorado River has shaped the most spectacular gorge on earth, the Grand Canyon. It plunges up to 1,828 metres (6,000 feet) deep and spans as much as 24 kilometres (15 miles) wide. It is home to numerous rare, endemic, and protected (threatened or endangered) plant and animal species.

Thus the Grand Canyon is a land of song. Mountains of music swell in the rivers, hills of music billow in the creeks, and meadows of music murmur in the rills that ripple over the rocks. Altogether it is a symphony of multitudinous melodies. All this is the music of waters.

John Wesley Powell
first Grand Canyon expedition,
1869

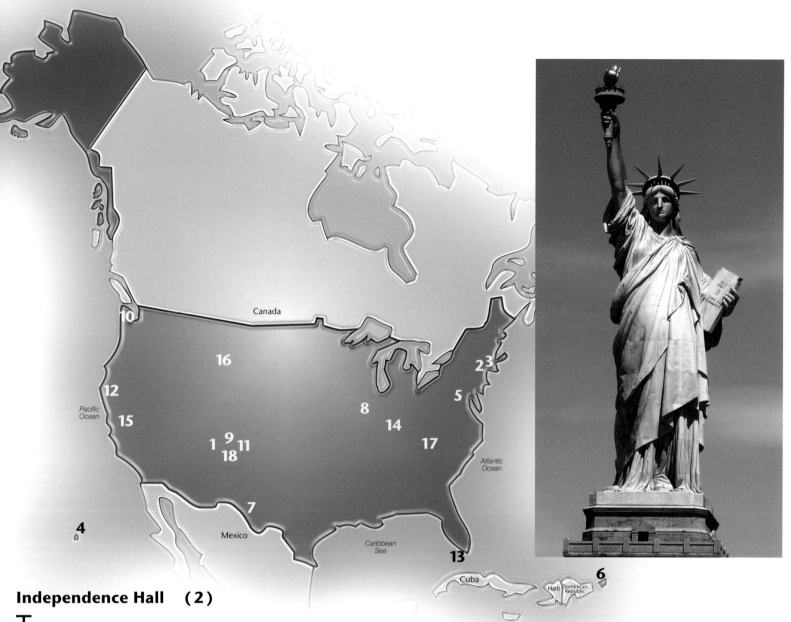

Canada

Pacific
Ocean

Atlantic
Ocean

Mexico

Caribbean
Sea

Cuba

Haiti Dominican
Republic

Independence Hall   (2)

This is the heart and soul of the United States. The Declaration of Independence (1776) and the Constitution of the United States (1787) were both signed in this building in Philadelphia. The universal principles of freedom and democracy set forth in these documents are of fundamental importance to American history and have also had a profound impact on lawmakers around the world.

Statue of Liberty   (3)

Symbol of freedom and democracy, the Statue of Liberty was a gift from the people of France to the people of the United States in 1886. It was made by the French sculptor Bartholdi, in collaboration with Gustave Eiffel. It stands on the 5-hectare (12-acre) Liberty Island in New York Harbor, and has welcomed millions of immigrants since it was first erected.

"Not like the brazen giant of Greek fame, With conquering limbs astride from land to land; Here at our sea-washed, sunset gates shall stand A mighty woman with a torch, whose flame. Is the imprisoned lightning, and her name Mother of Exiles"

Excerpt of Emma Lazarus' poem "The New Colossus", written for the statue in 1883

"The Liberty Bell is a very significant symbol for the entire democratic world."

Nelson Mandela, 1993, speaking of the famous bell which rang on July 8, 1776, for the reading of the Declaration of Independence

Hawaii Volcanoes National Park   (4)

This site contains two of the most active volcanoes in the world, Mauna Loa and Kilauna. Hawaii Volcanoes National Park was established in 1916 and displays the results of 70 million years of volcanism, migration, and evolution. Because of its unique environment, the site hosts rare birds and endemic species.

"There was a time in the mysterious past when the air was surrounded with spiritual beings and a thin veil divided the living from the dead, the natural from the supernatural. During that time, Pele, goddess of the volcano, came to Hawaii."

Hawaiian legend

Monticello and the University of Virginia in Charlottesville   (5)

This site was developed by the author of the American Declaration of Independence and third president of the United States, Thomas Jefferson. It is now the heart of the University of Virginia, with an architectural style representing the new American Republic as the inheritor of European traditions.

La Fortaleza and San Juan Historic Site in Puerto Rico   (6)

This fortress is a great example of European military architecture adapted to harbour sites in the Caribbean. It was built by the Spanish to protect their colonies in Puerto Rico and the San Juan Bay.

Carlsbad Caverns National Park (7)

This New Mexico park includes over 100 caves. They are outstanding not only for their size, but also for the profusion, diversity and beauty of their mineral formation.

"...I am wholly conscious of the feebleness of my efforts to convey in the deep conflicting emotions, the feeling of fear and awe, and the desire for an inspired understanding of the Divine Creator's work which presents to the human eye such a complex aggregate of natural wonders..."

*Inspector Robert Holley,
investigating Carlsbad Cavern
in 1923*

Cahokia Mounds State Historic Site (8)

North of Saint-Louis, Missouri, Cahokia Mounds is the largest pre-Columbian settlement north of Mexico. It was mainly occupied between the years 800 and 1400. It is the largest prehistoric earthwork in the Americas, covering over 5 hectares (12 acres) and standing 30 metres high (98 feet).

Mesa Verde (9)

Sitting on a plateau in south-western Colorado, Mesa Verde is a concentration of ancestral Pueblo Indian dwellings, built from the 6th to the 12th centuries. This nation first used caves as shelter, but later built sophisticated apartments, including multi-story complexes such as the "Cliff Palace".

"The falling snowflakes sprinkling the piñons gave it a special kind of solemnity. It was more like sculpture than anything else ... preserved ... like a fly in amber."

*Richard Wetherill,
cowboy who discovered Mesa Verde
in 1888*

Olympic National Park　(10)

With mountains crushed up against the coast of the Pacific Ocean, Olympic National Park is renowned for its spectacular ecosystems, including glacier-capped mountains, Pacific coastline and temperate rain forests. Because the park sits on an isolated peninsula in Washington state, with a high mountain range dividing it from the land to the south, the region developed many unique plant and animal species that can't be found anywhere else in the world.

> *"In closing, I would state that while the country on the outer slope of these mountains is valuable, the interior is useless for all practicable purposes. It would, however, serve admirably for a national park..."*
>
> Lieutenant Joseph O'Neil, 1890

Pueblo de Taos　(11)

Pueblo de Taos is located in the valley of a small tributary of the Rio Grande in New Mexico. It features spectacular examples of dwelling and ceremonial buildings of the Pueblo Indians of Arizona and New Mexico. Taos has been a centre of Native-American culture since the 17th century.

Redwood National Park　(12)

Home to the world's tallest trees, just a few miles north of San Francisco, California, this costal forest has some unique marine and land life. The redwood trees can live for up to 2,000 years and grow as high as 90 metres (300 feet).

Everglades National Park (13)

The everglades, in southern Florida, near the Gulf of Mexico, is called the River of Grass by Native Americans. It is formed by a river of fresh water 15 centimetres (6 inches) deep and 80 kilometres (50 miles) wide. It is home to more than 300 bird species and well known for its alligators. Unfortunately, Everglades Park is a fragile ecosystem threatened by urban development in Miami. The park is on the World Heritage Sites endangered list.

"Here are no lofty peaks seeking the sky, no mighty glaciers or rushing streams wearing away the uplifted land. Here is land, tranquil in its quiet beauty, serving not as the source of water, but as the receiver of it. To its natural abundance we owe the spectacular plant and animal life that distinguishes this place from all others in our country."

U.S. President Harry S. Truman, 1947

Mammoth Cave National Park (14)

This Kentucky Park features the world's largest natural caves and underground passageways. The underground network extends more than 560 kilometres (348 miles) and is home to a unique and varied fauna and flora. Mammoth Cave is home to the endangered Kentucky cave shrimp, a sightless albino shrimp.

Yosemite National Park   (15)

In the heart of California, nestled in the Sierra Nevada mountain range, the park features spectacular valleys, cliffs, granite reliefs, domes, lakes and waterfalls. It is home to a diversified flora and fauna, including giant sequoias, which are the world's tallest trees. Impressive granite domes, such as the Sentinel Dome and Half Dome, rise 3,000 feet and 4,800 feet (900 and 1450 m), respectively, above the Yosemite valley floor.

"The level bottom seemed to be dressed like a garden, sunny meadows here and there, and groves of pine and oak; the river of Mercy sweeping in majesty through the midst of them and flashing back the sunbeams."

Environmentalist John Muir (1838 –1914), describing the site in 1869

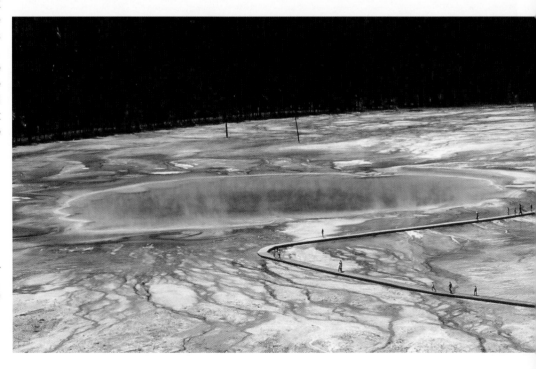

Great Smoky Mountains National Park (17)

The "Smokies" cover over 200,000 hectares (494,210 acres) on the border between North Carolina and Tennessee. This exceptional park, located in the south-eastern United States, features over 3,500 plant species, including 130 tree species. This park is also well known for the beauty of its mountains, the Appalachians,and the "smoke" surrounding them.

"Some historians say the Ulster-Scots settled in the mountains because the area was so isolated; others believe it was because it reminded them of the Highlands they left behind."

Smoky Mountain Host of North Carolina, explaining that in the early 1600s, the Scot-Irish became the prominent settlers in the Great Smokies

Chaco Culture National Historical Park (18)

Chaco Park is the pride of New Mexico. Its ruins are a heritage from the Pueblo peoples, who occupied this region for over 2,000 years. Chaco is remarkable for its monumental public and ceremonial buildings, and its distinctive architecture.

Yellowstone (16)

The first park to be designated a world national park, Yellowstone is located in Wyoming and touches two other states, Montana and Idaho. It contains half of all the world's known geothermal features, with more than 10,000 examples. It is also well known for its concentration of geysers, the largest on the planet.

"Yellowstone would forever be dedicated and set apart as a public park or pleasuring ground for the benefit and enjoyment of the people."

U.S. President Ulysses S. Grant, 1871

Mexico

Pre-Hispanic City of Chichen-Itza (1)

Chichen-Itza is located in the south of Mérida, in the state of Yucatán, in the midst of fabulous natural surroundings where the deep blue skies contrast with the lush green vegetation. This sacred site was one of the greatest Mayan centres. Throughout its nearly 1,000-year history, different peoples have left their mark on the city. The Maya, Toltec and Iztec vision of the world and the universe is revealed in their stone monuments and art works.

"At the mouth of the wells of the Itza people"

Meaning of "Chichen Itza" in Maya

Historic Centre of Morelia   (2)

Construction of the city of Valladolid began on May 18, 1541, on the initiative of the first viceroy of New Spain, Antonio de Mendoza, in a place known as Guayangeo. This city is an outstanding example of urban planning which combines the ideas of the Spanish Renaissance with the Mesoamerican experience. Since the 19th century, the capital of Michoacán has been called Morelia, in honour of one of the most important figures in the struggle for Mexico's independence, José Maria Morelos.

Historic Centre of Mexico City and Xochimilco   (3)

Capital of Mexico, second most populated city of the world, Mexico City was build by the Spanish in the 16th century on the ruins of the old Aztec capital Tenochtitlan. The city is home to five Aztec temples and the continent's largest cathedral. Its characteristic urban and rural structures, built in the 16th century and duringthe colonial period, have been exceptionally well preserved.

Historic Town of Guanajuato and Adjacent Mines (4)

Established by the Spanish in the early 16th century, Guanajuato became the world's leading silver-extraction centre in the 18th century. The history can be seen in its subterranean streets and the "Boca del Inferno", a mineshaft that plunges a breathtaking 600 m (1,968 feet). The town's fine Baroque and neoclassical buildings, built thanks to the prosperity of the mines, have influenced architecture throughout central Mexico.

"Doña Carmen, the only daughter of a willful and violent man, was locked up in her room. Her lover, Don Luis, bought the house across the alley to talk to her. The houses were so close they could exchange kisses. Doña's father found out and stabbed her in the chest."

Legend of the Callejón del Beso (the Alley of the Kiss)

Historic Monuments Zone of Tlacotalpan   (5)

Founded in the mid-16th century, Tlacotalpan is a Spanish colonial river port on the Gulf Coast of Mexico. Its urban layout and architecture represent a fusion of Spanish and Caribbean traditions of exceptional importance and quality. Its outstanding character lies in the townscape of wide streets, modest houses in an exuberant variety of styles and colours, and many mature trees in public and private open spaces.

Earliest 16th-Century Monasteries on the Slopes of Popocatepetl (6)

In the southern portion of southeast Mexico City, 14 monasteries stand on the slopes of Popocatepetl. They are still in an excellent state of conservation and are good examples of the architectural style adopted by the first missionaries – Franciscans, Dominicans and Augustinians – who converted the indigenous populations to Christianity in the early 16th century.

Whale Sanctuary of El Vizcaino   (7)

This sanctuary in the central part of the Baja California peninsula contains some exceptionally interesting ecosystems. The coastal lagoons of Ojo de Liebre and San Ignacio are important reproduction and wintering sites for the grey whale, harbour seal, California sea lion, northern elephant-seal and blue whale.

"It's a unique site on a world-wide scale, for species habitat and for its natural beauty, which is also a value to be preserved."

Ernesto Zedillo,
President of Mexico,
March 2000

Archaeological Monuments Zone of Xochicalco   (8)

Located in the south-western part of Morelos, Xochicalco is an exceptionally well-preserved example of a fortified political, religious and commercial centre from the troubled period of 650–900. The architecture and art of Xochicalco represent the fusion of cultural elements from different parts of Mesoamerica.

Pre-Hispanic City and National Park of Palenque   (9)

Discovered in the 19th century in dense jungle, Palenque is a prime example of a Mayan sanctuary of the classical period. Palenque was at its peak between AD 500 and 700, when its influence extended throughout the basin of the Usumacinta River. The elegance and craftsmanship of the buildings, as well as the lightness of the sculpted reliefs with their Mayan mythological themes, attest to the creative genius of this civilization.

"Palenque, the most enigmatically moving of all Maya sites, has held its secrets for over twelve hundred years."

Gillett G. Griffin,
faculty curator of pre-Columbian and Native American art, Princeton University

Pre-Hispanic City of Teotihuacan (10)

The Aztecs described this site as "the city where the gods are born". Teotihuacan is roughly 50 km (31 miles) north-east of Mexico City. It was built between the 1st and 7th centuries AD, and it is characterized by the vast size of its monuments – in particular, the Temple of Quetzalcoatl and the Pyramids of the Sun and the Moon, laid out on geometric and symbolic principles.

"In Teotihuacán, here were created the sun, the moon and the universe."

Aztec mythology

Historic Centre of Oaxaca and Archaeological Site of Monte Albán (11)

Inhabited over a period of 1,500 years by a succession of peoples – Olmecs, Zapotecs and Mixtecs – the terraces, dams, canals, pyramids and artificial mounds of Monte Albán were literally carved out of the mountain and are the symbols of a sacred topography. The nearby city of Oaxaca, which is built on a grid pattern, is a good example of Spanish colonial town planning.

Historic Monuments Zone of Querétaro (12)

The old colonial town of Querétaro is unusual in having retained the geometric street plan of the Spanish conquerors side by side with the twisting alleys of the Indian quarters. The city was built in 1531. It is an exceptional example of a colonial town whose layout symbolizes its multi-ethnic population.

Rock Paintings of the Sierra de San Francisco   (13)

The Sierra de San Francisco, in Baja California's El Vizcaino reserve, features some of the world's most outstanding collections of rock paintings, dating from 100 BC to AD 1300. They represent human figures and many animal species, illustrating their relationships.

"... they doubtless belong to another ancient nation, although we cannot say which it was. The Californians unanimously affirm that it was a nation of giants who came from the north."

Francisco Javier Clavigero, describing the paintings in his 1789 Historia de la Antigua o Baja California

Historic Centre of Zacatecas (14)

Zacatecas was founded in 1546 after the discovery of a rich silver lode. The city is built on the steep slopes of a narrow valley. Zacatecas is an example of the splendour of the colonial era. The pink stone filigree used in its cathedral and monasteries dates from this period. It is notable for its harmonious design and the Baroque profusion of its façades, where European and indigenous decorative elements are found side by side.

Franciscan Missions in the Sierra Gorda of Querétaro (15)

The five Franciscan missions were built during the last phase of the conversion to Christianity in the interior of Mexico during the mid-18th century. The Sierra Gorda Missions exhibit an important interchange of values in the process of evangelizing central and northern Mexico, and the western United States.

Ancient Maya City of Calakmul, Campeche   (16)

Calakmul is an important Maya site set deep in the tropical forest of the Tierras Bajas of southern Mexico. It played a key role in the history of this region for more than twelve centuries. Its imposing structures and its characteristic overall layout are remarkably well preserved and give a vivid picture of life in an ancient Maya capital.

"In Maya, 'ca' means 'two', 'lak' means adjacent', and 'mul' signifies any artificial mound or pyramid, so 'Calakmul' is the 'City of the Two Adjacent Pyramids'."

Biologist Cyrus L. Lundell, who discovered the site on December 29, 1931

Sian Ka'an   (17)

This biosphere reserve on the east coast of the Yucatán peninsula contains tropical forests, mangroves and marshes, as well as a large marine section that intersects a barrier reef. It provides a habitat for a remarkably rich flora and a fauna including over 300 species of birds, as well as a large number of the region's characteristic terrestrial vertebrates.

Historic Fortified Town of Campeche (18)

The city of Campeche, built in 1540 on the site of the estate of Ah Kim Pech (Lord Tick) was the first Spanish settlement on the Yucatán Peninsula. The city became one of the most important ports in America for shipping the immense wealth produced in the inland forests. The historic centre has kept its outer walls and fortification system, designed to defend this Caribbean port against attacks from the sea.

"Campeche spent decades in terror as it became wealthier and even more irresistible to buccaneers, until Spain finally agreed to fortify the city."

Writer Beatriz Martí,
Mundo Maya Online

Archeological Zone of Paquimé, Casas Grandes (19)

Paquimé reached its apogee in the 14th and 15th centuries. The area played a key role in trade and cultural contacts between the Pueblo culture of the south-western United States and northern Mexico, and the more advanced civilizations of Mesoamerica. The extensive remains of the archaeological site of Paquimé Casas Grandes provide exceptional evidence of the development of adobe architecture in North America.

Pre-Hispanic Town of Uxmal (20)

In this Mayan town founded c. AD 700, the layout of the buildings reveals a knowledge of astronomy. The Pyramid of the Soothsayer, as the Spanish called it, dominates the ceremonial centre, which has well-designed buildings decorated with a profusion of symbolic motifs and sculptures depicting Chaac, the god of rain.

"...The place of which I am now speaking was beyond all doubt once a large, populous, and highly civilized city. Who built it, why it was located away from water or any of those natural advantages which have determined the sites of cities whose histories are known, what led to its abandonment and destruction, no man can tell."

John Lloyd Stephens,
Incidents of Travel in Central America,
Chiapas & Yucatán, 1843

Pre-Hispanic City of El Tajin   (21)

Located in the state of Veracruz El Tajin was at its most prosperous from the early 9th to the early 13th century. Its archi-tecture, which is unique in Mesoamerica, is characterized by elaborately carved reliefs on the columns and frieze. El Tajin has survived as an outstanding example of the grandeur and importance of the pre-Hispanic cultures of Mexico.

"I gave myself over to being in a place with so much life and history, such a strong feeling of people of the past. It was grand to be there, and also a reminder of how short my own time will be, in the great scheme of things."

Publisher and writer Rosana Hart

Hospicio Cabañas, Guadalajara (22)

Located in a fertile valley in the foothills of the Sierra Madre Occidental, the Hospicio Cabañas is a unique architectural complex, designed to respond to social and economic requirements for housing the sick, the aged, the young, and the needy, which provides an outstanding solution showing great subtlety and humanity. It also houses one of the acknowledged masterpieces of mural art.

"What really makes every visit to Guadalajara special for me are the José Clemente Orozco murals in the Instituto Cultural Cabañas."

Writer and editor Wendy Luft, from Mexico City

Agave Landscape and Ancient Industrial Facilities in Tequila, Jalisco (23)

The process of fermenting juices from various agave species was discovered in central Mexico, and was common practice during pre-Hispanic times. Around 1600, Pedro Sinchez de Tagle, Marquis of Altamira, introduced the European distillation process into the production of agave liquor or mescal wine, which were the names originally used to describe the drink. Ultimately, it was named after its place of origin: Tequila.

"Tequila is Mexico. It's the only product that identifies us as a culture."

Carmelita Roman,
widow of the late tequila producer
Jesus Lopez Roman

Luis Barragán House and Studio (24)

Built in 1948, the house and studio of architect Luis Barragán, in a suburb of Mexico City, represent an outstanding example of the architect's creative work in the post-Second World War period. The work of Luis Barragán exhibits the integration of modern and traditional influence.

"My architecture is autobiographical...
underlying all that I have achieved such as it."

Mexican architect Luis Barragan
(1902 - 1988)

Historic Centre of Puebla   (25)

Founded ex nihilo in 1531, Puebla is situated about 100 km (62 miles) east of Mexico City, at the foot of the Popocatepetl volcano. It has preserved its great religious structures such as the 16th–17th-century cathedral and fine buildings like the old archbishop's palace, as well as a host of houses with walls covered in tiles (azulejos).

Islands and Protected Areas of the Gulf of California   (26)

The site – locally known in the Spanish language as Mar de Cortés – comprises 244 islands, islets and coastal areas in the Gulf of California, in north-eastern Mexico. The region has been called a natural laboratory for the investigation of speciation. Moreover, almost all major oceanographic processes occurring in the planet's oceans are present in the property, giving it extraordinary importance for study.

Guatemala

Tikal National Park　(1)

In the heart of the jungle, surrounded by lush vegetation, lies one of the major sites of Mayan civilization, inhabited from the 6th century BC to the 10th century AD. The ceremonial centre contains superb temples and palaces, and public squares accessed by means of ramps.

"Many people recognize the magic of Tikal. And yes, there is great magic.
We are not creating experiences. We are given experiences as a gift…"

Mercedes Barrios Longfellow,
Mayan Shaman and Priestess
from the highlands of Guatemala

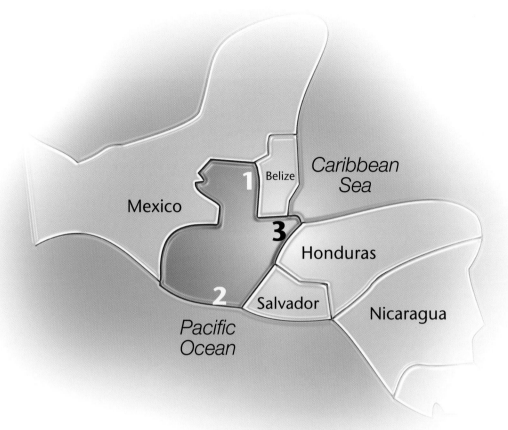

Antigua, Guatemala (2)

Capital of the Captaincy-General of Guatemala, Antigua was founded in the early 16th century. Built 1,500 metres (4,920 feet) above sea level, in an earthquake-prone region, it was largely destroyed by a quake in 1773, but its principal monuments are still preserved as ruins.

Archaeological Park and Ruins of Quirigua (3)

Quirigua has been inhabited since the 2nd century AD. During the reign of Cauac Sky (723–84), it had become the capital of an autonomous and prosperous state. The ruins of contain some outstanding 8th-century monuments and an impressive series of carved stelae and sculpted calendars that constitute an essential source for the study of Mayan civilization.

"We are not myths of the past, ruins in the jungle or zoos. We are people and we want to be respected, not to be victims of intolerance and racism."

Guatemalian Nobel Peace Prize winner Rigoberta Menchú Tum, member of the indigenous Quiché Maya group

Belize

Belize Barrier Reef Reserve System (1)

The coastal area of Belize is an outstanding natural system consisting of the largest barrier reef in the northern hemisphere, offshore atolls, several hundred sand cays, mangrove forests, coastal lagoons, and estuaries. It is a significant habitat for threatened species, including marine turtles, manatees and the American marine crocodile.

"It is one of the few places left where you can observe nature at its best, but it is nonetheless under threat."

*Coral reef researcher
Julianne Robinson,
National Geographic News*

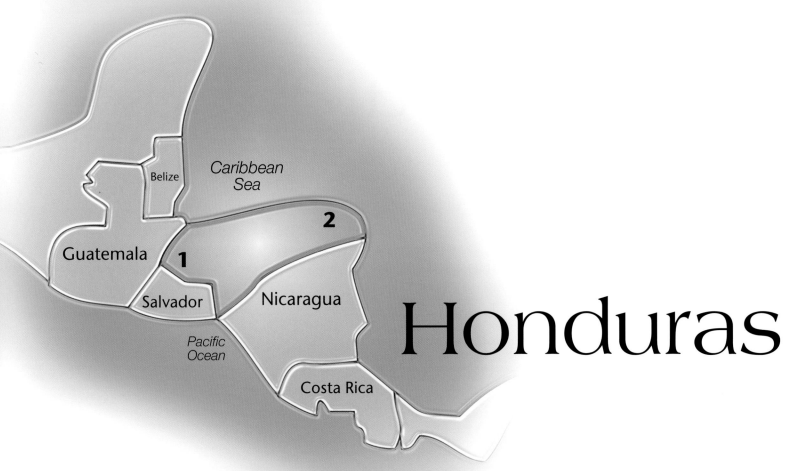

Honduras

Río Plátano Biosphere Reserve (2)

The reserve is one of the few remains of a tropical rainforest in Central America and has abundant and varied plant and wildlife. In its mountainous landscape sloping down to the Caribbean coast, over 2,000 indigenous people have preserved their traditional way of life. This site is now threatened on its west side by the advancing agricultural frontier, led by small farmers and cattle ranchers. This has already reduced the reserve's forest area.

Maya Site of Copan (1)

Discovered in 1570 by Diego García de Palacio, the ruins of Copán, one of the most important sites of the Mayan civilization, were not excavated until the 19th century. The ruined citadel and imposing public squares reveal the three main stages of development before the city was abandoned in the early 10th century.

"For its relatively small size, the amount of inscribed materials at Copán is truly astounding, suggesting that in some way the elite culture of this ancient kingdom was particularly interested in literate culture and whatever that entailed."

David Stuart,
expert on the written language of the ancient Maya,
Peabody Museum of Archaeology and Ethnology,
Harvard University

Nicaragua

Ruins of León Viejo   (1)

León Viejo is one of the oldest Spanish colonial settlements in the Americas. The form and nature of early Spanish settlement in the New World, adapting European architectural and planning concepts to the material potential of another region, are uniquely preserved in León Viejo's archaeological site.

"This is the best-preserved lowland Spanish colonial site in the hemisphere. No shopping centres were built over the place, no highways, no condos. The city wasn't torn down, it just disappeared."

American anthropologist
Fred Lange

Joya de Ceren Archaeological Site (1)

Joya de Cerén is a pre-Hispanic farming community that, like Pompeii and Herculaneum in Italy, was buried under a volcanic eruption c. AD 600. Because of their exceptional condition, the remains provide insight into the daily lives of the Central American populations who worked the land at that time.

El Salvador

Guatemala

Honduras

1

Nicaragua

Pacific Ocean

Costa Rica

Talamanca Range-La Amistad Reserves / La Amistad National Park (1)
(Site shared with Panama)

Along the Talamanca Mountain Range, in southern Costa Rica, La Amistad National Park spans 194,129 hectares (479,703 acres) of spectacular tropical rainforest. Its wide altitudinal range, deep climatic changes, and impressive variety of soil contribute to create diverse ecosystems and a high endemism. It is home to four different Indian tribes.

"You don't need to venture far to experience the nation's full panoply of magnificent wildlife. Costa Rica is nature's live theatre where the actors aren't shy."

*Travel and natural sciences writer
Christopher Baker*

Coco's Island National Park (2)

Isolated in the Pacific Ocean, 532 kilometres (330 miles) southwest of White Cape (Cabo Blanco), Coco's Island rises like a pearl in the middle of the ocean. It is the only island in the tropical eastern Pacific with a tropical rainforest. This site provides critical habitats for marine wildlife including large pelagic species, especially sharks.

"This is the most beautiful island of the world."

Jacques Cousteau

Area de Conservación Guanacaste (3)

This region contains important natural habitats for the conservation of biological diversity, including the best dry forest habitats from Central America to northern Mexico, and key habitats for endangered or rare plant and animal species. The site demonstrates significant ecological processes in both its terrestrial and marine-coastal environments.

Panama

Nicaragua

Caribbean Sea

Costa Rica

Pacific Ocean

Colombie

Venezuela

1
4
2
3

Fortifications on the Caribbean Side of Panama: Portobelo-San Lorenzo   (1)

It was here that Spanish galleons loaded their treasures for the voyage back to Europe. Standing as magnificent examples of 17th- and 18th-century military architecture, these Panamanian forts on the Caribbean coast form part of the defence system built by the Spanish Crown to protect transatlantic trade. The pirates of the Caribbean all had their eyes on the treasures of Portobelo.

"We took our canoes, twenty-three in number and rowing along the coast, landed at three o'clock in the morning and made our way into the town, and seeing that we could not refresh ourselves in quiet, we were enforced to assault the castle..."

Captain Henry Morgan,
in May of 1668, writing about his capture
of Puerto Bello, which he plundered
with his buccaneers for 14 days

Darien National Park (2)

Forming a bridge between the two continents of the New World, Darien National Park contains an exceptional variety of habitats – sandy beaches, rocky coasts, mangroves, swamps, and lowland and upland tropical forests containing remarkable wildlife. The park is home to the national bird of Panama, the Harpy Eagle. Three Amerindian ethnic groups live within the park: Embera, Waunana and Kuna.

Coiba National Park and its Special Zone of Marine Protection (3)

Off the southwest coast of Panama, Coiba National Park protects Coiba Island, 38 smaller islands and the surrounding marine areas within the Gulf of Chiriqui. Protected from the cold winds and effects of El Niño, Coiba's Pacific moist tropical forest maintains exceptionally high levels of endemism of mammals, birds and plants due to the ongoing evolution of new species. It is also the last refuge for a number of threatened animals such as the crested eagle.

"Coiba is a key link in the Pacific island ring that includes the Coco's and the Galapagos, and, as the member of the group closest to he continent, a protected nursery for juvenile fish that will migrate as adults."

Sandra Mayson,
editor of Oceana Magazine

Archaeological Site of Panamá Viejo and Historic District of Panamá (4)

Founded in 1519 by the conquistador Pedrarías Dávila, Panamá Viejo is the oldest European settlement on the Pacific coast of the Americas. The Historic District preserves the original street pattern intact, along with a substantial number of early domestic buildings, which are exceptional testimony to the nature of this early settlement.

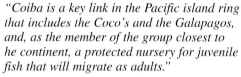

San Pedro de la Roca Castle, Santiago de Cuba   (1)

Commercial and political rivalries in the Caribbean region in the 17th century resulted in the construction of this massive series of fortifications on a rocky promontory, built to protect the important port of Santiago. They constitute the largest and most comprehensive example of the principles of Renaissance military engineering adapted to the Caribbean.

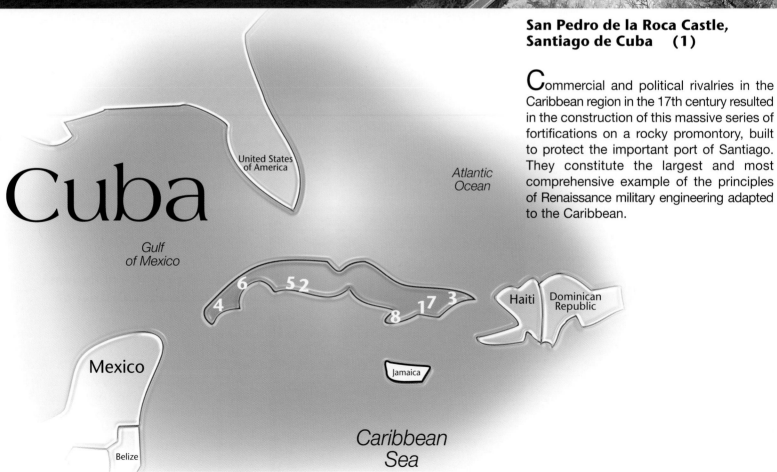

Cuba

Gulf
of Mexico

United States
of America

Atlantic
Ocean

Haiti   Dominican
          Republic

Mexico

Jamaica

Caribbean
Sea

Belize

Honduras

Trinidad and the Valley de los Ingenios   (2)

Founded in 1514 by the Spanish conquistadors in honour of the Holy Trinity, the city was a bridgehead for the conquest of the American continent. Its 18th- and 19th-century buildings, such as the Palacio Brunet and the Palacio Cantero, were built in the prosperous days of the sugar trade.

Alejandro de Humboldt National Park   (3)

This site is one of the most biologically diverse tropical island sites on earth. It boasts a diversity of ecosystems and species unmatched in the insular Caribbean. Many of the underlying rocks are toxic to plants, so species have had to adapt to survive in these hostile conditions. Endemism of flora, vertebrates and invertebrates is very high in this area. The local flora includes five species of carnivore plants.

Viñales Valley (4)

The valley is surrounded by mountains and its landscape is interspersed with dramatic rocky outcrops. The valley presents an outstanding karst landscape in which traditional methods of agriculture (notably tobacco growing) have survived unchanged for several centuries.

"I started to work for a rising young American politician named John Kennedy, who liked to smoke Petit Upmann Cuban cigars. Working around him, I felt I had no choice but to upgrade my smoke of choice to a Cuban."

Pierre Salinger (1925–2004),
White House Press Secretary
to U.S. President John F. Kennedy

Urban Historic Centre of Cienfuegos (5)

Founded in 1819 on the southern coast of Cuba, in the Spanish territory, the colonial town of Cienfuegos was initially settled by immigrants of French origin. It became a trading place for sugar cane, tobacco and coffee. Cienfuegos is the first, and still an outstanding example of an architectural ensemble representing the new ideas of modernity, hygiene and order in urban planning, as developed in Latin America from the 19th century.

"Cienfuegos is the city that I like the most."

Cuban singer Benny Moré
(1919 – 1963)

Old Havana and its Fortifications (6)

Havana was established in 1519 by Spanish settlers. By the 17th century, the city became a depository for treasures that Spanish fleets brought to the New World. It also became the centre of trade and commerce between the old and new worlds. Its old centre retains an interesting mix of Baroque and neoclassical monuments.

"In Habana Vieja, where we are preserving the values of the architecture of another century…"

Cuban President
Fidel Castro

Archaeological Landscape of the First Coffee Plantations in Southeast Cuba (7)

The remains of the 19th-century coffee plantations in the foothills of the Sierra Maestra are unique evidence of a pioneer form of agriculture in this virgin forest. The production of coffee in eastern Cuba during the 19th and early 20th centuries resulted in the formation of a unique cultural landscape.

Desembarco del Granma National Park   (8)

Located in and around Cabo Cruz in southwest Cuba, the park includes spectacular terraces and cliffs, as well as some of the most pristine and impressive coastal cliffs bordering the western Atlantic. It represents a globally significant example of geomorphologic and physiographic features and ongoing geological processes.

*"This is the most beautiful land
that human eyes saw."*

*Explorer Christopher Columbus,
upon arrival to the Cuban coasts
on October 27, 1492*

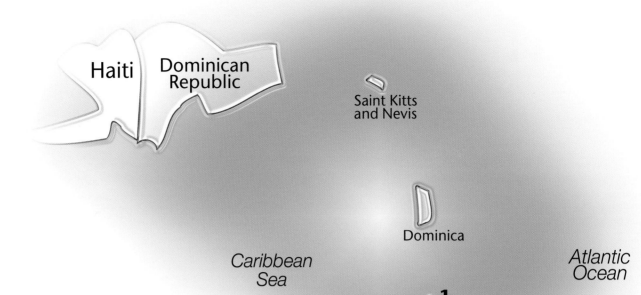

Haiti

Dominican Republic

Saint Kitts and Nevis

Dominica

Caribbean Sea

Atlantic Ocean

D^1

Saint Lucia

Pitons Management Area   (1)

Near the town of Soufriere, Pitons are two volcanic spires rising side by side from the sea, linked by the Piton Mitan ridge. The volcanic complex includes a geothermal field with sulphurous fumaroles and hot springs. Coral reefs cover almost 60% of site's marine area. At least 148 plant species have been recorded on Gros Piton, and 97 on Petit Piton and the intervening ridge, among them eight rare tree species.

"The two peaks, Gros Piton and Petit Piton, made a striking couple. They also recall Saint Lucia's chequered colonial past, reminding the visitor that many locals still speak a French patois…"

Robert H. Mohlenibrock,
Professor Emeritus of plant biology
at Southern Illinois University

Haiti

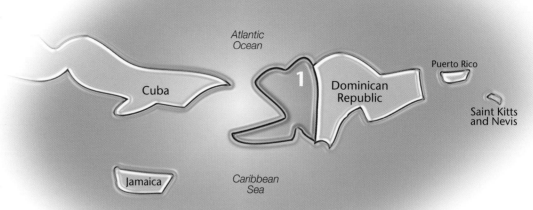

Atlantic Ocean

Cuba

1

Dominican Republic

Puerto Rico

Saint Kitts and Nevis

Jamaica

Caribbean Sea

National History Park - Citadel, Sans Souci, Ramiers   (1)

These Haitian monuments date from the beginning of the 19th century, when Haiti proclaimed its independence. The Palace of Sans Souci, the buildings at Ramiers and, in particular, the Citadel serve as universal symbols of liberty, being the first monuments to be built by black slaves who had gained their freedom.

"Sans Souci, a magnificent palace of brick and mortar … symbolized the early effort of the benevolent monarch to provide primitive Haiti with a lasting emblem of cultural leisure and good living."

Writer Seldon Rodman

Colonial City of Santo Domingo (1)

After Christopher Columbus' arrival on the island in 1492, Santo Domingo became the site of the first cathedral, hospital, customs house and university in the Americas. This colonial town, founded in 1498, was laid out on a grid pattern that became the model for almost all town planners in the New World.

"First City of the Indies"

Coat of arms and emblem given to the city by King Ferdinand II of Aragon in 1508

Dominican republic

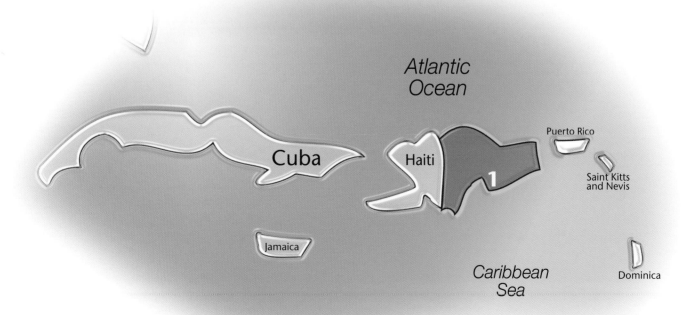

Atlantic Ocean

Cuba

Haiti

Puerto Rico

Saint Kitts and Nevis

Jamaica

Caribbean Sea

Dominica

Morne Trois Pitons National Park (1)

This 6,872-hectare park (16,980 acres) is a luxuriant natural tropical forest. Morne Trois Pitons National Park presents a rare combination of natural features of World Heritage value, including endemic species of vascular plants, hot springs, three freshwater lakes, a "boiling lake", five volcanoes and 50 fumaroles.

Dominica

Haiti

Dominican Republic

Puerto Rico

Saint Kitts and Nevis

Atlantic Ocean

Caribbean Sea

Saint Lucia

Puerto Rico

Dominican
Republic

*Atlantic
Ocean*

*Caribbean
Sea*

Dominica

Saint Kitts and Nevis

Brimstone Hill Fortress National Park (1)

The Fortress, constructed intermittently between the 1690s and 1790s, is of singular importance as the remains of a large and complete 18th-century military community. Designed by the British and built by African slave labour, the fortress is testimony to European colonial expansion, the African slave trade and the emergence of new societies in the Caribbean.

Panama

Colombie

Pacific Ocean

1

2

4

3

Peru

Ecuador

Galapagos Islands   (1)

Situated in the Pacific Ocean, some 1,000 km (620 miles) from the South American continent, these nineteen islands and their sur-rounding marine reserve have been called a unique "living museum and showcase of evolution." This is a largely self-contained ecological region and home to many spectacular species such as the marine and land iguanas, giant tortoises, Galapagos penguins and the Galapagos short-eared owl.

"The natural history of this archipelago is very remarkable: it seems to be a little world within itself; the greater number of its inhabitants, both vegetable and animal, being found nowhere else."

Charles Robert Darwin, Voyage of the Beagle, 1831

City of Quito   (2)

Capital of Ecuador, Quito was founded in the 16th century on the ruins of an Inca city, at an altitude of 2,850 m. Quito is located in a long narrow valley in the Andes, between the base of the Pichincha Volcano and the canyon of the river Machéangara. Despite the 1917 earthquake, the city has the best-preserved, least-altered historic centre in Latin America.

Historic Centre of Santa Ana de los Ríos de Cuenca   (3)

Santa Ana is set in a valley surrounded by the Andean Mountains in southern Ecuador. This former Inca town was conquered by the Spanish in 1533 and founded in 1557. Cuenca illustrates the successful implantation of the principles of Renaissance urban planning in the Americas.

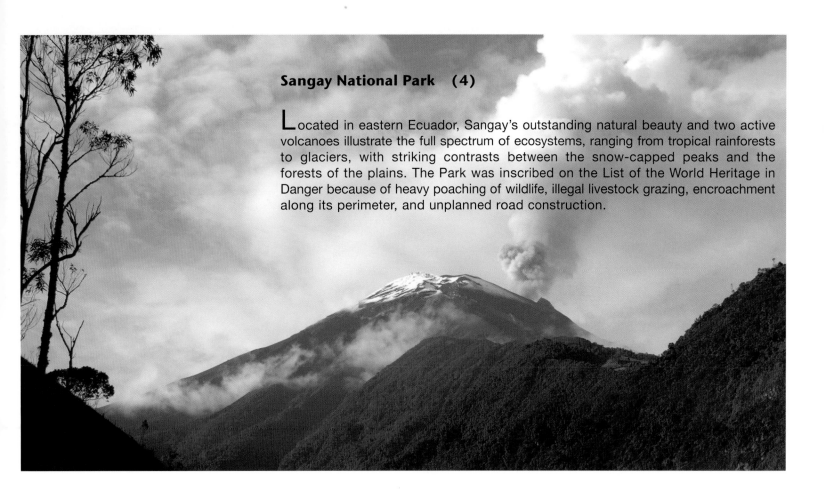

Sangay National Park   (4)

Located in eastern Ecuador, Sangay's outstanding natural beauty and two active volcanoes illustrate the full spectrum of ecosystems, ranging from tropical rainforests to glaciers, with striking contrasts between the snow-capped peaks and the forests of the plains. The Park was inscribed on the List of the World Heritage in Danger because of heavy poaching of wildlife, illegal livestock grazing, encroachment along its perimeter, and unplanned road construction.

Peru

Ecuador

Brazil

Pacific
Ocean

Bolivia

Chile

1

3

9 8

2

4

10 5

7

6

Rio Abiseo National Park   (1)

This park, with a surface of 274,520 hectares (678,353 acres), is located in the department of San Martín, province Mariscal Caceres, district Hurcungo. It was created in 1983 to protect the fauna and flora of the rainforests that are characteristic of this region of the Andes. There is a high level of endemism among the wildlife found in the park. The yellow-tailed woolly monkey, previously thought extinct, is found only in this area.

Historic Centre of Lima   (2)

The "City of the Kings" was, until the middle of the 18th century, the capital and most important city of the Spanish dominions in South America. Many of its buildings, such as the Convent of San Francisco (the largest of its type in this part of the world), are the result of collaboration between local crafts-people and others from the Old World.

"Peru is from this moment free and independent by the wish of the people and the justness of the cause which God defends."

José de San Martín, Protector del Peru, proclaiming the country's indepedence in Lima, 1821

Chan Chan Archaeological Zone (3)

The Chimu Kingdom, with Chan Chan as its capital, reached its apogee in the 15th century, not long before falling to the Incas. It was the largest urban centre in pre-Columbian America. Its adobe, or earthen, structures are quickly damaged by natural erosion as they become exposed to air and rain.   It is on the List of World Heritage in Danger.

Manú National Park   (4)

Manú is a biosphere reserve located in the heat of the Amazonian rainforest. This huge, 1.5 million-ha park (3,706,580 acres) has successive tiers of vegetation rising from 150 to 4,200 m (492 to 13,780 feet) above sea level. The tropical forest in the lower tiers is home to an unrivalled variety of animal and plant life. Some 850 species of birds have been identified, and rare creatures such as the giant otter and giant armadillo also find refuge there.

"Manu protects a greater number of plant and animal species than any other such South American park (with the exception of remote Madidi in Bolivia)."

Charles A. Munn, Ph.D., Senior Conservation Zoologis

City of Cuzco   (5)

Situated in the Peruvian Andes, Cuzco developed, under the Inca ruler Pachacutec, into a complex urban centre with distinct religious and administrative functions. When the Spanish conquered it in the 16th century, they preserved the basic structure, but built Baroque churches and palaces over the ruins of the Inca city.

Historical Centre
of the City of Arequipa   (6)

Arequipa is at an altitude of 2,325 m (7,627 feet) in the Desert Mountains of the Andes. Its historic centre is built from volcanic sillar rock, a kind of white volcanic stone. This is why Arequipa is called the white city. It integrates European and native building techniques and characteristics, challenged by natural conditions.

"When the moon separated from the Earth, it forgot to take Arequipa."

Local Arequipa legend

Lines and Geoglyphs
of Nasca and Pampas de Jumana
(7)

In the arid Peruvian coastal plain, some 400 km (250 miles) south of Lima, the geo-glyphs of Nasca and the pampas of Jumana cover about 450 sq. km (111,200 acres). These lines, which were scratched on the surface of the ground between 500 BC and AD 500, are among archaeology's greatest enigmas because of their quantity, nature, size and continuity.

Chavin (8)

Chavín was once compared to the Olmecs and depicted as the Mother Civilization of the Andes. The archaeological site gave its name to the culture that developed between 1500 and 300 BC in this high valley of the Peruvian Andes. This former place of worship is one of the earliest and best-known pre-Columbian sites.

"Chavín de Huántar was among the most famous religious centres of the 'gentiles', comparable to Rome or Jerusalem in the Old World."

Antonio Vásquez de Expinosa,
early 17th century.

Huascaran National Park (9)

The park was established on July 1, 1975. In the Cordillera Blanca, the world's highest tropical mountain range, Mount Huascarán rises 6,768 m (22,205 feet) above sea level. The deep ravines watered by numerous torrents, the glacial lakes and the variety of the vegetation make it a site of spectacular beauty.

Historic Sanctuary of Machu Picchu (10)

Machu Picchu stands 2,430 m (7,972 feet) above sea level, in the middle of a tropical mountain forest, in an extraordinarily beautiful setting. At its height, it was probably the most amazing urban creation of the Inca Empire. Its giant walls, terraces and ramps seem to have been cut naturally in the continuous rock escarpments. The natural setting, on the eastern slopes of the Andes, encompasses the upper Amazon basin, with its rich diversity of flora and fauna.

"It fairly took my breath away.
What could this place be?
Why had no one given us any idea of it?"

Explorer Hiram Bingham III,
who rediscovered the Inca settlement
in 1911

Colombia

National Archaeological Park of Tierradentro (1)

Several monumental statues of human figures can be seen in the park, which also contains many hypogea dating from the 6th to the 10th century. These huge underground tombs are decorated with motifs that reproduce the internal decor of period homes. They reveal the social complexity and cultural wealth of a pre-Hispanic society in the northern Andes.

Los Katíos National Park (2)

Los Katíos National Park lies in the Chocó biogeographical ecoregion, encompassing the Darien Mountains, which straddle the Panamanian and Colombian border. The area comprises low hills, forests and humid plains. Exceptional biological diversity is found in the park, which is home to many threatened animal species, as well as many endemic plants.

San Agustín Archaeological Park (3)

Located between the high mountains of the Central and Western Cordilleras in the Río Magdalena Valley, San Agustín is the largest group of religious monuments and megalithic sculptures in South America. Gods and mythical animals are skilfully represented in styles ranging from abstract to realist. These works of art display the creativity and imagination of a northern Andean culture that flourished from the 1st to the 8th century.

Gorgona and Malpelo Islands (4)

The only protected oceanic area in the Pacific Colombian Ocean, the Sanctuary of Flora and Fauna of Malpelo Island is the summit of a submerged volcanic range. The archipelago originated in the Miocene Period, about 20 million years ago. Gorgona National Park is a continental island with well-developed coral reefs, tropical rain forests, important seabird areas and several habitats for the conservation of endangered species, including whales and sea turtles.

Port, Fortresses and Group of Monuments, Cartagena   (5)

Nestled in a bay in the Caribbean Sea, Cartagena boasts the most extensive fortifications in South America. The city was founded in 1533 and became one of the chief ports of the Spanish treasure fleet, which made it a prime target for English and French pirates and privateers. Many of Cartagena's fortifications, such as the Castle of San Felipe de Barajas and the walls around the Old City, still stand today.

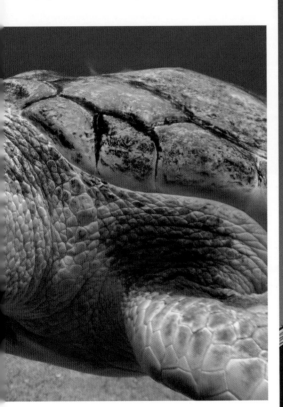

Historic Centre of Santa Cruz de Mompox   (6)

Founded in 1540 on the banks of the River Magdalena, Mompox played a key role in the Spanish colonization of northern South America. From the 16th to the 19th century, the city developed parallel to the river, with the main street acting as a dyke. The historic centre has preserved the harmony and unity of the urban landscape.

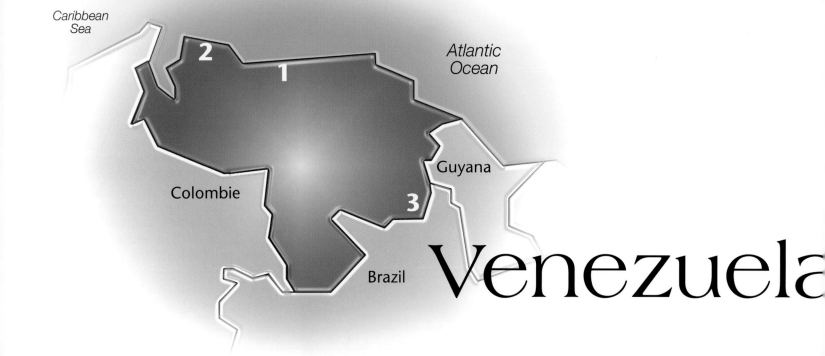

Caribbean
Sea

Atlantic
Ocean

2
1

Guyana

Colombie

3

Brazil

Venezuela

Ciudad Universitaria de Caracas (1)

Ciudad Universitaria was built between 1940 and 1960 according to the design of architect Carlos Raúl Villanueva. It is an outstanding example of the Modern Movement in architecture and it constitutes an ingenious interpretation of the concepts and spaces of colonial traditions, as well as an example of an open and ventilated solution, appropriate for its tropical environment.

Coro and its Port (2)

On the Caribbean coast at the base of the Península de Paraguaná stands Coro, one of Venezuela's oldest cities. Founded in 1527 by Juan de Ampies, it is the only surviving example of a rich fusion of local traditions with Spanish Mudéjar and Dutch architectural techniques. It features some 602 historic buildings.

Canaima National Park   (3)

On the Caribbean coast at the base of the Península de Paraguaná stands Coro, one of Venezuela's oldest cities. Founded in 1527 by Juan de Ampies, it is the only surviving example of a rich fusion of local traditions with Spanish Mudéjar and Dutch architectural techniques. It features some 602 historic buildings.

"While on a solo flight November 14, 1933, Angel flew into Devil's Canyon and saw for first time what was to become known to the world as Angel Falls."

Niece of Jimmie Angel and President of the Jimmie Angel Historical Project

Brazil

Brazilian Atlantic Islands: Fernando de Noronha and Atol das Rocas Reserves   (1)

Peaks of the Southern Atlantic submarine ridge form the Fernando de Noronha Archipelago and Rocas Atoll off the coast of Brazil. They represent a large proportion of the island surface of the South Atlantic, and their rich waters are extremely important for the breeding and feeding of tuna, sharks, turtles and marine mammals. The islands are home to the largest concentration of tropical seabirds in the Western Atlantic.

Historic Centre of the Town of Goiás   (2)

Located in the state that bears the same name, Goiás was called Vila Boa (Portuguese for "good village") in colonial times. The town is a testament to the occupation and colonization of the lands of central Brazil in the 18th and 19th centuries. Although modest, both public and private architecture form a harmonious whole.

Discovery Coast Atlantic Forest Reserves   (3)

The Discovery Coast, in the states of Bahia and Espírito Santo, consist of eight separate protected areas containing 112,000 ha (276,758 acres) of Atlantic forest and associated shrub (restingas). The site contains large numbers of rare and endemic species. Only these few scattered remnants of a once vast forest remain, making them an irreplaceable part of the world's forest heritage.

"Brazil's Atlantic forest is one of the richest areas in the world, but unfortunately it is a hot spot in terms of environmental threat."

Russell Mittermeier, President of U.S.-based Conservation International

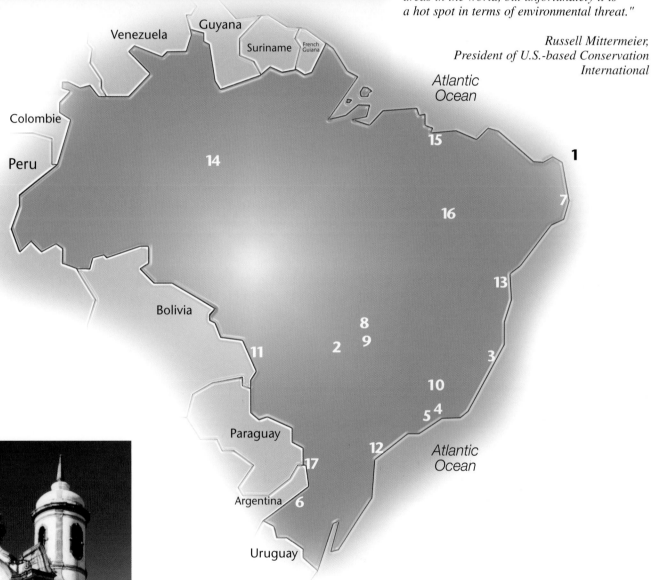

Historic Town of Ouro Preto   (4)

Founded at the end of the 17th century, Ouro Preto (Black Gold) was the focal point of the gold rush and Brazil's golden age in the 18th century. Completely preserved, the colonial architecture is a testament to past prosperity, with little signs of modern urban life.

"Paulista adventurer Antônio Dias pitched camp underneath a mountain the Indians called Itacolomi, with a thumb-shaped rock on its summit. Panning the streams nearby, he found 'black gold' (Ouro Prerto) and named his camp after it."

The legend of Ouro Preto's birth

Sanctuary of Bom Jesus do Congonhas (5)

This sanctuary in Minais Gerais, south of Belo Horizonte, was built in the second half of the 18th century. It consists of a church with a magnificent Rococo interior of Italian inspiration; an outdoor stairway decorated with statues of the prophets; and seven chapels illustrating the Stations of the Cross, in which the polychrome sculptures by Aleijadinho are masterpieces of a highly original, moving, expressive form of Baroque art.

Jesuit Missions of the Guaranis: San Ignacio Mini, Santa Ana, Nuestra Señora de Loreto and Santa Maria Mayor (Argentina), Ruins of Sao Miguel das Missoes (6)
(Site shared with Argentina)

The ruins lie at the heart of a tropical forest. They are the impressive remains of five Jesuit missions, built in the land of the Guaranis during the 17th and 18th centuries. Each is characterized by a specific layout and a different state of conservation.

Historic Centre of the Town of Olinda (7)

Olinda (meaning "oh beautiful") was founded in the 16th century by the Portuguese. Its history is linked to the sugarcane industry. Rebuilt after being looted by the Dutch, the town's basic urban fabric dates from the 18th century. The harmonious balance between the buildings, gardens, 20 Baroque churches, convents and numerous small passos (chapels) all contribute to Olinda's particular charm.

Cerrado Protected Areas: Chapada dos Veadeiros and Emas National Parks (8)

Cerrado, the central region of Brazil, is a true mosaic of different types of vegetation, soils, climates, and topographical features. It covers more than two million square kilometres (494,210,000 acres), spread out through ten states of the federation. It is one of the world's oldest and most diverse tropical ecosystems and home to 400 bird species, 67 mammal genera and 30 types of bats.

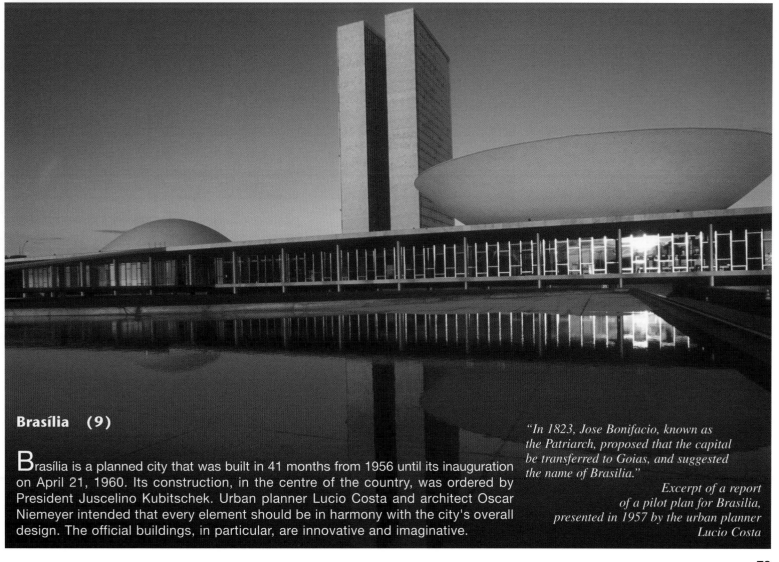

Brasília (9)

Brasília is a planned city that was built in 41 months from 1956 until its inauguration on April 21, 1960. Its construction, in the centre of the country, was ordered by President Juscelino Kubitschek. Urban planner Lucio Costa and architect Oscar Niemeyer intended that every element should be in harmony with the city's overall design. The official buildings, in particular, are innovative and imaginative.

"In 1823, Jose Bonifacio, known as the Patriarch, proposed that the capital be transferred to Goias, and suggested the name of Brasilia."

Excerpt of a report of a pilot plan for Brasilia, presented in 1957 by the urban planner Lucio Costa

Historic Centre of the Town of Diamantina (10)

Diamantina, a colonial village set like a jewel in a necklace of inhospitable rocky mountains, recalls the exploits of diamond prospectors in the 18th century and testifies to the triumph of human cultural and artistic endeavour over the environment.

Pantanal Conservation Area (11)

The Pantanal is one of the world's largest freshwater wetland ecosystems, covering 200,000 square kilometres (49,421,000 acres) in Brazil, Paraguay, and Bolivia. The association of the Amolar Mountains with the dominant freshwater wetland ecosystems confers to the site a uniquely important ecological gradient, as well as a dramatic landscape.

"The Pantanal has the greatest concentration of fauna in the Americas. People outside Brazil know only the Amazon ... it's a shame because the Pantanal is a very important ecological place."

Dr. Maria Tereza Jorge Pádua, former Director, Brazil's National Parks

Atlantic Forest Southeast Reserves (12)

The Reserves, in the states of Paraná and São Paulo, contain some of the best and most extensive examples of Atlantic forest in Brazil. The 25 protected areas that make up the site display the biological wealth and evolutionary history of the last remaining Atlantic forests. With its "mountains to the sea" attitudinal gradient, its estuary, wild rivers, karst and numerous waterfalls, the site also has exceptional scenic value.

Historic Centre of Salvador de Bahia   (13)

Located in the northeast coast of Brazil, Salvador de Bahia was the country's first capital, from 1549 to 1763. The city witnessed the blending of European, African and Amerindian cultures. It was also, from 1558, the first slave market in the New World, with slaves arriving to work on the sugar plantations. The city has managed to preserve many outstanding Renaissance buildings.

Central Amazon Conservation Complex   (14)

The Central Amazon Conservation Complex makes up the largest protected area in the Amazon Basin (over 6 million hectares, or 15 million acres) and is one of the planet's richest regions in terms of biodiversity. It is considered to be part of the planet's "lungs". The site protects key threatened species, including giant arapaima fish, the Amazonian manatee, the black caiman and two species of river dolphin. The rainforest in the Amazon Basin is under threat from logging, the clearing of land for farming and ranches, and water pollution.

"Today the world has come to realize the Amazon rainforest problems and everywhere, people are concerned about what they should do to help avoid its destruction."

The Amazon Rainforest Organization

Historic Centre of São Luis   (15)

The city is on an island at the delta of the Pindaré and Itapecuru rivers, in a bay just off the Atlantic Ocean. The late 17th-century core of this historic town, founded by the French and occupied by the Dutch before coming under Portuguese rule, has preserved its original rectangular street plan in its entirety.

"He who falls asleep in São Luís,
wakes up as a poet."

Local Sao Luis legend

Serra da Capivara National Park (16)

In the north-east of Brazil, the park has many ancient caves bearing cave paintings, some of which are more than 25,000 years old. They are an outstanding testimony to one of the oldest human communities in South America.

Iguaçu National Park   (17)

(Site shared with Argentina)

The area covered by this park includes one of the world's largest and most impressive waterfalls: Iguaçu Falls, extending over some 2,700 m (8,858 feet). The park is home to many rare and endangered species of flora and fauna, among them the giant otter and the giant anteater. The clouds of spray produced by the waterfall are conducive to the growth of lush vegetation.

"I had seen photographs many
years ago, but no one can know how
it is without coming here and seeing it.
It is unbelievably beautiful."

U. S. President Bill Clinton, after visiting
Iguaçu Falls in August 2001

Suriname

Central Suriname Nature Reserve (1)

This reserve comprises 1.6 million ha (3,953,686 acres) of primary tropical forest in west-central Suriname. It protects the upper watershed of the Coppename River and the headwaters of the Lucie, Oost, Zuid, Saramaccz, and Gran Rio rivers. The site contains a rich diversity of plant and animal species, many of which are endemic to the Guyana Shield and are globally threatened.

"This area may contain answers to questions we have not yet learned to ask."

James Thorcell,
site explorer for UNESCO

Historic Inner City of Paramaribo (2)

Capital of Suriname, Paramaribo is found on the Suriname River, approximately 15 km inland from the Atlantic Ocean. This former Dutch colonial town from the 17th and 18th centuries is rooted on the northern coast of tropical South America. Its buildings illustrate the gradual fusion of Dutch architectural influence with traditional local techniques and materials.

Chile

Peru

Bolivia

5

Pacific
Ocean

Argentina

2

1
4

3

Atlantic
Ocean

Historic Quarter of the Seaport City of Valparaíso (1)

Valparaiso played an important geopolitical role in the second half of the 19th century, when it served as a major stopover for ships travelling between the Atlantic and Pacific oceans via the Straights of Magellan. It bears exceptional witness to the early phase of globalization. Situated in its natural amphitheatre-like setting, Valparaiso presents an excellent example of late 19th-century urban and architectural development in Latin America.

Rapa Nui National Park   (2)

In the remote southern Pacific Ocean, 3,515 km (2,184 miles) west of continental Chile, Rapa Nui, also known as Easter Island bears witness to a unique cultural phenomenon. A society of Polynesian origin settled there c. AD 300 and established a powerful, imaginative and original tradition of monumental sculptures and architecture, free from any external influence.

"The stone images at first caused us to be struck with astonishment, because we could not comprehend how it was possible that these people … had been able to erect such images."

Dutch explorer Jacob Roggeveen, first European to visit the island, 1772

Churches of Chiloé   (3)

Second largest island of South America, Chiloé is home to churches that stand as a unique example in Latin America of an outstanding form of ecclesiastical wooden architecture. They represent a tradition initiated by the Jesuit Peripatetic Mission in the 17th and 18th centuries, maintained and enriched by the Franciscans during the 19th century and still prevailing today.

Sewell Mining Camp (4)

In 1905, the Chilean government granted official authorization to the Braden Cooper Co. to operate El Teniente copper deposit. Until the middle of the following century, the established camp was small and developed in a scattered manner, lacking an ordering core. This first sector was called "Pueblo Hundido" (Sunken Town). Then, another section arose, known as "El Establecimiento" (The Establishment). By 1909, the first sulfuric acid factory was constructed. The majority of the workers lived in "colectivos" (collective houses) for single men, although there were some houses for married ones.

"This site is a national monument, and the government hopes to do everything in its power to have it declared a World Heritage Site soon, because it holds a special place in our history. Here, a culture of work and struggle was formed - a way of life that formed various generations and marked people's memories indelibly."

Michelle Bachelet,
President of Chile,
May 2006

Humberstone and Santa Laura Saltpeter Works (5)

Out in the remote desert of Pampa in northern Chile, one of the driest places on earth, Humberstone and Santa Laura contain over 200 former saltpetre works where employees from Chile, Peru and Bolivia lived in company towns and forged a distinctive communal pampinos culture. The site was placed on the List of World Heritage in Danger to help mobilize resources for its conservation.

Bolivia

Fuerte de Samaipata (2)

The archaeological site of Samaipata consists of two parts: the hill, with its many carvings, believed to have been the ceremonial centre of the old town (14th–16th century), and the area to the south of the hill, which formed the administrative and residential district. The huge sculptured rock dominating the town below is a unique testimony to pre-Hispanic traditions and beliefs, and has no parallel anywhere in the Americas.

Noel Kempff Mercado National Park (1)

Located in north-eastern Bolivia, this national park is one of the largest and most intact in the Amazon Basin. The site contains an array of habitat types including evergreen rainforests, palm forests, cerrado, swamps, savannahs, gallery forests, and semi-deciduous dry forests. The cerrado habitats found on the Huanchaca Meseta have been isolated for millions of years, providing an ideal living laboratory for the study of the evolution of these ecosystems.

City of Potosi (3)

Founded in 1545, at an altitude of 3,967 meters (13,015 feet), Potosi is claimed to be the highest city in the world. It lies beneath the Cerro Rico ("Rich Mountain"), a mountain of silver ore that has always dominated the city. In the 16th century, this area was regarded as the world's largest industrial complex. The extraction of silver ore relied on a series of hydraulic mills.

"The Cantumarca natives were convinced that the devil had hidden in a gulch called The Door near Potosí. It was said that any person who walked there died.
The religious and Spaniards spread the rumour that Saint Bartolomé went to The Door and defeated Satan."

Myth of San Bartolomé and Ch'utillos Festivity

Jesuit Missions of the Chiquitos (4)

Between 1696 and 1760, six ensembles of reducciones (settlements of Christianized Indians), inspired by the "ideal cities" of the 16th-century philosophers, were founded by the Jesuits in a style that married Catholic architecture with local traditions. The six that remain make up a living heritage on the former territory of the Chiquitos.

Historic City of Sucre   (5)

Lying at an altitude of 2,800 m (9,200 ft), Sucre, the first capital of Bolivia, was founded by the Spanish in the first half of the 16th century. Its many well-preserved 16th-century religious buildings, such as San Lázaro, San Francisco and Santo Domingo, illustrate the blending of local architectural traditions with styles imported from Europe.

"At its installation on July 5, 1825, in the city of Chuquisaca, the Assembly proclaimed their independence, changing the name of Chuquisaca to 'Sucre' and that of Alto Perú to 'Bolivia'."

In honour of independence leader and President Antonio José de Sucre (1795 - 1830) Excerpt of Glory on Simón Bolívar, The South-American Washington

Tiwanaku: Spiritual and Political Centre of the Tiwanaku Culture (6)

The city of Tiwanaku, capital of a powerful pre-Hispanic empire that dominated a large area of the southern Andes and beyond, reached its apogee between 500 and 900 AD. Its monumental remains testify to the cultural and political significance of this civilisation, which is distinct from any of the other pre-Hispanic empires of the Americas. The ruins of the ancient city are on the eastern shore of Lake Titicaca, about 72 km (44 miles) west of La Paz.

"Although dozens of national and international projects began to unlock Tiwanaku's secrets during the last century, we are only recently beginning to piece together the puzzle..."

The University of Pennsylvania Museum of Archaeology and Anthropology

Paraguay

Jesuit Missions of La Santisima Trinidad de Parana and Jesus de Tavarangue   (1)

In addition to their artistic interest, these missions are a reminder of the Jesuits' Christianization of the Río de la Plata basin in the 17th and 18th centuries, with the accompanying social and economic initiatives.

Historic Quarter of the City of Colonia del Sacramento (1)

Colonia del Sacramento, facing Buenos Aires, is the oldest town in Uruguay. Founded by the Portuguese in 1680 on the Río de la Plata, the city was of strategic importance in resisting the Spanish. After being disputed for a century, it was finally lost by its founders. The well-preserved urban landscape illustrates the successful fusion of the Portuguese, Spanish and post-colonial styles.

Uruguay

Paraguay

Brazil

Argentina

1

Atlantic Ocean

Argentina

Los Glaciares (1)

Part of Patagonia, Los Glaciares National Park comprises an area of about 6000 km2 (1,482,630 acres). It is an area of exceptional natural beauty, with rugged, towering mountains and numerous glacial lakes, including Lake Argentino, which is 160 km (100 miles) long. At its farthest end, three glaciers meet to dump their effluvia into the milky grey glacial water, launching massive igloo icebergs into the lake with thunderous splashes.

"In my wanderings in the south during those years, I saw exceptionally beautiful places and more than once pondered on the importance that the Nation set aside portions for present and future generations."

Argentine Explorer Dr. Francisco Pascacio Moreno (1852 – 1919)

Cueva de las Manos, Río Pinturas (2)

This site contains an exceptional assemblage of cave art, executed between 13,000 and 9,500 years ago. It takes its name ("Cave of the Hands") from the stencilled outlines of human hands in the cave, but there are also many depictions of animals, such as guanacos (Lama guanicoe), still commonly found in the region, as well as hunting scenes.

Ischigualasto / Talampaya Natural Parks (3)

These two contiguous parks, extending over 275,300 ha (680,280 acres) in the desert region on the western border of the Sierra Pampeanas, in central Argentina, contain the most complete continental fossil record known from the Triassic Period (245-208 million years ago). Six geological formations in the parks feature fossils of a wide range of ancestors of mammals, dinosaurs and plants.

Jesuit Block and Estancias of Córdoba (4)

Located at the foothills of the Sierra Chica mountains on the Suquía River, Córdoba contains the core buildings of the Jesuit system: the university, the church and residence of the Society of Jesus, and the college. This site is an exceptional example of the fusion of European and indigenous values and cultures during the 17th and 18th centuries in South America.

Quebrada de Humahuaca   (5)

Quebrada de Humahuaca follows the line of a major cultural route, the Camino Inca, along the spectacular valley of the Rio Grande, from its source in the cold high desert plateau of the High Andean lands to its confluence with the Rio Leone some 150 km (95 miles) to the south. This route has been used over the past 10,000 years as a crucial passage for the transport of people and ideas from the high Andean lands to the plains.

"I've been guiding groups through these paths for the last ten years and each new travel is like the first one. Seeing how people are astonished by the wild and incredible sightseeing, the local food and the ancient traditional holidays…"

Local guide and explorer Hubert Alem

Península Valdés   (6)

This peninsula covers about 3,625 km2 (895,757 acres) in Patagonia. It is a site of global significance for the conversation of marine mammals. Península Valdés contains very important natural habitats for the in-situ conservation of several threatened species of outstanding universal value.

"Nature in these desolate scenes … moves us more deeply than in others."

British-Argentine author
Henry Hudson
(1841 - 1922)

Europe

The Old Continent is the cradle of many significant empires and cultures that have changed and moulded the face of our planet. No other region in the world can boast such a concentrated wealth of human heritage. In many places, the heart and soul of glory days and dark ages still linger in vestiges of the past. Indeed, Europe speaks to us with stories of great and courageous people who, through centuries of amazing engineering achievements, built solid forts, meticulous castles and splendid cities. Every culture and every nation of Europe offers a rich and distinctive past.

Travelling through Europe is like taking a fabulous cultural journey through centuries of human achievement and human folly. It is also a study in geographical contrasts, where natural borders have played significant historical roles: the Alps, Pyrenees and Carpathian Mountains have acted as geopolitical barriers; magnificent coastlines have been tainted by the blood of valiant soldiers; and the crystal waters of lakes, rivers and seas have nourished mythology and countless legends. So the stories of Old Europe are told not only through its Baroque and Renaissance monuments, but also with its natural wonders.

While fierce combat amongst Europeans has resulted in irreplaceable losses in terms of cultural heritage, many gems of our collective history have been saved by the grace of enlightened warriors who recognized the work of past builders. Europe now seems more united than ever, as borders have fallen and East and West continue to come together. All of these nations and peoples now seem to be advancing in the same direction, with different pasts building one common future.

Iceland

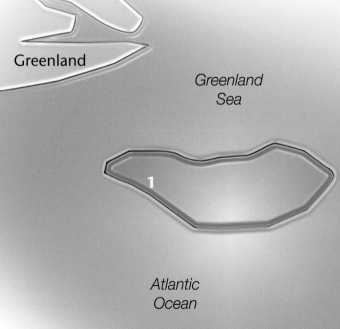

Greenland

Greenland
Sea

1

Atlantic
Ocean

United
Kingdom

Ireland

Thingvellir National Park   (1)

Tingvellir is located in south-western Iceland, near the peninsula of Reykjanes and the Hengill volcanic area. This is the national park where the Althing – an open-air assembly that represented the whole of Iceland – was established in 930 and continued to meet until 1798. Over two weeks a year, the assembly set laws, seen as a covenant between free men, and settled disputes. The Althing has deep historical and symbolic associations for the people of Iceland.

"Tingvellir brings together some of the most striking and beautiful aspects of Icelandic nature, while also being the site of many of the most important events in Icelandic history."

*Icelander teacher Guomundur Davíosson
about Thingvellir, in 1913,
before it became a national park*

Ireland

Atlantic Ocean

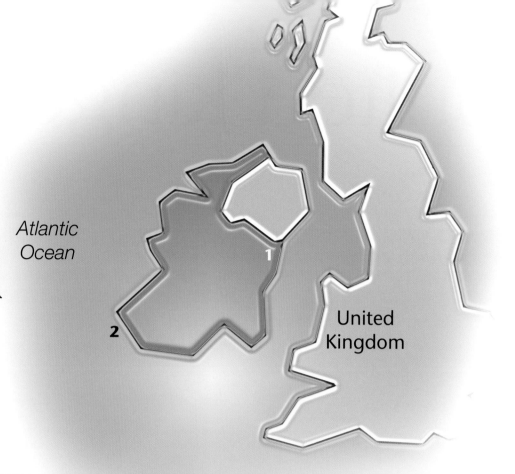

1

2

United Kingdom

Archaeological Ensemble of the Bend of the Boyne (1)

The three main prehistoric sites of the Brú na Bóinne Complex – Newgrange, Knowth and Dowth – are situated on the north bank of the River Boyne, 50 km (30 miles) north of Dublin. This is Europe's largest and most important concentration of prehistoric megalithic art. The monuments there had social, economic, religious and funerary functions.

Skellig Michael (2)

Also known as Great Skellig, this monastic complex, perched since 588 on the steep sides of the rocky island of Skellig Michael, some 12 km (7 miles) off the coast of south-west Ireland, illustrates the very Spartan existence of the first Irish Christians. This site is exceptionally well preserved.

*"An incredible, impossible, mad place.
I tell you, the thing does not belong to any
world that you and I have lived and worked in;
it is part of our dream world."*

*Irish playwright and Nobel Prize
for Literature winner
George Bernard Shaw (1856 – 1950),
about Skellig Michael in 1910*

United kingdom

Hadrian's Wall, frontiers of the Roman Empire   (1)

Hadrian's Wall was a stone and turf fortification, built on the orders of the Emperor Hadrian by the Romans across the width of Great Britain to prevent military raids by the Pictish tribes of Scotland to the north. Construction started in 122 and was largely completed within ten years, with soldiers from all three of the occupying Roman legions participating in the work. The 118-km-long (73 miles) wall is a striking example of the defensive techniques and geopolitical strategies of ancient Rome. This World Heritage site includes also the " Roman Limes ", stretching from the Atlantic Coast to Black Sea in Europe and vestiges in North Africa.

*"Just when you think you are at the world's end, you see smoke rising from east to west as far as
the eye can turn... one long, low, rising and falling, and hiding and showing line of towers... that is the wall."*

*British author Rudyard Kipling,
from "Puck of Pook's Hill"*

Durham Castle and Cathedral (2)

In the north-east of England, Durham Cathedral was built in the late 11th and early 12th centuries. It attests to the importance of the early Benedictine monastic community and is the largest and finest example of Norman architecture in England. Behind the cathedral stands the castle, an ancient Norman fortress that served as the residence of the prince-bishops of Durham.

"Durham is one of the great experiences of Europe to the eyes of those who appreciate architecture, and to the minds of those who understand architecture."

German-born British art historian Sir Nikolaus Pevsner (1902 – 1983)

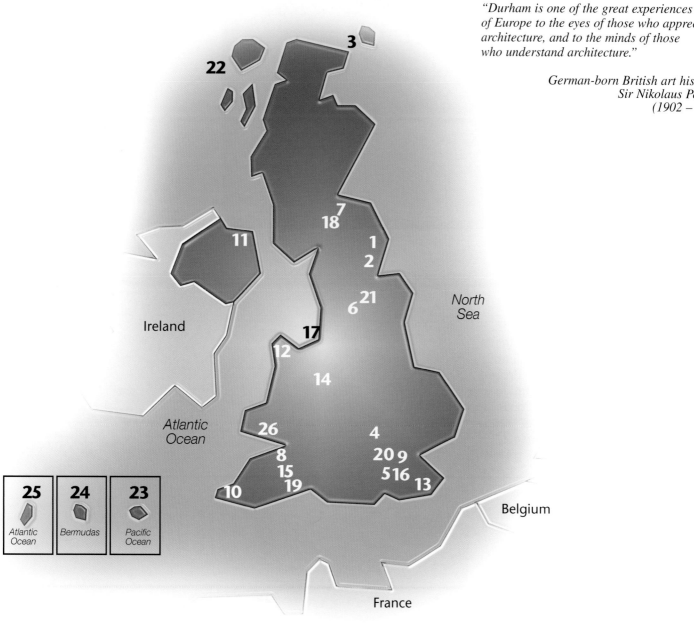

Heart of Neolithic Orkney　(3)

Located in the region of Orkney – 200 small islands 16 kilometres (10 miles) north of Caithness, in northern Scotland – this group of Neolithic monuments consists of a large chambered tomb, two ceremonial stone circles and a settlement, together with a number of unexcavated burial, ceremonial and settlement sites. The group constitutes a major prehistoric cultural landscape providing a graphic depiction of life in this remote archipelago some 5,000 years ago.

Blenheim Palace　(4)

Near Oxford, Blenheim Palace stands in a romantic park created by the famous landscape gardener, "Capability" Brown. It was presented by the English nation to John Churchill, first Duke of Marlborough, in recognition of his victory in 1704 over French and Bavarian troops. Built between 1705 and 1722 and characterized by an eclectic style and a return to national roots, it is a perfect example of an 18th-century princely dwelling.

"...as we passed through the entrance archway and the lovely scenery burst upon me, Randolph (Churchill) said with pardonable pride: This is the finest view in England."

*Jeanette Jerome
(Lady Randolph Churchill, 1854 – 1921),
mother of British Prime Minister
Winston Churchill, about Blenheim*

Royal Botanic Gardens, Kew (5)

Often referred to simply as Kew Gardens, this historic landscape located in southwest London features elements that illustrate significant periods of the art of gardens from the 18th to the 20th century. The gardens house botanic collections that have been considerably enriched through this period. Since their creation in 1759, the gardens have made a significant and uninterrupted contribution to the study of plant diversity and economic botany.

Saltaire (6)

Saltaire, West Yorkshire, is a complete and well-preserved industrial village of the second half of the 19th century. It was founded by Sir Titus Salt to provide better sanitary arrangements for his workers. Its textile mills, public buildings and workers' housing are built in a harmonious style of high architectural standards. The urban plan survives intact, giving a vivid impression of Victorian philanthropic paternalism.

> *"...that would enjoy the beauties of the neighbourhood, and who would be a well fed, contented, and happy*
> *body of operatives... nothing should be spared to render the dwellings of the operatives a pattern to the country."*
>
> *Sir Titus Salt*
> *(1803 - 1876),*
> *about building a model village*

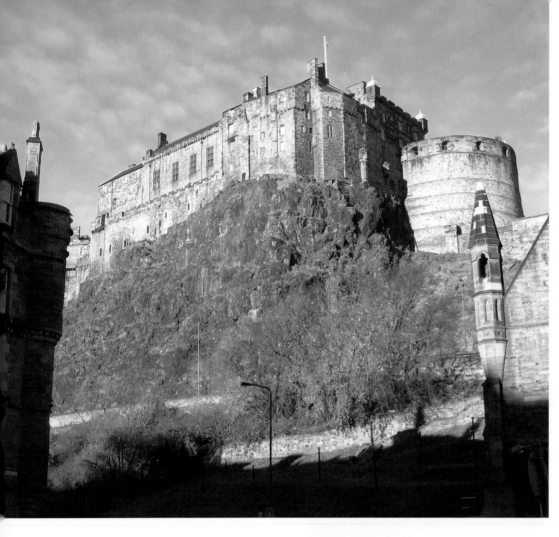

Old and New Towns of Edinburgh (7)

Edinburgh has been the Scottish capital since the 15th century. It has two distinct areas: the Old Town, dominated by a medieval fortress, and the neoclassical New Town, whose development from the 18th century onwards had a far-reaching influence on European urban planning. The New Town was a solution to the problem of an increasingly crowded Old Town. The harmonious juxtaposition of these two contrasting historic areas, each with many important buildings, is what gives the city its unique character.

City of Bath (8)

Founded by the Romans as a thermal spa in southwest England, close to the city of Bristol, Bath became an important centre of the wool industry in the Middle Ages. In the 18th century, under George III, it developed into an elegant town with neoclassical Palladian buildings, which blend harmoniously with the Roman baths.

Tower of London (9)

The massive White Tower is a typical example of Norman military architecture, whose influence was felt throughout the kingdom. In 1078, William the Conquero ordered this White Tower to be built on the River Thames to protect London and assert his power. The Tower of London – an imposing fortress with many layers of history, which has become one of the symbols of royalty – was built around the White Tower.

"...a citadel to defend or command the city, a royal palace for assemblies or treaties, a prison of state for the most dangerous offenders; the only place of coinage for all England."

British historian John Stow
(1525 - 1605),
about the Tower during
the reign of Elizabeth I

Cornwall and West Devon Mining Landscape (10)

This part of the United Kingdom was transformed in the 18th and early 19th centuries as a result of the rapid growth of pioneering copper and tin mining. In the early 19th century, the region was producing two thirds of the world's supply of copper. The substantial remains are a testimony to the contribution Cornwall and West Devon made to the industrial revolution in the rest of Britain, and to the fundamental influence the area had on the mining world at large. Cornwall was locked into the global economy at an early stage. By the 1820s, Cornish miners were being recruited for work in Latin America. Within a generation, a flourishing culture of emigration had been created and links with North America and Australia were forged.

Giant's Causeway and Causeway Coast (11)

The Giant's Causeway lies at the foot of the basalt cliffs, along the seacoast on the edge of the Antrim plateau in Northern Ireland. It is made up of some 40,000 massive black basalt columns sticking out of the sea. The dramatic sight has inspired legends of giants striding over the sea to Scotland. This striking landscape was caused by volcanic activity during the Tertiary, some 50-60 million years ago.

"The giant Finn McCool built the causeway to walk to Scotland to fight his Scottish equivalent Benandonner."

Irish legend

Castles and Town Walls of King Edward in Gwynedd (12)

The castles of Beaumaris and Harlech and the fortified complexes of Caernarfon and Conwy are located in the former principality of Gwynedd, in northern Wales. These extremely well preserved monuments are examples of the colonization and defence projects carried out throughout the reign of Edward I (1272–1307). They are largely the work of the greatest military engineer of the time, James of St. George.

Canterbury Cathedral, Saint Augustine's Abbey, and Saint Martin's Church   (13)

Canterbury, in Kent, has been the seat of the spiritual head of the Church of England for nearly five centuries. The cathedral is one of the oldest and most famous Christian structures in England. Canterbury's other important monuments are the modest Church of St. Martin – the oldest church in England – and the ruins of the Abbey of St. Augustine.

Ironbridge Gorge   (14)

Originally called the Severn Gorge, it now takes its name from the village of Ironbridge, which is in turn named after its famous iron bridge, the first of its kind in the world and a monument to the Industrial Revolution. Built in 1779, the bridge had a considerable influence on developments in technology and architecture.

*"After the Bridge survived the great floods
of 1795, cast iron was used widely
and imaginatively in construction of bridges,
buildings and aqueducts."*

Ironbridge Gorge Museums

Stonehenge, Avebury and Associated Sites   (15)

Stonehenge and Avebury, in Wiltshire, are among the most famous groups of megaliths in the world. The two sanctuaries consist of circles of menhirs arranged in a pattern whose astronomical significance is still being explored. These holy places and the nearby Neolithic sites are an incomparable testimony to prehistoric times.

Maritime Greenwich   (16)

The ensemble of buildings at Greenwich (an outlying district of London) and the park in which they are set symbolize English artistic and scientific endeavour in the 17th and 18th centuries. The Queen's House (by Inigo Jones) was the first Palladian building in England, while the complex that was until recently the Royal Naval College was designed by Christopher Wren.

Liverpool -
Maritime Mercantile City   (17)

Six areas in the historic centre and docklands of the Maritime Mercantile City of Liverpool bear witness to the development of one of the world's major trading centres in the 18th and 19th centuries. Liverpool played an important role in the growth of the British Empire. The city was a pioneer in the development of modern dock technology, transport systems, and port management.

"I have heard of the greatness of Liverpool but the reality far surpasses the expectations "

Prince Albert
at the dock,
July 30, 1846

New Lanark   (18)

New Lanark was founded in 1784 around its new mills next to the town of Lanark. The small 18th-century village is set in a sublime Scottish landscape where the philanthropist and Utopian idealist Robert Owen moulded a model industrial community in the early 19th century. The imposing cotton mill buildings, the spacious and well-designed workers' housing, and the dignified educational institute and school still testify to Owen's humanism.

Dorset and East Devon Coast (19)

The cliff exposures along the Dorset and East Devon coast provide an almost continuous sequence of rock formations spanning the Mesozoic Era, or some 185 million years of the Earth's history. The area's important fossil sites and classic coastal geomorphologic features have contributed to the study of earth sciences for over 300 years. The region is also famous for its picturesque coastline.

"The coast provides a unique walk through time with an amazing wealth of fossil sites and landforms."

Devon County Councillor
David Morrish

Westminster Palace, Westminster Abbey and Saint Margaret's Church   (20)

Also known as the Houses of Parliament, the Palace lies on the west bank of the River Thames in London. The oldest extant part of the Palace, Westminster Hall, dates to 1097. Most of the present structure dates to the nineteenth century. The Palace was rebuilt after it was almost entirely destroyed by fire in 1834. It is a fine example of neo-Gothic architecture. The exterior of the Palace of Westminster, especially the clock tower called "Big Ben", is one of the most visited tourist attractions in London.

Studley Royal Park, Including the Ruins of Fountains Abbey (21)

A striking landscape was created around the ruins of the Cistercian Fountains Abbey and Fountains Hall Castle, in Yorkshire. The 18th-century landscaping, gardens and canal, the 19th-century plantations and vistas, and the neo-Gothic castle of Studley Royal Park, make this an outstanding site.

Saint Kilda (22)

St. Kilda is an island group that has fascinated travellers, historians and dreamers for centuries. It is a volcanic archipelago with spectacular landscapes, situated off the coast of the Hebrides. The group comprises the islands of Hirta, Dun, Soay and Boreray. It has some of the highest cliffs in Europe, inhabited by large colonies of rare and endangered species of birds, especially puffins and gannets.

"Whatever he studies, the future observer of St. Kilda will be haunted the rest of his life by the place, and tantalized by the impossibility of describing it to those who have not seen it."

British naturalist James Fisher, 1947

Henderson Island (23)

Lying in the eastern South Pacific, Henderson is one of the few atolls in the world whose ecology has been practically untouched by a human presence. Its isolated location provides the ideal context for studying the dynamics of insular evolution and natural selection. Although Henderson is virtually uninhabitable, in 1957, a man lived the life of a castaway on the island for approximately two months, accompanied by a pet chimpanzee.

"The most memorable feature of the island was the coral reef, not the island itself, though it was beautiful in a stark and desolate way."

Larry McCabe,
who visited the island in 1978

Historic Town of Saint George and Related Fortifications, Bermuda (24)

St. George was the first settlement on the island of Bermuda, and is today the oldest continuously inhabited English-speaking settlement in the New World. It is now in large part a museum town. Founded in 1612, the town is an outstanding example of the earliest English urban settlements in the New World. Its fortifications illustrate the development of English military engineering from the 17th to the 20th century.

Gough and Inaccessible Islands (25)

Two isolated volcanic islands of the south Atlantic Ocean, Inaccessible Island and Gough Island are wildlife reserves. The spectacular cliffs of each island, towering above the ocean, are free of introduced mammals and home to one of the world's largest colonies of sea birds. Gough Island features two endemic species of land birds, the Gough Moorhen and the Gough Bunting , as well as 12 endemic species of plants. For its part, Inaccessible Island boasts two birds, eight plants and at least ten invertebrates that are endemic to the island.

"House mice, introduced accidentally on Gough by sealers during the 19th century, have become extremely abundant in all the habitats of the island. They have evolved a large body size and are thought to have a significant impact on the island's invertebrates and plants. But even more frightening, it has recently been shown that they predate on chicks of winter breeding sea birds, amongst which is the globally threatened and almost endemic Tristan Albatross."

Marie-Helene Burle,
overwintering research biologist for
the Royal Society for the Protection of Birds
and the University of Cape Town

Blaenavon Industrial Landscape (26)

The area around Blaenavon is evidence of the pre-eminence of South Wales as the world's major producer of iron and coal in the 19th century. The Blaenavon landscape constitutes an exceptional illustration in material form of the social and economic structure of 19th century industry.

"At Blaenavon, the parallel development of coal mining and iron making represented one of the key dynamic forces of the Industrial Revolution, which has self-evidently changed and moulded the way all peoples of the world now live."

British Arts Minister
Alan Howarth,
December 5, 2000

Netherlands

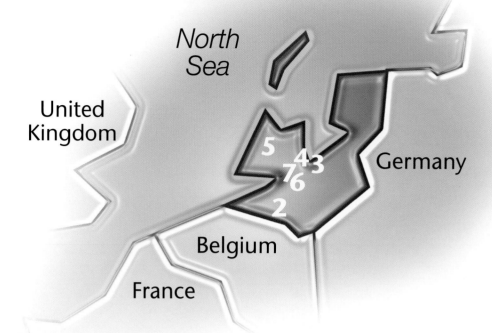

North Sea

United Kingdom

5 4 3
7 6
2

Germany

Belgium

France

Venezuela

Historic Area of Willemstad, Inner City and Harbour, Netherlands Antilles   (1)

This town was established in 1634, when the Dutch captured the island from Spain, under the name of Punda. The Dutch established a trading settlement at this fine natural harbour on the Caribbean island of Curaçao in 1634. The historic area of Willemstad is a European colonial ensemble of outstanding value and integrity in the Caribbean, illustrating the organic growth of a multicultural community over three centuries.

Mill Network at Kinderdijk-Elshout (2)

This mill network is an outstanding man-made landscape that bears powerful testimony to human ingenuity and fortitude over nearly a millennium in draining and protecting an area by the development and application of hydraulic technology. Construction of hydraulic works for the drainage of land for agriculture and settlement purposes began in the Middle Ages, and it has continued non-stop to the present day.

"During the Saint Elizabeth flood of 1421, the cradle with a child on the waves was kept in balance by a cat and stranded on the slope of a dike."

Legend behind the name Kinderdijk
(Child's Dike)

Schokland and Surroundings (3)

Schokland was a peninsula that, by the 15th century, had become an island. Occupied and then abandoned as the sea encroached, it had to be evacuated in 1859. But following the draining of the Zuider Zee, it has, since the 1940s, formed part of the land reclaimed from the sea. Schokland has vestiges of human habitation going back to prehistoric times. It symbolizes the heroic, age-old struggle of the people of the Netherlands against the encroachment of the waters.

Ir.D.F. Woudagemaal - D.F. Wouda Steam Pumping Station   (4)

Opened in 1920, this is the largest steam-pumping station ever built and it is still in operation. It represents the high point of the contribution made by Dutch engineers and architects in protecting their people and land against the natural forces of water.

Droogmakerij de Beemster - Beemster Polder -   (5)

Located in north-western Netherlands, the Beemster Polder, dating from the early 17th century, is the oldest area of reclaimed land in the Netherlands. It has preserved intact its well-ordered landscape of fields, roads, canals, dykes and settlements, laid out in accordance with classical and Renaissance planning principles.

Rietveld Schröderhuis - Rietveld Schröder House   (6)

Designed by the architect Gerrit Thomas Rietveld and built in Utrecht in 1924, Rietveld Schröder House is an icon of the Modern Movement in architecture. This small family house is a pioneer in flexible spatial arrangement, and it is the only building to have been built completely in accordance with the architectural principles of De Stijl.

"The opposites that as living beings we are most interested in, perhaps, are tranquillity and excitement, or repose and stir. Tranquillity or repose by itself is boredom, uselessness. Excitement or stir by itself is uncertainty, sloppiness, fidgetiness, indecisiveness, the plague of unwilling motion. Tranquillity and excitement are one in all art."

Dutch designer and architect
Gerrit Rietveld, (1888 – 1964)

Defence Line of Amsterdam   (7)

Extending 135 km (84 miles) around the city of Amsterdam, this defence line, built between 1883 and 1920, is the only example of a fortification based on the principle of controlling the waters. Since the 16th century, the people of the Netherlands have used their expert knowledge of hydraulic engineering for defence purposes.

"In 1672, the Prince of Orange made inundations and defence works around Amsterdam, and because of these, Louis XIV thought the position was impossible to attack."

René G.A. Ros,
Military Heritage Greater-Amsterdam
Foundation

Belgium

Flemish Béguinages (1)

The Béguines were women who dedicated their lives to God without retiring from the world. In the 13th century, they founded the béguinages, enclosed communities designed to meet their spiritual and material needs. The Flemish béguinages are architectural ensembles composed of houses, churches, ancillary buildings and green spaces, with a layout of either urban or rural origin and built in styles specific to the Flemish cultural region.

The Four Lifts
on the Canal du Centre and
their Environs, La Louvière
and Le Roeulx, Hainault   (2)

The four hydraulic boatlifts on this short stretch of the historic Canal du Centre are industrial monuments of the highest quality. Together with the canal itself and its associated structures, they constitute a remarkably well-preserved and complete example of a late-19th-century industrial landscape.

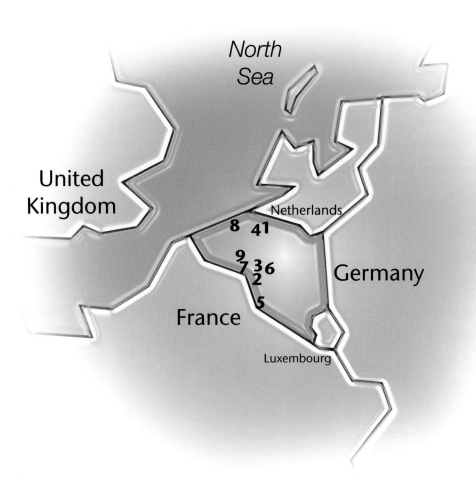

Grand-Place, Brussels　(3)

The heart of Brussels, the Grand-Place is a remarkably homogeneous body of public and private buildings, dating mainly from the late 17th century. It represents an outstanding example of the eclectic and highly successful blending of architectural and artistic styles that characterizes the culture and society of this region.

"The most beautiful theatre in the world."

French cinematographer
Jean Cocteau (1889 -1963),
speaking of the Grand-Place

Plantin-Moretus House-Workshops-Museum Complex　(4)

Situated in Antwerp, one of the three leading cities of early European printing along with Paris and Venice, the Plantin-Moretus Complex is associated with the history of typography, from its invention to its expansion throughout the world. The name of the complex refers to the greatest printer-publisher of the second half of the 16th century, Christophe Plantin (1520-1589). The monument is of outstanding architectural value. It contains exhaustive evidence of the life and work of what was the most prolific printing and publishing house in Europe in the late 16th century.

"Here lies Christopher Plantin,
not only typographer of kings,
but king of typographers."

Christopher Plantin's epitaph
in Antwerp

Neolithic Flint Mines at Spiennes, Mons (5)

Covering more than 100 ha (247 acres), these are the largest and earliest concentration of ancient mines in Europe. They are also remarkable for the diversity of technological solutions used for extraction, and for the fact that they are directly linked to a settlement of the same period.

"The men who started to dig mines in Spiennes, some 6,000 years ago, are regarded as the oldest miners in the world."

La Société de recherche préhistoriqueen Hainaut (SRPH)

Belfries of Belgium and France (7)

(Site shared with France)

The 30 belfries in Flanders and Wallonia, found in an urban setting, are imposing bell-towers of medieval origin, generally attached to the town hall and occasionally to a church. They are potent symbols of the transition from feudalism to the mercantile urban society that played a vital role in the development of late medieval Europe.

Major Townhouses of the Architect Victor Horta, Brussels (6)

Victor Horta (1861 - 1947) was a Belgian architect famous for working in the Art Nouveau style. Located in Brussels, the four major townhouses – Hôtel Tassel, Hôtel Solvay, Hôtel van Eetvelde, and Maison & Atelier Horta – are some of the most remarkable pioneering works of late-19th-century architecture. The townhouses of Victor Horta in Brussels bear exceptional witness to his radical new approach.

Historic Centre of Brugge (8)

Brugge is an outstanding example of a medieval settlement that has maintained its historic fabric as it has evolved over the centuries, and where original brick Gothic constructions form part of the town's identity. The city is closely associated with the school of Flemish Primitive painting.

"Somewhere within the dingy casing lay the ancient city like a notorious jewel, too stared at, talked of, trafficked over."

English novelist Graham Greene (1904 - 1991)

Notre-Dame Cathedral in Tournai (9)

The Cathedral of Notre-Dame was built in the first half of the 12th century. In its imposing dimensions, it is an outstanding example of the great edifices of the school of the northern Seine, precursors to the vastness of the Gothic cathedrals.

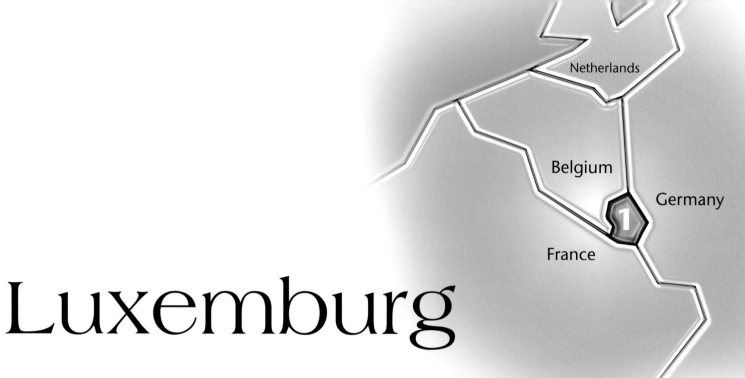

Netherlands

Belgium

Germany

1

France

Luxemburg

City of Luxembourg (1)

Strategically positioned – bordered by France, Germany and Belgium – Luxembourg was, from the 16th century until 1867, one of Europe's greatest fortified sites. It was repeatedly reinforced as it passed from one great European power to another. Today, 10% of the original fortifications still remain visible.

"Here is a spot where so much grandeur and grace, so much serenity combined with loveliness are found side by side that one only wishes that Poussin could have used his wonderful talent in such beautiful surroundings."

German writer Johann Wolfgang von Goethe, in a quotation engraved on a wall of the city of Luxembourg

The Loire Valley between Sully-sur-Loire and Chalonnes   (1)

The Valley is noteworthy for the quality of its architectural heritage in such historic towns as Blois, Chinon, Orléans, Saumur and Tours, and in particular in its world-famous castles, such as the Château de Chambord. The region is also known as the garden of France because of its cultural landscape of great beauty.

"The Loire is a queen and kings have loved her."

French saying about the Loire

Decorated Grottoes of the Vézère Valley   (2)

The Valley contains 147 prehistoric sites dating from the Palaeolithic period and 25 decorated caves. It is particularly interesting from an ethnological and anthropological point of view, as well as froman aesthetic standpoint because of its cave paintings. The hunting scenes show some 100 animal figures, which are remarkable for their detail, rich colours and lifelike quality.

France

United Kingdom

Netherlands

Belgium

Luxembourg

Germany

Switzerland

Italy

Atlantic Ocean

Spain

Mediterranean Sea

Roman Theatre and its Surroundings and the "Triumphal Arch" of Orange (3)

Situated in the Rhone valley in the south of France, the ancient theatre of Orange, with its 103-m-long facade (338 feet), is one of the best preserved of all the great Roman theatres. Built between AD 10 and 25, the Roman arch is one of the most beautiful and interesting surviving examples of a provincial triumphal arch from the reign of Augustus.

Mont-Saint-Michel and its Bay   (4)

Perched on a rocky islet between Normandy and Brittany is a Gothic-style Benedictine abbey dedicated to the archangel Saint Michael, and the village that grew up in the shadow of its great walls. Built between the 11th and 16th centuries, the abbey is a technical and artistic tour de force, having had to adapt to the challenges posed by this unique natural site.

"The archangel Michael appeared to St. Aubert, bishop of Avranches, in 708 and instructed him to build a church on the rocky islet. Aubert repeatedly ignored the angel's instruction, until Michael burned a hole in the bishop's skull with his finger."

The legend of Mont-Saint-Michel

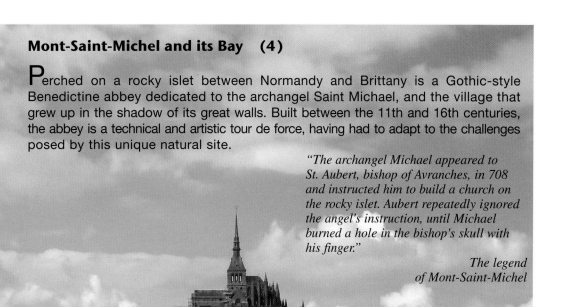

Historic Site of Lyons   (5)

This capital of the Rhône-Alpes region has a long history. Lyons was founded by the Romans in the 1st century BC as the capital of the Three Gauls and has continued to play a major role in Europe's political, cultural and economic development ever since. The city bears exceptional testimony to the continuity of urban settlement over more than two millennia on a site of great commercial and strategic significance.

Historic Centre of Avignon (6)

In the 14th century, this city in the south of France was the seat of the papacy. The Palais des Papes, an austere-looking fortress lavishly decorated by Simone Martini and Matteo Giovanetti, dominates the city. Beneath this outstanding example of Gothic architecture, the Petit Palais and the Romanesque Cathedral of Notre Dame-des-Doms complete an exceptional group of monuments that testify to the leading role played by Avignon in 14th-century Christian Europe.

"The most beautiful and the strongest house in the world..."

Jean Froissart, important chronicler of medieval France, speaking of the Palais des Papes

Routes of Santiago de Compostela in France (7)

(Site shared with Spain)

Santiago de Compostela was the supreme goal for countless thousands of pious pilgrims who converged there from all over Europe throughout the Middle Ages. To reach it, Spanish pilgrims had to go through France, and the group of important historical monuments included in this inscription marks out the four routes by which they travelled.

Bourges Cathedral (8)

Built between 1195 and 1255, the Cathedral of Saint Étienne of Bourges is one of the great masterpieces of Gothic art and is admired for its proportions and the unity of its design. The tympanum, sculptures and stained-glass windows are particularly striking. Apart from the beauty of the architecture, it attests to the power of Christianity in medieval France.

Strasbourg - Grande Île   (9)

Strasbourg is situated in the Ill River, at the point where it flows into the Rhine on the border with Germany. The city boasts an outstanding complex of monuments within a fairly small area known as the Petite-France district. The cathedral, the four ancient churches and the Palais Rohan form a neighbourhood that is characteristic of a medieval town and illustrates Strasbourg's evolution from the 15th to the 18th century.

"Strasbourg, oh, it is a rich heritage from Louis XIV, it is the certainty of mutual happiness"

Honoré de Balzac,
December 12, 1845

Notre-Dame Cathedral, Reims (10)

Reims is home to an outstanding masterpiece of Gothic art: Notre-Dame de Reims Cathedral. The former abbey still has its beautiful 9th-century nave, in which lie the remains of Archbishop Saint Rémi (440–533), who instituted the Holy Anointing of the kings of France. The former archiepiscopal palace known as the Tau Palace, which played an important role in religious ceremonies, was almost entirely rebuilt in the 17th century.

Royal Saltworks of Arc-et-Senans (11)

The Royal Saltworks of Arc-et-Senans, near Besançon, was built by Claude-Nicolas Ledoux. Its construction, begun in 1775 during the reign of Louis XVI, was the first major achievement of industrial architecture, reflecting the Enlightenment's ideal of progress.

"Ledoux wanted the form of the Saltworks to be as pure as the course of the sun."

Institut
Claude-Nicolas Ledoux

123

Amiens Cathedral   (12)

Amiens Cathedral, in the heart of Picardy, 120 km (75 miles) north of Paris, is one of the largest "classic" Gothic churches of the 13th century It is notable for the coherence of its plan, the beauty of its three-tiered interior elevation, and the particularly fine display of sculptures on the principal facade and in the south transept.

"This cathedral is an adorable woman, a virgin. What a joy and rest for the artist to find her back so beautiful!"

Auguste Rodin

Pyrenees - Mont Perdu   (13)
(Site shared with Spain)

The region of Mount Perdu, located on the French-Spanish border in the Pyrenees, displays classic geological land forms, including two of Europe's largest and deepest canyons and spectacular cirque walls. This site also has its roots in the past and illustrates a mountain-dwelling way of life that has become rare in Europe.

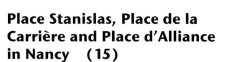

Cistercian Abbey of Fontenay (14)

This stark Burgundian monastery was founded by Saint Bernard in 1119. With its church, cloister, refectory, sleeping quarters, bakery and ironworks, it is an excellent illustration of the ideal of self-sufficiency as practised by the earliest communities of Cistercian monks.

Place Stanislas, Place de la Carrière and Place d'Alliance in Nancy (15)

Nancy, located in Lorraine, in north-eastern France, was the temporary residence of a king without a kingdom, Stanislas Leszczynski. The city is paradoxically the oldest and most typical example of a modern capital where an enlightened monarch proved to be sensitive to the needs of the people.

Paris, Banks of the Seine (16)

From the Louvre to the Eiffel Tower, from the Place de la Concorde to the Grand and Petit Palais, the evolution of Paris and its history can be seen from the River Seine. Notre-Dame Cathedral and the Sainte Chapelle are architectural masterpieces, while Haussmann's wide squares and boulevards influenced late 19th- and 20th-century town planning the world over. City of Light and capital of France, Paris is renowned worldwide for the beauty of its architecture, its urban perspectives and avenues, as well as the wealth of its museums.

"Yes, Fuhrer. Paris is burning."

Lied Dietrich von Choltitz, the Nazi commandant of Paris, having decided to spare this wondrous city from Hitler's vindictive order to blow up the ancient bridges and timeless landmarks

Jurisdiction of Saint-Émilion (17)

Saint-Émilion, a small town near Bordeaux, is famous for its wine. Viticulture was introduced to this fertile region of Aquitaine by the Romans, and intensified in the Middle Ages. This site is an outstanding example of an historic vineyard landscape that has survived intact and is still active to the present day.

"It is in Saint-Emilion that was set up for the first time the practice of quality control by tasting."
City of Saint-Emilion

Palace and Park of Fontainebleau (18)

Used by the kings of France from the 12th century, the medieval royal hunting lodge of Fontainebleau, standing at the heart of a vast forest on the Île-de-France, was transformed, enlarged and embellished in the 16th century by François I, who wanted to make a "New Rome" out of it. It is now the largest of the French royal châteaux. Surrounded by an immense park, the Italianate palace combines Renaissance and French artistic traditions.

"Here is the real abode of the kings, the house of centuries."

Emperor Napoléon Bonaparte (1769 – 1821), speaking of the Palace of Fontainebleau, a symbol of his grandeur

Cape Girolata, Cape Porto, Scandola Nature Reserve and the Piana Calanches in Corsica (19)

The nature reserve occupies the Scandola peninsula, an impressive, porphyritic rock mass. The vegetation is an outstanding example of scrubland. The region is home to seagulls, cormorants and sea eagles. The clear waters, with their islets and inaccessible caves, host a rich marine life. This natural park protects thousands of rare species of fauna and flora.

Roman and Romanesque Monuments of Arles (20)

Arles, situated in the Bouches-du-Rhône region in southern France, is an extremely ancient town established by the Greeks as early as the 6th century BC under the name of Theline. The city reached its peak during the 4th and 5th centuries, when it was frequently used as headquarters for Roman emperors during military campaigns. Arles is a good example of the adaptation of an ancient city to medieval European civilization. It has some impressive Roman monuments, of which the earliest date back to the 1st century BC.

"Julius Caesar settled the veterans of his Roman legions here in 46 BC. This would be the first Golden Age of the city known as 'Little Rome in Gaul'."

City of Arles

Canal du Midi (21)

This 360-km (224 miles) network of navigable waterways linking the Mediterranean and the Atlantic through 328 structures (locks, aqueducts, bridges, tunnels, etc.) is one of the most remarkable feats of civil engineering in modern times. Built between 1667 and 1694, it paved the way for the industrial revolution. Some 12,000 workers toiled for fifteen years under the supervision of Pierre Paul Riquet to create the canal.

"Of all the methods of travelling I have ever tried, this is the pleasantest."

U.S. President Thomas Jefferson,
speaking of the Canal in 1787

Provins, Town of Medieval Fairs (22)

The fortified medieval town of Provins is situated in the former territory of the powerful counts of Champagne. At the beginning of the 2nd millennium, this small city hosted some of the biggest fairs in Champagne. Today, Provins still preserves the architecture and urban layout that characterize these great medieval fair towns.

"Homage to a city where princes write song, where history becomes poems."
André Miquel,
Professor and Administrator
of the Collège de France

Historic Fortified City of Carcassonne (23)

Since the pre-Roman period, a fortified settlement has existed on the hill where Carcassonne now stands. In its present form, it is an outstanding example of a medieval fortified town. The city is also of exceptional importance because of the lengthy restoration campaign undertaken by Viollet-le-Duc, one of the founders of the modern science of conservation.

"As the oldest town in France, and the only one whose restoration has been a world event, it is the common heritage of all the great countries at war…"

French author Joë Bousquet during World War II

Chartres Cathedral (24)

Located about 80 kilometres (50 miles) from Paris, Notre-Dame de Chartres cathedral is considered the finest example in France of the "high Gothic" style of architecture. The cathedral was partly built starting in 1145, and then reconstructed over a 26-year period after a fire in 1194.

"The other cathedrals of the Christian world haven't succeeded to express as many things as Chartres does. There is nothing comparable to Chartres. Chartres is the manifestation of the Middle Age spirit."

French art historian Émile Mâle

Pont du Gard   (25)

The bridge is thought to have been built around 19 BC. It was part of a nearly 50-km (31 miles) aqueduct, bringing water from springs near Uzès to the Roman city of Nemausus (Nîmes). Built on three levels, the bridge is 49 m (160 feet) high, and the longest level is 275 m (902 feet) long. The Roman architects and hydraulic engineers who designed it created a technical – as well as an artistic – masterpiece.

"The engineers who built Pont du Gard, with its triple tier of graceful arches, were concerned with more than functionality. They also had an eye for the aesthetics."

American traveller
Bob Christman

Church of Saint-Savin-sur-Gartempe (26)

Known as the "Romanesque Sistine Chapel", the Abbey-Church of Saint-Savin contains many beautiful 11th- and 12th-century murals, which are still in a remarkable state of preservation.

Palace and Park of Versailles (27)

Just a few miles from the centre of Paris, the Palace of Versailles was the principal residence of the French kings from the time of Louis XIV to Louis XVI. Embellished by several generations of architects, sculptors, decorators and landscape architects, it provided Europe with a model of the ideal royal residence for over a century.

"There is an intimate relation between
the King and his château.
The idol is worthy of the temple,
the temple of the idol …
For a cathedral, it is the idea of God.
For Versailles, it is the idea of the King.
Its mythology is but a magnificent allegory
of which Louis XIV is the reality."

Baron Arthur Léon Imbert
de Saint-Amand

Le Havre, the City Rebuilt by Auguste Perret (28)

In Normandy, northern France, on the English Channel at the mouth of the River Seine, the city of Le Havre was severely bombed during the Second World War. The destroyed area was rebuilt according to the plan of a team headed by Auguste Perret, from 1945 to 1964. Among many reconstructed cities, Le Havre is exceptional for its unity and integrity.

"Perret is not a revolutionary, he is a
continuator. His whole personality lives
in the continuation of the great, noble
and elegant truths of French architecture. "

Swiss architect Le Corbusier
(1887–1965)

Vézelay, Church and Hill   (29)

Shortly after its foundation in the 9th century, the Benedictine abbey of Vézelay acquired the relics of Saint Mary Magdalene and since then it has been an important place of pilgrimage. With its sculpted capitals and portal, Madeleine of Vézelay – a 12th-century monastic church – is a masterpiece of Burgundian Romanesque art and architecture.

Switzerland

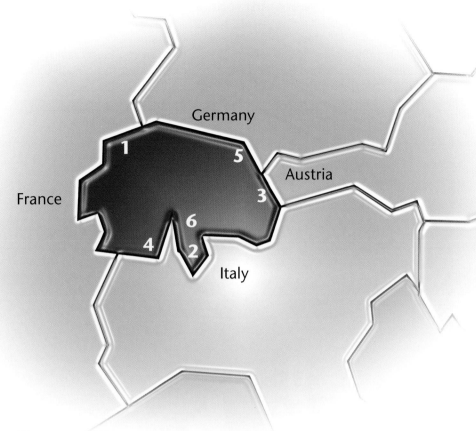

Old City of Berne   (1)

Founded in the 12th century, Berne, capital of Switzerland, was developed over the centuries in line with an exceptionally structured planning concept. The buildings in the Old City, dating from a variety of periods, include 15th-century arcades and 16th-century fountains. Most of the medieval town was restored in the 18th century, but it has still retained its original character.

"It is great here in Bern, an ancient, thoroughly comfortable city, in which one can live just as in Zurich. Both sides of the roads are completely lined by old arcades, so that one can stroll from one end of the city to the other in the worst downpour without getting noticeably wet…"

Albert Einstein, writing a letter to Mileva Maric, February 4, 1902

Monte San Giorgio   (2)

Monte San Giorgio is the single best-known record of marine life from the Triassic period, and it holds important remains of life on land as well. The sequence reflects life in a tropical lagoon environment, sheltered and partially separated from the open sea by an offshore reef.

Benedictine Convent of Saint John at Müstair   (3)

Located in Val Müstair, a spectacular mountain valley in the Swiss Alps, the Convent of Müstair is a good example of Christian monastic renovation during the Carolingian period. It has Switzerland's greatest series of figurative murals, painted in AD 800, along with Romanesque frescoes and stuccoes.

Jungfrau-Aletsch-Bietschhorn   (4)

This is the most glaciated part of the Alps, containing Europe's largest glacier and a range of classic glacial features such as U-shaped valleys, cirques, horn peaks and moraines. The diversity of flora and wildlife, represented in a range of Alpine and sub-Alpine habitats and plant colonization in the wake of retreating glaciers, provides an outstanding example of plant succession.

"The Aletsch is the grandest glacier in the Alps: over it we now stood, while the bounding mountains poured vast feed into the noble stream."

Physicist and glacier explorer
John Tyndall, 1860

Convent of Saint Gall   (5)

This Carolingian monastery was, from the 8th century to its secularization in 1805, one of the most important in Europe. Its library is one of the richest and oldest in the world and contains precious manuscripts such as the earliest-known architectural plan drawn on parchment. From 1755 to 1768, the convent area was rebuilt in Baroque style.

Bellinzone   (6)

The Bellinzone site consists of a series of fortifications grouped around the castle of Castelgrande, which stands on a rocky peak looking out over the entire Ticino valley. Running from the castle, a series of fortified walls protect the ancient town and block the passage through the valley. A second castle, Montebello, forms an integral part of the fortifications, while a third but separate castle, called Sasso Corbaro, was built on an isolated rocky promontory south-east of the other fortifications.

"They are the doors and keys of Italy."

War Officer Azzo Visconti, describing the Bellizone castles in 1475

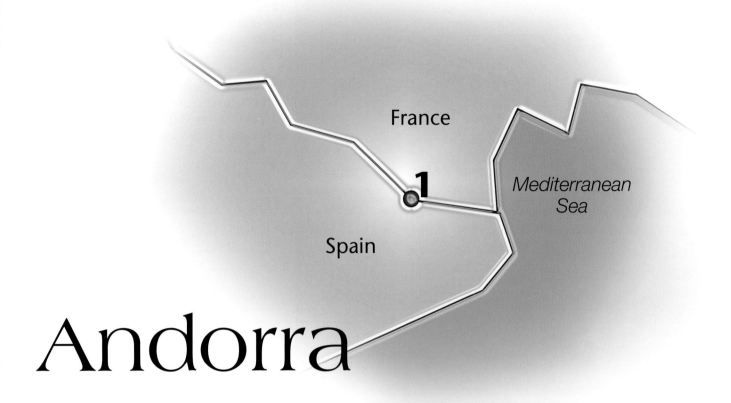

Andorra

France

1

Spain

Mediterranean Sea

Madriu-Perafita-Claror Valley (1)

The valley offers a microcosmic perspective of the way people have harvested the resources of the high Pyrenees over millennia. Its dramatic glacial landscapes of craggy cliffs and glaciers, with high open pastures and steep wooded valleys, covers an area of 4,247 ha (10,494 acres), or 9% of the total area of Andorra. The Valley is a reflection of an ancient communal system of land management that has survived for over 700 years.

Vatican City (1)

Vatican City is a sovereign, landlocked enclave surrounded by Rome, and one of the most sacred places in Christendom. A unique collection of artistic and architectural masterpieces lies within the boundaries of this small state. At its centre is St. Peter's Basilica, with its double colonnade and circular piazza, bordered by palaces and gardens. The basilica, erected over the tomb of St. Peter the Apostle, is the largest religious building in the world.

"One of the most important doors of the Holy See open on the world, expressing the renewed will of the Church to seek dialogue with humanity in the sign of art and culture, putting at the disposal of everybody the heritage with which history entrusted her."

Pope John Paul II on February 7, 2000, while inaugurating the new entrance to the Vatican Museum

Holy See

Italy

○1

Adriatic Sea

Mediterranean Sea

Spain

Portugal

France

Andorra

Mediterranean Sea

Atlantic Ocean

Algeria

Morocco

Alhambra, Generalife and Albayzin, Granada   (1)

Rising above the modern lower town, the Alhambra and the Albaycín, situated on two adjacent hills, form the medieval part of Granada. To the east of the Alhambra fortress and residence are the magnificent gardens of the Generalife, the former rural residence of the emirs who ruled this part of Spain in the 13th and 14th centuries.

"This piece of art has come to decorate the Alhambra, which is the home of the peaceful and of the warriors."

Extract of Epigraphic poems of the walls of the Alhambra

Historic City of Toledo   (2)

Successively a Roman municipium, the capital of the Visigothic Kingdom, a fortress of the Emirate of Cordoba, an outpost of the Christian kingdoms fighting the Moors and, in the 16th century, the temporary seat of supreme power under Charles V, Toledo is the repository of more than 2,000 years of history. The city was famed for its production of swords and is still a centre for the manufacture of knives and other steel implements.

"Rocky gravity, glory of Spain
and light of her cities."

Spanish author
Miguel de Cervantes y Saavedra
(1547 – 1616),
describing Toledo

Historic Walled Town of Cuenca   (3)

This beautiful and ancient city of central Spain was built by the Moors in a defensive position at the heart of the Caliphate of Cordoba. Cuenca is an unusually well-preserved medieval fortified city. Conquered by the Castilians in the 12th century, it became a royal town and bishopric endowed with important buildings, such as Spain's first Gothic cathedral, and the famous casas colgadas (hanging houses), suspended from sheer cliffs overlooking the Huécar River.

Parque Güell, Palacio Güell and Casa Mila in Barcelona   (4)

These works by Antonio Gaudí (1852–1926) may be seen as truly universal in view of the diverse cultural sources that inspired them. They represent an eclectic as well as a very personal style, which was given free reign not only in the field of architecture but also in gardens, sculpture and all forms of decorative art.

"The temple grows slowly, but this has been the case with everything destined to have a long life. Hundred-year-old oak trees take many years to grow tall; on the other hand, reeds grow quickly, but in autumn the wind knocks them down and there is no more to be said."

Catalan architect
Antoni Gaudí
(1852 –1926)

University and Historic Precinct of Alcalá de Henares   (5)

Alcalá de Henares was founded by Cardinal Jiménez de Cisneros in the early 16th century, 30 km (19 miles) northeast of Madrid. It was the first city to be designed and built solely as the seat of a university, and was to serve as the model for other centres of learning in Europe and the Americas. The city suffered severe damage during the Spanish Civil War.

"In the sixteenth and seventeenth centuries, the University of Alcalá became the pre-eminent centre of academic excellence ... At the same time, the prestige of its learning and teaching soon converted it into the model to be followed by the new universities in the Americas."

Universidad de Alcalá

142

Las Médulas   (6)

In the 1st century AD, the Roman Imperial authorities began to exploit the gold deposits of this region in northwest Spain, using a technique based on hydraulic power. After two centuries of working the deposits, the Romans withdrew, leaving a devastated landscape. Since there was no subsequent industrial activity, the dramatic traces of this remarkable ancient technology are visible everywhere as sheer faces in the mountainsides.

Palau de la Musica and Hospital de San Pau   (7)

Masterpieces of the imaginative and exuberant Art Nouveau style that flourished in early 20th century Barcelona. These are two of the finest contributions to Barcelona's architecture by the Catalan Art Nouveau architect Lluís Domènech i Montaner.

"...that the needy should find refuge at all times in this shelter intended for them."

Excerpt of banker Pau Gil i Serra's will, who donated the funds to build the Hospital de Sant Pau

Monastery and Site of the Escurial, Madrid (8)

Built at the end of the 16th century, on a plan in the form of a grill, the instrument of the martyrdom of St. Lawrence, the Escurial Monastery, stands in an exceptionally beautiful site in Castile. Its austere architecture, a break with previous styles, had a considerable influence on Spanish architecture for more than half a century.

"Spain has an ambiguous attitude: its golden ages are also its dark past. But this often troubled tale, soaked in both blood and glory, has bequeathed an unequalled wealth of castles and palaces, monuments, monasteries and museums."

Robert Elms, author of Spain: A Portrait After The General, while visiting El Escorial

Historic Centre of Cordoba (9)

Located in southern Spain, Cordoba was founded in ancient Roman times as Corduba by Claudius Marcellus. Cordoba's period of greatest glory began in the 8th century after the Moorish conquest, when some 300 mosques and innumerable palaces and public buildings were built to rival the splendours of Constantinople, Damascus and Baghdad. In the 13th century, under Ferdinand III, the Saint, Cordoba's Great Mosque was turned into a cathedral and new defensive structures.

Monuments of Oviedo and the Kingdom of the Asturias (10)

In the 9th century, the flame of Christianity was kept alive in the Iberian Peninsula in the tiny Kingdom of the Asturias, in northern Spain. Here, an innovative pre-Romanesque architectural style was created that was to play a significant role in the development of the religious architecture of the peninsula.

Old Town of Segovia and its Aqueduct (11)

The old city is spectacularly perched atop a long, narrow promontory. Its Roman aqueduct, probably built c. AD 50, is remarkably well preserved. This impressive construction, with its two tiers of arches, forms part of the setting of the magnificent historic city of Segovia.

"Despite its high profile and Segovia's inscription as a World Heritage Site, the aqueduct is threatened by lack of maintenance, differential decay of stone blocks, water leakage from the upper viaduct, and in some areas pollution..."

World Monuments Watch
100 Most Endangered Sites, 2005

Rock-Art of the Mediterranean Basin on the Iberian Peninsula (12)

The corpus of late prehistoric mural paintings in the Mediterranean basin of eastern Spain, in the Iberian Peninsula, is the largest group of rock-art sites anywhere in Europe, and provides an exceptional portrait of life in a seminal period of human cultural evolution.

Santiago de Compostela (13)

Santiago is only a few miles inland from the westernmost coast of mainland Europe facing the Atlantic, so prior to Christopher Columbus' voyage of 1492, it was considered the edge of the known world. This famous pilgrimage site in north-western Spain became a symbol in the Spanish Christians' struggle against Islam. Destroyed by the Muslims at the end of the 10th century, it was completely rebuilt in the following century. The Old Town of Santiago is one of the world's most beautiful urban areas.

"The body of Saint James was buried at a place where now stands the cathedral of Santiago de Compostela. Saint James appeared on earth and helped the Spanish Christian army win a decisive victory over the Moors."

Story of Saint James' appearance in 834

Old Town of Avila with its Extra-Muros Churches (14)

Founded in the 11th century to protect the Spanish territories from the Moors, this "City of Saints and Stones", the birthplace of St. Teresa and the burial place of the Grand Inquisitor Torquemada, has kept its medieval austerity. This purity of form can still be seen in the Gothic cathedral and the fortifications which, with their 82 semicircular towers and nine gates, are the most complete in Spain.

Poblet Monastery (15)

This Cistercian abbey in Catalonia is one of the largest in Spain. At its centre is a 12th-century church. The austere, majestic monastery, which has a fortified royal residence and contains the pantheon of the kings of Catalonia and Aragon, is an impressive sight.

Garajonay National Park (16)

Laurel forest covers some 70% of this park, situated in the middle of the island of La Gomera, the second smallest of the Canary Islands, in the Atlantic Ocean off the coast of Africa. The presence of springs and numerous streams assures lush vegetation resembling that of the Tertiary, which, due to climatic changes, has largely disappeared from southern Europe.

Old Town of Cáceres (17)

This city in western Spain has a history of battles between Moors and Christians, which is reflected in its architecture – a blend of Roman, Islamic, Northern Gothic and Italian Renaissance styles. Of the 30 or so towers from the Muslim period, the Torre del Bujaco is the most famous. The old town is also well known for its multitude of storks' nests, home to a large, long-legged and long-necked wading bird.

Doñana National Park (18)

Doñana National Park in Andalusia, southwestern Spain, occupies the right bank of the Guadalquivir River at its estuary on the Atlantic Ocean. It is notable for the great diversity of its biotopes, especially lagoons, marshlands, fixed and mobile dunes, scrub woodland and maquis. It shelters wildlife including thousands of European and African migratory birds, and endangered species such as the Spanish Imperial Eagle and Iberian Lynx.

"At 3:30 a.m. on Saturday, April 25, 1998, the south coast of Spain was host to what has been dubbed the worst environmental disaster in Europe. A supporting wall of the reservoir containing the toxic wastes of the Aznalcollar mine burst ... The toxic waste entered the Agrio River, a tributary of the Guadiamar River, which feeds the swamps of the Guadalquivir situated within Doñana National Park."

Commission of Protected Natural Areas,
IUCN, Spain

Archaeological Ensemble of Mérida (19)

The colony of Augusta Emerita, which became present-day Mérida in Estremadura, was founded in 25 BC at the end of the Spanish Campaign and was the capital of Lusitania. The well-preserved remains of the old city include, in particular, a large bridge over the Guadiana, an amphitheatre, a theatre, a vast circus and an exceptional water-supply system. Mérida preserves more important ancient Roman monuments than any other city in Spain.

La Lonja de la Seda de Valencia (20)

Built between 1482 and 1533 on the east coast of Spain, this group of buildings was originally used for trading in silk (hence its name, the Silk Exchange) and it has always been a centre for commerce. It is a masterpiece of late Gothic architecture. The grandiose Sala de Contratación (Contract or Trading Hall), in particular, illustrates the power and wealth of a major Mediterranean mercantile city in the 15th and 16th centuries.

"Year of the foundation of Rome 616. Junius Brutus, consul of Spain, gave those who had fought under the orders of Viriathus plots of land and a city, which they called Valencia."

Roman writer Titus Livius, also knowns as Livy, (59 BC – AD 17), about the foundation of Valencia

San Millán Yuso and Suso Monasteries (21)

Monasteries of Suso and Yuso at San Millán de la Cogolla are exceptional testimony to the introduction and continuous survival of Christian monasticism, from the 6th century to the present day. The property is also of outstanding associative significance as the birthplace of the modern written and spoken Spanish language.

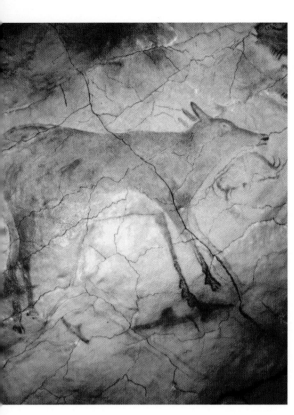

Altamira Cave (22)

Altamira (Spanish for "high view") is located near the town of Santillana del Mar in Cantabria, Spain, 30 km (19 miles) west of the city of Santander. In 1879, Marcelino Sanz de Sautuola was led by his daughter to discover that the cave contains Upper Paleolithic drawings and polychrome rock paintings depicting wild mammals and human hands. This prehistoric site was inhabited in the Aurignacian period and then in the Solutrean and Magdalenian periods.

Burgos Cathedral (23)

In northwestern Spain, Our Lady of Burgos was begun in the 13th century at the same time as the great cathedrals of the Île-de-France, and was completed in the 15th and 16th centuries. The entire history of Gothic art is summed up in its superb architecture and its unique collection of art.

Ibiza, Biodiversity and Culture (24)

One of the Balearic Islands located in the Mediterranean Sea, Ibiza provides an excellent example of the interaction between the marine and coastal ecosystems. The dense prairies of oceanic Posidonia (seagrass), an important endemic species found only in the Mediterranean basin, contain and support a diversity of marine life. Ibiza also preserves considerable evidence of its long history.

Catalan Romanesque Churches of the Vall de Boí (25)

The narrow Vall de Boí is situated in the high Pyrenees, in the Alta Ribagorça region, and is surrounded by steep mountains. Each village in the valley contains a Romanesque church, which collectively offer a pure and consistent example of Romanesque art in an untouched rural setting.

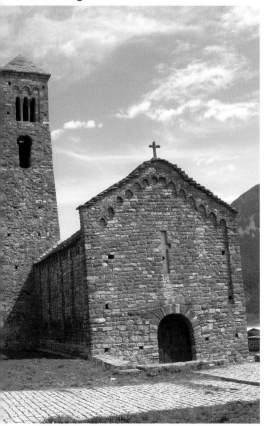

Mudejar Architecture of Aragon (26)

The development in the 12th century of Mudéjar art in Aragon, in northeastern Spain, resulted from the particular political, social and cultural conditions that prevailed after the Reconquista. Present until the early 17th century, this art is characterized by an extremely refined and inventive use of brick and glazed tiles in architecture, especially in the belfries.

Cathedral, Alcazar and Archivo de Indias in Seville (27)

Together, these three buildings form a remarkable monumental complex in the heart of Seville, the artistic and cultural capital of southern Spain. The cathedral and the Alcázar are an exceptional testimony to the civilization of the Almohads, as well as that of Christian Andalusia. The Giralda minaret is a masterpiece of Almohad architecture.

"Let us build a church so big that those who see it will think us mad."

Said in 1401 by architects and workers who decided to build the cathedral

Old City of Salamanca (28)

This ancient university town, northwest of Madrid, was first conquered by the Carthaginians in the 3rd century BC. It then became a Roman settlement, before being ruled by the Moors until the 11th century. The city's historic centre has important Romanesque, Gothic, Moorish, Renaissance and Baroque monuments. The Plaza Mayor, the central square, is one of the finest in Europe.

Archaeological Ensemble of Tárraco   (29)

Tárraco (modern-day Tarragona) was a major administrative and mercantile city in Roman Spain and the centre of the Imperial cult for all the Iberian provinces. Tárraco provides eloquent and unparalleled testimony to a significant stage in the history of the Mediterranean lands in antiquity.

"In 218 BC, during the Second Punic War between Romans and Carthaginians ... Tarraco was founded, as the main winter base for the Roman troops in Hispania, thus beginning the long and complex process of the incorporation of Peninsula territory into the new political, cultural and economic order of the Romans..."

Museu Nacional Arqueològic de Tarragona

Royal Monastery of Santa Maria de Guadalupe (30)

The monastery is an outstanding repository of four centuries of Spanish religious architecture. It symbolizes two significant events in world history that occurred in 1492: the Reconquest of the Iberian Peninsula by the Catholic Kings, and Christopher Columbus' arrival in the Americas. Its famous statue of the Virgin became a powerful symbol of the Christianization of much of the New World.

Palmeral of Elche (31)

This landscape of date palm groves was formally laid out, with elaborate irrigation systems, at the time the Muslim city of Elche was erected, towards the end of the tenth century AD, when much of the Iberian peninsula was Arab. The Palmeral is an oasis, a system for agrarian production in arid areas. It is also a unique example of Arab agricultural practices on the European continent.

Archaeological Site of Atapuerca (32)

The earliest and most abundant evidence of humankind in Europe is to be found in the caves of the Sierra de Atapuerca. The fossil remains of this region constitute an exceptional reserve of information about the physical nature and the way of life of the earliest human communities in Europe.

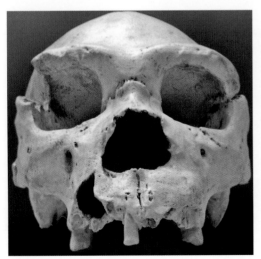

"Human fossils are not that common ... this particular site is the most astonishing concentration of human fossils than has been found anywhere in the world."

Ian Tattersall,
Curator in the Division of Anthropology,
American Museum of Natural History

Renaissance Monumental Ensembles of Úbeda and Baeza (33)

The urban morphology of the two small cities of Úbeda and Baeza in southern Spain dates back to the Moorish 9th century and to the Reconquista in the 13th century. The region constitutes outstanding early examples of Renaissance civic architecture and urban planning in Spain in the early 16th century.

San Cristóbal de La Laguna (34)

San Cristóbal de La Laguna, in the Canary Islands, was the first non-fortified Spanish colonial town, and its layout provided the model for many colonial towns in the Americas. Its wide streets and open spaces feature a number of fine churches and public and private buildings dating from the 16th to the 18th century.

Vizcaya Bridge (35)

The bridge was designed by the Basque architect Alberto de Palacio and completed in 1893. It merges 19th-century ironwork traditions with the then new, lightweight technology of twisted steel ropes. It was the first bridge in the world to carry people and traffic on a high suspended gondola, and it was used as a model for many similar bridges in Europe, Africa and the Americas - only a few of which survive.

Aranjuez Cultural Landscape   (36)

Located just 48 km south of Madrid, the Aranjuez cultural landscape is an entity of complex relationships: between nature and human activity, between sinuous watercourses and geometric landscape design, between rural and urban, and between forest landscape and the delicately modulated architecture of its palatial buildings.

Roman Walls of Lugo   (37)

Lugo, located in northwestern Spain, is the only city in the country to be surrounded by completely intact Roman walls, which reach a height of 10 to 15 metres (32 to 50 feet) along a 3-km circuit ringed with 85 towers. Lugo is the finest example of late Roman fortifications in Western Europe.

"The Wall of Lugo was very subsequent to the birth of the Roman city Lucus Augusti. While the city was founded in the year 14 before Christ, the Wall was not built until the end of the 3rd century, when Rome felt the Barbarian threat."

City of Lugo

Portugal

Atlantic
Ocean

Spain

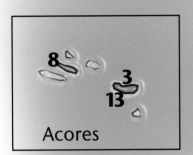

Acores

Alto Douro Wine Region (1)

Wine has been produced by traditional landholders in the Alto Douro region for some 2,000 years. Since the 18th century, its main product, port wine, has been world famous for its quality. This long tradition of viticulture has produced a cultural landscape of outstanding beauty that reflects its technological, social and economic evolution.

"Here the green tints outdo the colours of the rainbow"

Portuguese poet Miguel Torga (1907-1995), writing about the Douro region

Monastery of Alcobaça (2)

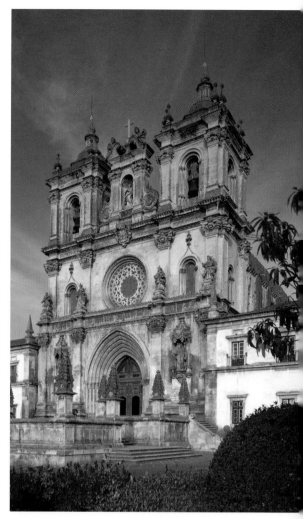

The Monastery of Santa Maria d'Alcobaça, north of Lisbon, was founded in the 12th century by King Alfonso I in memory to his victory against the Moors. The monastery is a masterpiece of Cistercian Gothic art. In its church are the tombs of King Pedro I and his murdered mistress Inês de Castro, and with it the story of the tragic liaison between Pedro and his ever-lasting love for Inês.

Central Zone of the Town of Angra do Heroismo in the Azores (3)

Situated on one of the islands in the Azores archipelago, this was an obligatory port of call from the 15th century until the advent of the steamship in the 19th century. The 400-year-old San Sebastião and San João Baptista fortifications are unique examples of military architecture.

*"Every street is handsomely paved . . .
and the surface is neat and true as a floor . . .
Everywhere are walls, walls, walls -- and all
of them are tasteful and handsome -- eternally
substantial . . . the town and the island are
miracles of cleanliness."*

*American writer Mark Twain
(1835 – 1910),
describing the urban setting
in the Azores*

Monastery of the Hieronymites and Tower of Belem in Lisbon (4)

Standing at the entrance to Lisbon harbour, the Monastery of the Hieronymites, construction of which began in 1502, exemplifies Portuguese art at its best. The nearby Tower of Belém, built to commemorate Vasco da Gama's expedition, is a reminder of the great maritime discoveries that laid the foundations of the modern world.

Historic Centre of Evora (5)

This museum-city in the south of Portugal, whose roots go back to Roman times, was wrested from the moors by Geraldo the Fearless (Sem Pavor) in 1166 and flourished as one of the most dynamic cities in the Kingdom of Portugal during the Middle Ages. It reached its golden age in the 15th century, when it became the residence of the Portuguese kings. Its monuments had a profound influence on Portuguese architecture in Brazil.

Convent of Christ in Tomar   (6)

Originally designed as a monument symbolizing the Reconquest, the Convent of the Knights Templar of Tomar (transferred in 1344 to the Knights of the Order of Christ) came to symbolize just the opposite during the Manueline period, the opening up of Portugal to other civilizations.

Monastery of Batalha   (7)

The Monastery of the Dominicans of Batalha was built to commemorate the victory of the Portuguese over the Castilians at the battle of Aljubarrota in 1385. It was to be the Portuguese monarchy's main building project for the next two centuries. Kings of Portugal wanted to leave their mark on this construction built in pale stone. As Capelas Imperfeitas (The Imperfect Chapels) remain as a testimony of the fact that the monastery was never actually finished.

Landscape of the Pico Island Vineyard Culture   (8)

This 987-ha (2,440-acre) site on the volcanic island of Pico, the second largest in the Azores archipelago, consists of a remarkable pattern of spaced-out, long linear walls running inland from, and parallel to, the rocky shore. The Pico Island landscape reflects a unique response to viniculture on a small island, and one that has been evolving since the arrival of the first settlers in the 15th century.

Historic Centre of Oporto   (9)

The city of Oporto, also known as Porto, built in the north of the country along the hillsides overlooking the mouth of the Douro River, is an outstanding urban landscape with a 1,000-year history. Its continuous growth, linked to the sea, can be seen in the many and varied monuments, from the cathedral with its Romanesque choir, to the neoclassical Stock Exchange and the typically Portuguese Manueline-style Church of Santa Clara.

"Cidade Invicta – The Unvanquished City"

Celebrated name of Oporto
after its brilliant and victorious resistance
to the Napoleonic Imperial army

Prehistoric Rock-Art Sites inthe Côa Valley   (10)

Located in northern Portugal, this exceptional concentration of rock carvings from the Upper Palaeolithic (22,000–10,000 BC) is the most outstanding example of early human artistic activity in this form anywhere in the world.

Cultural Landscape of Sintra (11)

Just northwest of Lisbon, Sintra became in the 19th century the first centre of European Romantic architecture. Ferdinand II turned a ruined monastery into a castle, where this new sensitivity was displayed in the use of Gothic, Egyptian, Moorish and Renaissance elements and in the creation of a park blending local and exotic species of trees.

"In all the land of Portugal, the whole
expanse of Europe, Sintra stands out as one
of the loveliest, rarest places that Nature's
prodigious hand has created."

Portuguese poet
Afonso Lopes Vieira,
(1878 - 1948)

Historic Centre of Guimarães (12)

Portugal was born in this small northwestern town. It is an exceptionally well-preserved and authentic example of the evolution of a Medieval settlement into a modern town. Its rich building typology exemplifies the specific development of Portuguese architecture from the 15th to the 19th century through the consistent use of traditional building materials and techniques.

Laurisilva of Madeira (13)

This Portuguese archipelago in the north Atlantic Ocean is an outstanding relict of a previously widespread laurel forest type. It is the largest surviving area of laurel forest and is believed to be 90% primary forest. It contains a unique suite of plants and animals, including many endemic species such as the Madeiran long-toed pigeon.

Norway

West Norwegian Fjords - Geirangerfjord and Nærøyfjord (1)

Northeast of Bergen, Geirangerfjord and Nærøyfjord, set 120 km (75 miles) from one another, are part of the west Norwegian fjord landscape, which stretches from Stavanger in the south to Andalsnes, 500 km (310 miles) to the northeast. The two fjords, among the world's longest and deepest, are considered as archetypical fjord landscapes and among the most scenically outstanding anywhere.

"It is very important to protect our environment. We need to protect the Nærøyfjord and Geirangerfjord for our children and all future generations. The fjords are precious and they inspire me. It's so wonderful that they will now b protected for posterity!"

Renowned British long-distance swimmer Lewis Gordon Pugh, commenting the fjords' inscription on the World Heritage List

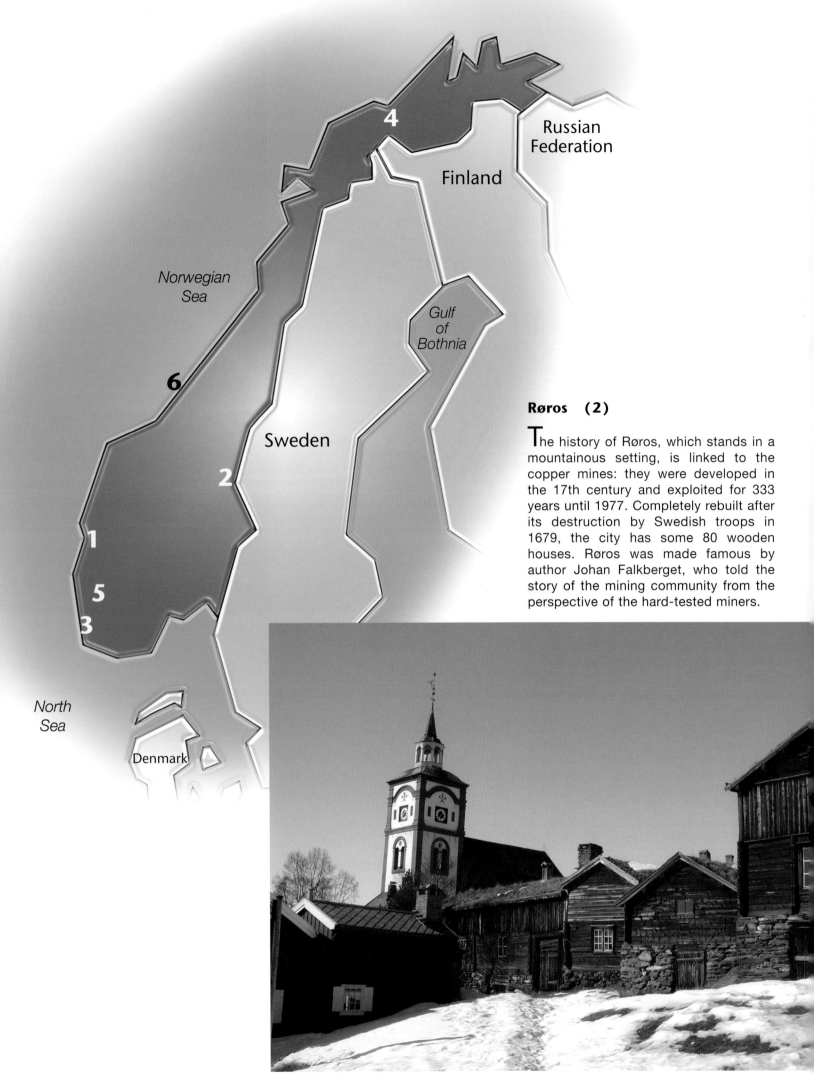

North
Sea

Norwegian
Sea

6

1

5

3

2

Sweden

Denmark

4

Finland

Russian
Federation

Gulf
of
Bothnia

Røros (2)

The history of Røros, which stands in a mountainous setting, is linked to the copper mines: they were developed in the 17th century and exploited for 333 years until 1977. Completely rebuilt after its destruction by Swedish troops in 1679, the city has some 80 wooden houses. Røros was made famous by author Johan Falkberget, who told the story of the mining community from the perspective of the hard-tested miners.

Bryggen (3)

Founded in 1070, Bryggen ("The Dock" in Norwegian), the old wharf of Bergen, is a reminder of the town's importance as part of the Hanseatic League's trading empire from the 14th to the mid-16th century. Many fires, the last in 1955, have ravaged the beautiful wooden houses of Bryggen, but its main structure has been preserved.

Rock Drawings of Alta (4)

Discovered in 1972, this group of petroglyphs in the Alta Fjord, near the Arctic Circle, bears the traces of a settlement dating from c. 4200 to 500 BC. The thousands of paintings and engravings add to our understanding of the environment and human activities on the fringes of the Far North in prehistoric times.

"Everywhere the view combines the majestic, the charming and the enchanting."

Leopold von Buch,
German traveller to Alta in 1807

Urnes Stave Church   (5)

Located near Lustrafjorden, the wooden church of Urnes (the stavkirke) stands in the natural setting of Sogn og Fjordane. It was built in the 12th and 13th centuries and is an outstanding example of traditional Scandinavian wooden architecture. It brings together traces of Celtic art, Viking traditions and Romanesque spatial structures. It is the oldest such building remaining in Norway.

Vegaøyan, The Vega Archipelago (6)

The archipelago reflects the way generations of fishermen and farmers have, over the past 1,500 years, maintained a sustainable living in an inhospitable seascape near the Arctic Circle, based on the now unique practice of eiderdown harvesting. It also celebrates the contribution made by women to the eiderdown process.

Sweden

Hanseatic Town of Visby   (1)

This former Viking site, located on the island of Gotland, was the main centre of the Hanseatic League in the Baltic from the 12th to the 14th century. Its 13th-century ramparts and more than 200 warehouses and wealthy merchants' dwellings from the same period make it the best-preserved fortified commercial city in northern Europe. Visby is sometimes referred as the "city of roses".

"...the city of Visby emerges like a dream. First you'll see the rambling medieval walls that still surround this ancient city; next, the red-tiled roofs of its quaint old buildings rising on the horizon; and last, you'll spot the green lawns and flower gardens that are Visby's pride."

Erika Fabian,
photographer and co-director
of Photographic Society International

Mining Area of the Great Copper Mountain in Falun (2)

The enormous mining excavation known as the Great Pit at Falun is the most striking feature of a landscape that illustrates the activity of copper production in this region since at least the 13th century. The 17th-century planned town of Falun provides a vivid picture of what was for centuries one of the world's most important mining areas.

Church Village of Gammelstad, Luleå (3)

Gammelstad, at the head of the Gulf of Bothnia in the north of Sweden, is the best-preserved example of a "church village", a unique kind of village formerly found throughout northern Scandinavia. The 424 wooden houses, huddled round the early 15th-century stone church, were used only on Sundays and at religious festivals to house worshippers from the surrounding countryside.

"They went from home to come here the day before Christmas Eve and at Christmas Eve they chop wood to heat their cottages during the weekend. All farmers have their cottages near the church at a place they call the hill."

First Antiquarius Regni in Sweden, Johannes Bureaus, visiting the Church town in Luleå at Christmas in 1600

169

Royal Domain of Drottningholm (4)

The domain stands on an island in Lake Mälar, in a suburb of Stockholm. With its castle, perfectly preserved theatre, Chinese pavilion and gardens, it is the finest example of an 18th-century northern European royal residence inspired by the Palace of Versailles.

Birka and Hovgården (5)

This archaeological site, located on Björkö Island in Lake Mälar, was occupied in the 9th and 10th centuries. Hovgården is situated on the neighbouring island of Adelsö. Together, they make up an archaeological complex illustrating the elaborate trading networks of Viking-Age Europe and their influence on the subsequent history of Scandinavia, which handled goods from Eastern Europe and the Orient, possibly as far as China.

Naval Port of Karlskrona (6)

Located in southeast Sweden, Karlskrona is an outstanding example of a late17th-century European planned naval city. The original plan and many of the buildings have survived intact, along with installations that illustrate its subsequent development up to the present day. Karlskrona is also known as the country's only baroque city.

Rock Carvings in Tanum (7)

The rock carvings in Tanum, in the north of Bohuslän in western Sweden, are a unique artistic achievement not only for their rich and varied motifs, but also for their cultural and chronological unity. They reveal the life and beliefs of people in Europe during the Bronze Age and are remarkable for their large numbers and outstanding quality.

Laponian Area (8)

The Arctic Circle region of northern Sweden is the home of the Saami, or Lapp people. It is the largest area in the world, and one of the last, with an ancestral way of life based on the seasonal movement of livestock. Every summer, the Saami lead their huge herds of reindeer towards the mountains through a natural landscape hitherto preserved, but now threatened by the advent of motor vehicles.

"As long as we have water for the fish to live in, as long as we have land for reindeer to graze and wander, as long as we have grounds for the wild beasts to hide in, there is comfort on this earth."

Sami poet Paulus Utsi
(1918-1975)

Agricultural Landscape of Southern Öland   (9)

The southern part of the island of Öland, in the Baltic Sea, is dominated by a vast limestone plateau. Human beings have lived here for some five thousand years and adapted their way of life to the physical constraints of the island. As a consequence, the landscape is unique, with abundant evidence of continuous human settlement from prehistoric times to the present day.

Varberg Radio Station   (10)

The Varberg Radio Station at Grimeton, in southern Sweden, was built in 1922-24. It is an exceptionally well-preserved monument to early wireless transatlantic communication, representing the process of development of communication technology in the period following the First World War.

"Today the unique radio transmitter at Grimeton meets a new millennium. My message today is the same as that sent by King Gustaf V seventy five years ago..."

King of Sweden
H. M. Carl XVI Gustaf,
January 1, 2000

Engelsberg Ironworks   (12)

Sweden's production of superior grades of iron made it a leader in this field in the 17th and 18th centuries. This site, located in middle the country, is the best-preserved and most complete example of this type of Swedish ironworks.

"The Eiffel Tower in Paris was built of iron bar manufactured in Sweden."

Ecomuseum Bergslagen

Skogskyrkogården   (11)

Skogskyrkogården (The Woodland Cemetery) came about following an international competition in 1915 for the design of a new cemetery in Enskede, in the southern part of Stockholm. It was created between 1917 and 1920 by two young architects, Asplund and Lewerentz, on the site of former gravel pits overgrown with pine trees. The design blends vegetation and architectural elements, taking advantage of irregularities in the site to create a landscape that is finely adapted to its function.

High Coast and Kvarken Archipelago   (13)

The High Coast is located on the western shore of the Gulf of Bothnia, a northern extension of the Baltic Sea. The irregular topography of the region has been largely shaped by the combined processes of glaciation, glacial retreat and the emergence of new land from the sea. Isostatic rebound is well illustrated in this region. Because of its unique topography, High Coast is notable for its beautiful scenery. In 2006, the Kvarken Archipelago was added to this site. The islands feature unusual ridged washboard moraines formed by the melting of the continental ice sheet.

Finland

Norway

Sweden

Russian federation

Gulf of Bothnia

2

4
1

3
5

Gulf of Finland

Baltic Sea

Estonia

Latvia

Bronze Age Burial Site of Sammallahdenmäki (1)

The Sammallahdenmäki cairn cemetery bears exceptional witness to the society of the Bronze Age of Scandinavia. This site features more than 30 granite burial cairns, providing unique insight into the funerary practices and social and religious structures in northern Europe more than three millennia ago.

Petäjävesi Old Church   (2)

Petäjävesi Old Church, in central Finland, was built of logs between 1763 and 1765. This Lutheran country church is a typical example of an architectural tradition that is unique to eastern Scandinavia. It combines the Renaissance conception of a centrally planned church with older forms deriving from Gothic groin vaults.

"...Custodian's priests can, according to the old ways, hold services on every fourth Sunday as well as bury their dead due to the fact that the inhabitants of Petäjävesi live at least nine new miles from the mother church. Given that distance, it becomes difficult to transport the dead, especially in the summer months."

Excerpt of the Royal Charter of the Congregation of Petäjävesi, signed by Friedrich O. Cederström on December 3, 1728

Verla Groundwood and Board Mill (3)

The Verla groundwood and board mill, and its associated residential area, are an outstanding, remarkably well-preserved example of the small-scale rural industrial settlements associated with pulp, paper and board production that flourished in northern Europe and North America in the 19th and early 20th centuries. Only a handful of such settlements survive to the present day.

Old Rauma   (4)

Situated on the Gulf of Botnia, Rauma is one of the oldest harbours in Finland. Built around a Franciscan monastery, where the mid-15th-century Holy Cross Church still stands, it is an outstanding example of an old Nordic city constructed in wood. There are approximately six hundred buildings and about 800 people living in the area.

Fortress of Suomenlinna   (5)

Built in the second half of the 18th century by the Swedes on six islands located at the entrance of Helsinki's harbour, this fortress is an especially interesting example of the European military architecture of the time. It took about 40 years to be completed. The fortress was surrendered to Russia in 1808. The Russians ruled there for 110 years but in 1918, the year following Finnish independence from Russia, it was officially renamed Suomenlinna, the Castle of Finland.

"What use do I have of titles and handsome ribbons? Should the king wish to show me his grace, then he should acquire the necessary funds for the building of the fleet and the fortress. Everything else is unnecessary."

Swedish General
Augustin Ehrensvärd,
1764

Struve Geodetic Arc (6)

The Struve Arc is a chain of survey triangulations stretching from Hammerfest, in Norway, to the Black Sea, over 2,820 km across 10 countries (Norway, Sweden, Finland, Estonia, Latvia, Lithuania, Russia, Belarus, Moldavia and Ukraine). These are points of a survey, carried out between 1816 and 1855, by the astronomer Friedrich Georg Wilhelm Struve, which represented the first accurate measuring of a long segment of a meridian. This helped establish the exact size and shape of our planet and marked an important step in the development of earth sciences and topographic mapping. The original arc consisted of 258 main triangles, with 265 main station points.

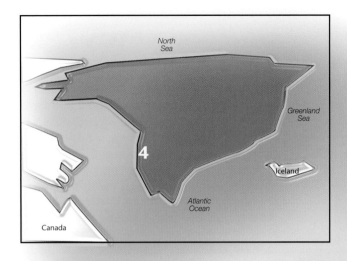

Denmark

Jelling Mounds, Runic Stones and Church   (1)

Jelling is the old Viking capital of Scandinavia. It is located near Vejle on the Jutland peninsula. The Jelling burial mounds and one of the runic stones are striking examples of pagan Nordic culture, while the other runic stone and the church illustrate the Christianization of the Danish people towards the middle of the 10th century.

Roskilde Cathedral   (2)

Roskilde is an ancient city in Denmark situated in the island of Zealand, 30 km (19 miles) west of Copenhagen. It was the capital of Denmark until about 1400, when that role transferred to Copenhagen. The city is home of Scandinavia's first Gothic cathedral to be built of brick and it encouraged the spread of this style throughout northern Europe.

Kronborg Castle (3)

Located on a strategically important site commanding the Sund, the stretch of water between Denmark and Sweden, the Royal castle of Kronborg at Helsingør (Elsinore) played a key role in the history of northern Europe in the 16th-18th centuries. Work began on the construction of this outstanding Renaissance castle in 1574, and its defences were reinforced according to the canons of the period's military architecture in the late 17th century. It is world-renowned as Elsinore, the setting of Shakespeare's Hamlet.

"People around here don't think of it as Hamlet's castle. It didn't happen.
It's a fairytale. The castle, for us, is the history of Denmark."

Camilla Kloster Larsson,
Manager at the Danhostel Helsingor Vandrerhjem

Ilulissat Icefjord (4)

On the west coast of Greenland, Ilulissat Icefjord is one of the few glaciers through which the Greenland ice cap reaches the sea. Sermeq Kujalleq is one of the fastest and most active glaciers in the world with around 20 billion tones of icebergs calved off and passing out of the fjord every year. The wild and highly scenic combination of rock, ice and sea, along with the dramatic sounds produced by the moving ice, combine to present a memorable natural spectacle.

"Greenland was perceived as this huge solid place that would never melt. In the U.S., global warming is a tomorrow issue.
For us working here, it hits you like a ton of bricks when you see it."

Robert Corell
of the American Meteorological Society,
2005

Germany

Castles of Augustusburg and Falkenlust at Brühl (1)

Set in an idyllic garden landscape, Augustusburg Castle and the Falkenlust hunting lodge are among the earliest examples of Rococo architecture in 18th-century Germany. The palaces were built in the beginning of the 18th century by the Archbishop of Cologne, Clemens August I.

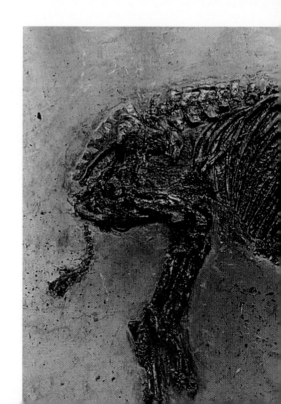

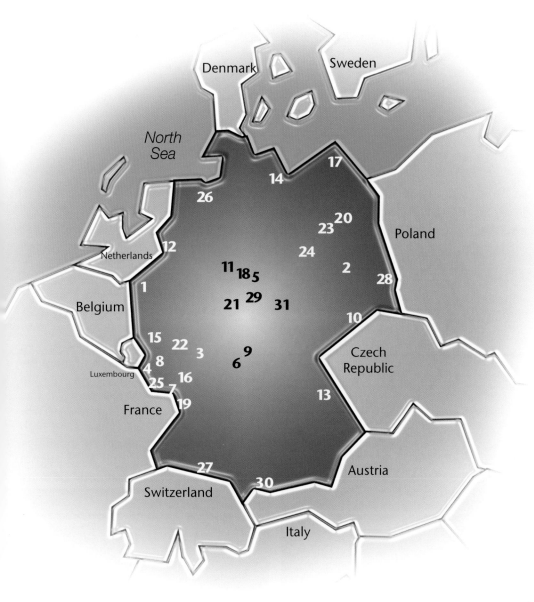

North Sea

Denmark
Sweden

17
14
26
20
23
Poland
24
2
12
Netherlands
11 18 5
1
28
21 29 31
Belgium
10
15 22 3
Czech
8 9
Republic
4 6
Luxembourg
25 7 16
19
13
France

27
Austria
30
Switzerland

Italy

Luther Memorials in Eisleben and Wittenberg   (2)

Martin Luther was a German theologian and an Augustinian monk whose teachings inspired the Protestant Reformation. These places in Saxony-Anhalt are all associated with the lives of Luther and his fellow reformer Melanchthon. They include Melanchthon's house in Wittenberg, the houses in Eisleben where Luther was born in 1483 and died in 1546, his room in Wittenberg, the local church, and the castle church where, on October 31, 1517, Luther posted his famous "95 Theses".

"I submit to no laws of interpreting the word of God."

> *Martin Luther's answer
> to the Exsurge Domine, a Papal bull
> issued on June 15, 1520
> at the Diet of Worms by Pope Leo X
> in response to the 95 Theses*

Messel Pit Fossil Site   (3)

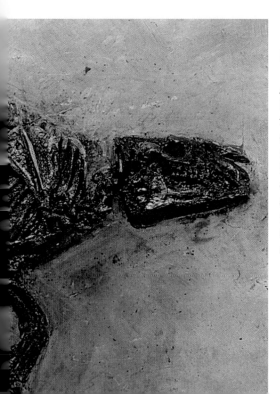

About 35 km (22 miles) southeast of Frankfurt, Messel Pit is the richest site in the world for understanding the living environment of the Eocene, between 57 million and 36 million years ago. In particular, it provides unique information about the early stages of the evolution of mammals and includes exceptionally well-preserved mammal fossils, ranging from fully articulated skeletons to the contents of stomachs of animals from this period.

Collegiate Church, Castle, and Old Town of Quedlinburg (5)

In the Land of Sachsen-Anhalt, Quedlinburg was a capital of the East Franconian German Empire at the time of the Saxonian-Ottonian ruling dynasty. It has been a prosperous trading town since the Middle Ages. The number and high quality of the timber-framed buildings make Quedlinburg an exceptional example of a medieval European town.

Aachen Cathedral   (4)

Located on the border with Belgium and the Netherlands, 65 km (40 miles) to the west of Cologne, Aachen is home to a palatine chapel built under the Emperor Charlemagne. Originally inspired by the churches of the Eastern part of the Holy Roman Empire, it was splendidly enlarged in the Middle Ages. The tombs of Charlemagne and Otto III rest in this magnificent cathedral.

"In Aachen I have seen the well-proportioned pillars, with their beautiful capitals from prophyry green and red and granite, which Carolus ordered to be taken from Rome and placed in this building."

Albrecht Dürer,
German artist, 1520

Würzburg Residence   (6)

The magnificent Baroque palace of Würzburg in Bavaria was created under the patronage of the prince-bishops Lothar Franz and Friedrich Carl von Schönborn. It was designed by the leading Baroque architect Balthasar Neumann. Venetian painter Giovanni Battista Tiepolo painted frescos in the building.

Speyer Cathedral   (7)

Founded on the Rhine by Conrad II in 1030, the cathedral was remodelled at the end of the 11th century. It is one of the most important Romanesque monuments from the time of the Holy Roman Empire. The cathedral was the burial place of the German emperors for almost 300 years.

Roman Monuments, Cathedral of St. Peter and Church of Our Lady in Trier   (8)

Trier, which stands on the Moselle River, was a Roman colony from the 1st century AD and then a great trading centre beginning in the next century. It became one of the capitals of the Tetrarchy at the end of the 3rd century, when it was known as the "second Rome". The number and quality of the surviving monuments are an outstanding testimony to Roman civilization.

Town of Bamberg   (9)

From the 10th century onwards, this Bavarian town became an important link with the Slav peoples, especially those of Poland and Pomerania. During its period of greatest prosperity, starting in the 12th century, the architecture of Bamberg strongly influenced northern Germany and Hungary. The Cathedral of Bamberg shelters the tombs of Emperor Henry II and Pope Clement II.

"In Bavaria, beer is considered as the fifth element along with earth, water, air and fire. After Bamberg was declared part of the World Cultural Heritage, everybody looked at Bamberg's traditional heritage: beer!"

City of Bamberg

Dresden Elbe Valley   (10)

This valley between Berlin and Prague has long been a European crossroads for culture, science and technology. The 18th- and 19th-century cultural landscape of Dresden Elbe Valley extends some 18 km along the river from Übigau Palace and Ostragehege fields in the northwest, to the Pillnitz Palace and the Elbe River Island in the southeast. It features low meadows and is crowned by the Pillnitz Palace and the centre of Dresden, with its numerous monuments and parks from the 16th to the 20th century.

St. Mary's Cathedral and St. Michael's Church at Hildesheim   (11)

Located in Lower Saxony, about 25 km (15 miles) southeast of Hannover, St. Michael's Church was built between 1010 and 1020 on a symmetrical plan with two apses, characteristic of Ottonian Romanesque art in Old Saxony. Its interior is of exceptional interest as an example of the Romanesque churches of the Holy Roman Empire.

"Hildesheim is so full of joy to the eye and imagination in audacity of colour and quaintness of timbered houses, that it is one of the most enchanting records of a past so unlike our own age that the very sight of its quaint beauty is a feast."

*American publisher
Hamilton Wright Mabie
(1845 - 1916)*

Zollverein Coal Mine Industrial Complex in Essen   (12)

The Zollverein industrial complex in Land Nordrhein-Westfalen consists of the complete infrastructure of a historical coal-mining site, with some 20th-century buildings of outstanding architectural merit. It constitutes remarkable material evidence of the evolution and decline of an essential industry over the past 150 years.

"Zollverein has kept its distinctive character with its famous 'Dopplebock' double rack, even if the facilities inside have fallen silent."

Museum Zeche Zollverein

Historic Old Town of Regensburg   (13)

The starting points for the town's development were the Roman camp "Castra Regina" (founded in AD 179). Regensburg is a vivid historical – as well as architectural – example of a medieval town that developed from a Roman military camp and was later dominated by dukes, bishops and merchants. The town became the capital of the East Franconian Empire and later of the Bavarian Duchy, of which the palaces of the seven dioceses as well as those of the many monasteries and counts give evidence. As capital of the East Franconian part of the Empire, Regensburg's importance went far beyond the Duchy of Bavaria.

Hanseatic City of Lübeck (14)

The former capital and Queen City of the Hanseatic League, Lübeck was founded in the 12th century and prospered until the 16th century as the major trading centre for northern Europe. Despite the damage it suffered during the Second World War, the basic structure of the old city, consisting mainly of 15th- and 16th-century patrician residences, public monuments, churches and salt storehouses, remains unaltered.

"Queen of the Hanseatic League"

Nickname of the city in the 14th century

Cologne Cathedral (15)

Cologne Cathedral (German: Kölner Dom) is one of the most well-known architectural monuments in Germany and has been Cologne's most famous landmark for centuries. Construction of this gothic masterpiece began in the 13th century and took, with interruptions, more than 600 years to complete. The cathedral suffered 14 hits by World War II aerial bombs, but luckily didn't collapse. Reconstruc-tion was completed in 1956. However, current urban development in Cologne threatens the cathedral.

"I sincerely hope that Cologne will not lose an important component of its historical legacy.

Francesco Bandarin,
Director of the World Heritage Centre,
2004

Abbey and Altenmünster of Lorsch (16)

One of the most renowned monasteries of the old Franco-German Empire is situated about ten miles east of Worms in the Grand Duchy of Hesse. The abbey is a rare architectural vestige of the Carolingian era. The sculptures and paintings from this period are still in remarkably good condition.

Historic Centres of Stralsund and Wismar (17)

Wismar and Stralsund are two small Hanseatic League towns in northern Germany on the Baltic Sea. They were major trading centres of the Hanseatic League in the 14th and 15th centuries. In the 17th and 18th centuries, they became Swedish administrative and defensive centres for the German territories. They contributed to the development of the characteristic building types and techniques of Brick Gothic in the Baltic region.

Mines of Rammelsberg and Historic Town of Goslar (18)

Goslar held an important place in the Hanseatic League because of the rich Rammelsberg metallic ore deposits. The town was founded in the 10th century after the discovery of silver deposits in the nearby Rammelsberg Mountain. It became a particularly rich town, which attracted the interest of the Holy Roman Emperor.

"In 938, a German nobleman was riding his horse, Ramelus. He tied the reins to a tree when he dismounted to hunt. Ramelus was impatient and pawed the earth. When the nobleman returned, he saw metals gleaming in the horse's little excavation. It is why the mine was named Rammelsberg, after the horse Ramelus."

Legend of the horse Ramelus

Maulbronn Monastery Complex (19)

Founded in 1147, this monastery is considered the most complete and best-preserved medieval monastic complex north of the Alps. Surrounded by fortified walls, the main buildings were constructed between the 12th and 16th centuries. The monastery's church had a major influence in the spread of Gothic architecture over much of northern and central Europe.

"Where the Eselsbrunnen ("mule fountain") stands today is where the mule was reputed to have stopped and quenched its thirst at a stream. The monks saw this as a sign from God and it was there that they decided to build the monastery."

Legend of the foundation of Maulbronn Monastery

Museumsinsel, Berlin   (20)

Museum Island (or, in German, Museumsinsel) in Berlin, Germany, is the name of the northern half of an island in the Spree River, in the centre of the city. The museum as a social phenomenon owes its origins to the Age of Enlightenment in the 18th century. These five museums, built between 1824 and 1930, are a unique ensemble of buildings illustrating the evolution of modern museum design over more than a century.

Wartburg Castle (21)

Wartburg Castle is situated on a 410-metre (1230 feet) precipitous hill to the southwest of and overlooking the town of Eisenach in Thuringia. The castle was founded in 1067 by the landgrave Ludwig the Springer. Wartburg Castle blends superbly into its forest surroundings and is in many ways "the ideal castle". Although it has retained some original sections from the feudal period, the form it acquired during the 19th-century reconstitution gives a good idea of what this fortress might have been at the height of its military and seigneurial power.

"Wait, mountain – you should become a castle for me!"

*Famous legendary words of Ludwig the Springer
in 1067, when he first laid his eyes
on the hill upon which the Wartburg now sits*

Upper Middle Rhine Valley   (22)

This 65-km (40-mile) stretch of the Middle Rhine Valley, with its castles, historic towns and vineyards, graphically illustrates the long history of human involvement with a dramatic and varied natural landscape. It is intimately associated with history and legend, and for centuries has exercised a powerful influence on writers, artists and composers.

"The river breaks through and the rocks recede and look down with astonishment and bewilderment..."

Prussian author and playwright
Heinrich von Kleist
during his 1803 Rhine journey

Palaces and Parks of Potsdam and Berlin   (23)

With 500 ha (1,235 acres) of parks and 150 buildings constructed between 1730 and 1916, Potsdam's complex of palaces and parks forms an artistic whole, whose eclectic nature reinforces its sense of uniqueness. The Cecilienhof palace was the scene of the Potsdam Conference from July 17 to August 2, 1945, as Franklin D. Roosevelt (followed by Harry S. Truman), Winston Churchill (followed by Clement Attlee) and Stalin met to decide the future of Germany.

"We, the President of the United States, the President of the National Government of the Republic of China, and the Prime Minister of Great Britain, representing the hundreds of millions of our countrymen, have conferred and agree that Japan shall be givenan opportunity to end this war."

Excerpt of the Declaration of Potsdam,
July 26, 1945

Garden Kingdom of Dessau-Wörlitz (24)

This huge garden complex was commissioned by prince Leopold III of Anhalt-Dessau in about 1750. It is strongly influenced by traditional English gardening. At 25 km (16 miles) in width, it is the largest garden of its kind in continental Europe.

Völklingen Ironworks (25)

The ironworks, which cover some 6 ha. (15 acres), dominate the city of Völklingen. Although they have recently gone out of production, they are the only intact example, in the whole of Western Europe and North America, of an integrated ironworks that was built and equipped in the 19th and 20th centuries.

Town Hall and Roland on the Marketplace of Bremen (26)

These two monuments of Bremen, in northwest Germany, are outstanding representations of civic autonomy and sovereignty, as these principles developed in the Holy Roman Empire in Europe. The old town hall was built as in the Gothic style in the early 15th century, after Bremen joined the Hanseatic League.

"Bremen Town Hall is considered to have preserved its authenticity ... Numerous German town halls were destroyed during the Second World War, and many have been modified. Bremen Town Hall, however, has been fully preserved in its original state.

*Mayor of Bremen,
Henning Scherf, 2005*

Monastic Island of Reichenau   (27)

The remains of Reichenau Island, located on Lake Constance in southern Germany, bear outstanding witness to the religious and cultural role of a great Benedictine monastery in the early Middle Ages. The churches of St. Mary and Marcus, St. Peter and St. Paul, and St. George, mainly built between the 9th and 11th centuries, provide a panorama of early medieval monastic architecture in central Europe.

Muskauer Park / Park Muzakowski   (28)
(Site shared with Poland)

Park Muzakowski is the biggest and most famous English-style park in Germany and Poland. It covers roughly 5.45 km (1,347 acres) of land on both sides of the Lusatian Neisse River, which constitutes the Polish-German border. It was created by Prince Hermann von Puckler-Muskau from 1815 to 1844. Muzakowski Park was the forerunner for new approaches to landscape design in cities.

Bauhaus and its Sites in Weimar and Dessau   (29)

Between 1919 and 1933, the Bauhaus School, based first in Weimar and then in Dessau, revolutionized architectural and aesthetic concepts and practices. The buildings put up and decorated by the school's professors launched the Modern Movement, which shaped much of 20th century architecture.

Pilgrimage Church of Wies   (30)

Miraculously preserved in the beautiful setting in the Steingaden, an Alpine valley of Bavaria, the Church of Wies was built in the late 1740s by the famous Domenikus Zimmermann. It is one of the most beautiful rococo churches in the world.

"The Wies is a bit of heaven
in this suffering world."

Writer Peter Dörfler

Classical Weimar   (31)

In the late 18th and early 19th centuries, the small Thuringian town of Weimar witnessed a remarkable cultural flourish, attracting many writers and scholars, notably Goethe and Schiller. This development is reflected in the high quality of many of the buildings and parks in the surrounding area.

"Where have I not been? Yet I am always glad to return to Weimar."

German novelist and philosopher
Johann Wolfgang von Goethe
(1749 – 1832)

Austria

Czech Republic

1

Germany

4 3

2

6

5

Switzerland

7

Hungary

Italy

Slovenia

Wachau Cultural Landscape   (1)

The Wachau is a stretch of the Danube Valley between Melk and Krems, a landscape of high visual quality. The architecture, the human settlements, and the agricultural use of the land in the Wachau vividly illustrate a basically medieval landscape that has evolved organically and harmoniously over time.

Historic Centre of the City of Salzburg (2)

Nestled at the northern boundary of the Alps, Salzburg has managed to preserve an extraordinary baroque architecture. Its Flamboyant Gothic art attracted many craftsmen and artists before the city became even better known through the work of the Italian architects Vincenzo Scamozzi and Santini Solari. This meeting point of northern and southern Europe perhaps sparked the genius of Salzburg's most famous son, Wolfgang Amadeus Mozart, whose name has been associated with the city ever since.

"Of all the lovely regions I have seen, none can compare to Salzburg's striking natural beauty."

Wolfgang Amadeus Mozart

Historic Centre of Vienna (3)

Vienna developed from early Celtic and Roman settlements into a medieval and Baroque city, the capital of the Austro-Hungarian Empire. It played an essential role as a leading European music centre, from the great age of Viennese Classicism through the early part of the 20th century. Three key periods of European cultural and political development – the Middle Ages, the Baroque period, and the Gründerzeit – are exceptionally well illustrated by the urban and architectural heritage of the Historic Centre of Vienna.

"Emperor Franz Joseph I's remarks and severe criticism from other circles drove architect Eduard van der Nüll to commit suicide. Only a few weeks after this tragic event, his partner August von Siccardsburg died from a heart attack."

Tragic legend of the Vienna Opera House architects

Palace and Gardens of Schönbrunn   (4)

The Schönbrunn Palace near Vienna is one of the most important cultural monuments in Austria. From the 18th century to 1918, Schönbrunn was the residence of the Habsburg emperors. It was designed by the architects Johann Bernhard Fischer von Erlach and Nicolaus Pacassi and is full of outstanding examples of decorative art.

"... the people have taken over the government through its representatives. I renounce any share in the affairs of state..."

Karl I, last Emperor of Austria, ending the rule of Habsburgs with this declaration in the Blue Chinese Room of Scönbrunn Palace, on November 11, 1918

Hallstatt-Dachstein Salzkammergut Cultural Landscape   (5)

Human activity in the magnificent natural landscape of the Salzkammergut, east of Salzburg, began in prehistoric times, with the salt deposits being exploited as early as the 2nd millennium BC. This resource formed the basis of the area's prosperity up to the middle of the 20th century, as reflected in the fine architecture of the town of Hallstatt.

Semmering Railway   (6)

The Semmering Railway, which starts at Gloggnitz and leads over the Semmering to Mürzzuschlag, is commonly referred to as the world's first mountain railway, especially given the very difficult terrain and difference in height. It was built over 41 km (25 miles) of high mountains between 1848 and 1854. It is one of the greatest feats of civil engineering from this pioneering phase of railway building.

City of Graz - Historic Centre   (7)

Situated on the Mur River, in the region of Styria, Graz is a particularly fine example of a central European urban complex that experienced many centuries of Habsburg rule. The historic centre of the city reflects artistic and architectural movements originating from the Germanic region, the Balkans, and the Mediterranean, for which it served as a crossroads for centuries.

"The devil promised the people of Graz to make their local mountain, the Schöckl. Satan flew over Graz with a huge rock from Africa in his hands. He threw the rock onto the town. The rock broke in two parts. Today, the smaller one is Austein with its Calvary. The bigger one is Schlossberg."

Legend of the Graz Mountains

Italy

Early Christian Monuments of Ravenna   (1)

In the Emilia-Romagna region, Ravenna was the seat of the Roman Empire in the 5th century and then of Byzantine Italy until the 8th century. It has a unique collection of early Christian mosaics and monuments. Eight buildings were constructed in the 5th and 6th centuries. They show great artistic skill, including a wonderful blend of Greco-Roman tradition, Christian iconography, and oriental and Western styles.

"Mysteriously secured by nature and doubly so after the failure of the Roman administration, Ravenna was the deathbed of the empire and its tomb."

Travel author Edward Hutton
(1875-1969)

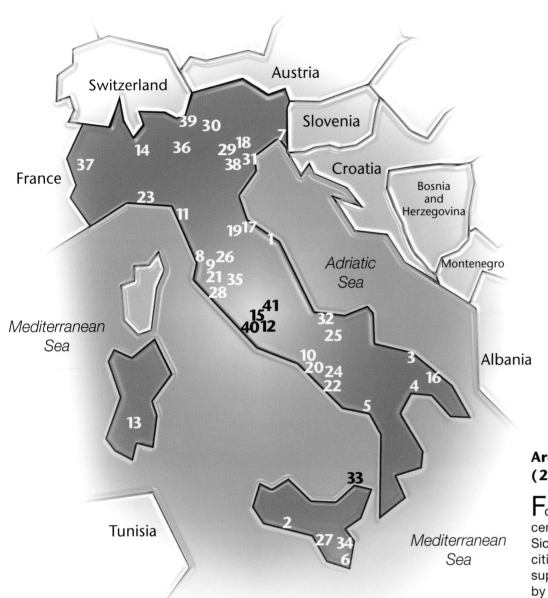

Archaeological Area of Agrigento (2)

Founded as a Greek colony in the 6th century BC on the southern coast of Sicily, Agrigento became one of the leading cities in the Mediterranean world. Its supremacy and pride are demonstrated by the remains of the magnificent Doric temples that dominate the ancient town, much of which still lies intact under today's fields and orchards.

Castel del Monte (3)

When the Emperor Frederick II built this castle near Bari in the 13th century, he imbued it with symbolic significance, as reflected in the location, the mathematical and astronomical precision of the layout, and the perfectly regular shape. A unique piece of medieval military architecture, Castel del Monte is a successful blend of elements from classical antiquity, the Islamic Orient and North European Cistercian Gothic.

I Sassi di Matera (4)

This is the most outstanding, intact example of a troglodyte settlement in the Mediterranean region, perfectly adapted to its terrain and ecosystem. The first inhabited zone dates from the Palaeolithic, while later settlements illustrate a number of significant stages in human history. Matera is in the southern region of Basilicata.

"Certain sections of the city are 2,000 years old, and the architecture, the blocks of stone, the surrounding areas and rocky terrain added a vista and backdrop that we used to create the backdrops for our lavish sets of Jerusalem ... In fact, the first time I saw it, I just went crazy, because it was so perfect."

Australian actor, director and producer Mel Gibson, speaking of the location of Sassi for the movie "The Passion of the Christ"

Cilento and Vallo di Diano National Park   (5)

During the prehistoric period, and again in the Middle Ages, the Cilento region served as a key route for cultural, political, and commercial communications, utilizing the crests of the mountain chains running east-west, and thereby creating a cultural landscape of outstanding significance and quality. The Cilento was the boundary between the Greek colonies of Magna Graecia and the indigenous Etruscan and Lucanian peoples. The remains of two major cities from classical times, Paestum and Velia, are found there.

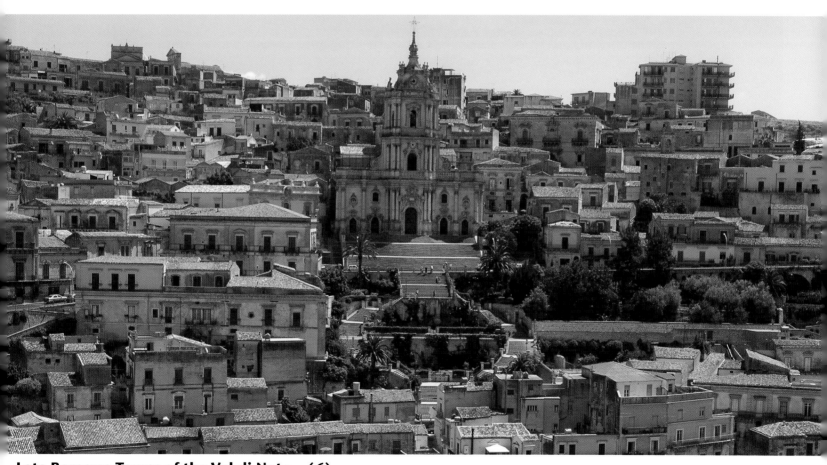

Late Baroque Towns of the Val di Noto   (6)

Eight towns in south-eastern Sicily – Caltagirone, Militello Val di Catania, Catania, Modica, Noto, Palazzolo, Ragusa and Scicli – were rebuilt after 1693 on or beside towns existing at the time of the earthquake which took place in that year. They represent a considerable collective undertaking, successfully carried out with a high level of architectural and artistic achievement.

Archaeological Area and the Patriarchal Basilica of Aquileia (7)

Aquileia, an ancient town at the head of the Adriatic, at the edge of the lagoons, was one of the largest and wealthiest cities of the Early Roman Empire. It was destroyed by Attila in the mid-5th century. Most of it still lies unexcavated beneath the fields, and as such it constitutes the greatest archaeological reserve of its kind. The Patriarchal Basilican Complex in Aquileia played a decisive role in the spread of Christianity into central Europe in the early Middle Ages.

Piazza del Duomo, Pisa (8)

Also known as the Campo dei Miracoli (Field of Miracles), Piazza del Duomo houses a group of monuments known the world over. These four masterpieces of medieval architecture – the cathedral, the baptistery, the campanile (the "Leaning Tower") and the cemetery – had a great influence on monumental art in Italy from the 11th to the 14th century.

"Italy's famed Leaning Tower of Pisa was last week in danger of being blown to marble bits. The Germans were reportedly using it as an artillery observation post."

Time Magazine,
August 7, 1944

Historic Centre of San Gimignano (9)

"San Gimignano delle belle Torri", a small but famous walled medieval town, is located in Tuscany, 56 km (35 miles) south of Florence. It served as an important relay point for pilgrims travelling to or from Rome on the Via Francigena. The patrician families who controlled the town built approximately 72 tower-houses as symbols of their wealth and power. Although only 14 have survived, San Gimignano has retained its feudal atmosphere and appearance.

"The train doesn't reach the city, nor does any major route. The town lives in superb isolation, above industrial smoke and noise, frozen in its barbarian luxury, unchanging in its rude Gothic architecture, resolved to keep for a long time its medieval atmosphere."

French wine grower Henry Aubert, 1922

18th-Century Royal Palace at Caserta (10)

Caserta, near Naples, was certainly the largest palace and probably the largest building erected in Europe in the 18th century. The monumental complex, created by the Bourbon King Charles III to rival Versailles and the Royal Palace in Madrid, is exceptional for the way in which it brings together a magnificent palace with its park and gardens, as well as natural woodland, hunting lodges and a silk factory.

Portovenere, Cinque Terre, and the Islands   (11)

The Ligurian coast between Cinque Terre and Portovenere, in north-western Italy, is a landscape of great scenic and cultural value. The layout and disposition of the small towns and the shaping of the surrounding landscape, overcoming the disadvantages of a steep, uneven terrain, encapsulate the continuous history of human settlement in this region over the past millennium.

"Noteworthy to see like a spectacle, the mountains not only in sweet incline but also quick so that even the birds flying over tire. Covered with stones that don't hold back water, vineyards cover the land, so meagre and delicate that they seem more like ivy than vines. From here comes wine for the table from a king."

G. Bracelli,
"De bello hispaniensi orae ligusticae descriptio", 1448

Villa Adriana - Tivoli   (12)

The Villa Adriana (at Tivoli, near Rome) is an exceptional complex of classical buildings created in the 2nd century AD by the Roman emperor Hadrian. It combines the best elements of the architectural heritage of Egypt, Greece and Rome in the form of an "ideal city".

204

Su Nuraxi di Barumini (13)

During the late 2nd millennium BC, in the Bronze Age, a special type of defensive structure known as nuraghi developed on the island of Sardinia. The complex consists of circular defensive towers in the form of truncated cones built of dressed stone, with corbel-vaulted internal chambers. It is the finest and most complete example of this remarkable form of prehistoric architecture.

Crespi d'Adda (14)

Crespi d'Adda, in Capriate San Gervasio, Lombardy, is an outstanding example of the 19th- and early 20th-century "company towns" built in Europe and North America by enlightened industrialists to meet workers' needs. The site is still remarkably intact and is partly used for industrial purposes, although changing economic and social conditions now threaten its survival.

Historic Centre of Rome (15)

Seat of the Roman Kingdom, Roman Republic, Roman Empire, Papal States, Kingdom of Italy and Italian Republic, Rome's history extends nearly 2,800 years. The World Heritage site, extended in 1990 to the walls of Urban VIII, includes some of the major monuments of antiquity such as the Forums, the Mausoleum of Augustus, the Mausoleum of Hadrian, the Pantheon, Trajan's Column and the Column of Marcus Aurelius, as well as the religious and public buildings of papal Rome.

As long as the Coliseum stands, so shall Rome
When the Coliseum falls, so shall Rome
When Rome falls, so shall the world

The Venerable Bede
(672 – 735)

The Trulli of Alberobello   (16)

The trulli, limestone dwellings found in the southern region of Puglia, are remarkable examples of drywall (mortarless) construction, a prehistoric building technique still in use in this region. The trulli are exceptional examples of a form of building deriving from prehistoric construction techniques that have survived intact and functioning into the modern world.

Ferrara, City of the Renaissance, and its Po Delta   (17)

This gorgeous city, which grew up around a ford over the River Po, became an intellectual and artistic centre that attracted the greatest minds of the Italian Renaissance in the 15th and 16th centuries. Here, Piero della Francesca, Jacopo Bellini and Andrea Mantegna decorated the palaces of the House of Este. The humanist concept of the "ideal city" also came to life here, in the neighbourhoods built from 1492 onwards by Biagio Rossetti.

City of Vicenza and the Palladian Villas of the Veneto (18)

Founded in the 2nd century BC in northern Italy, Vicenza prospered under Venetian rule from the early 15th to the end of the 18th century. The work of Andrea Palladio (1508–80), based on a detailed study of classical Roman architecture, gives the city its unique appearance. His work inspired a distinct architectural style known as Palladian, which spread to England and other European countries, and also to North America.

"Palladio is the Bible. You should get it and stick to it."

> *Third U.S. President and architect Thomas Jefferson, speaking of Palladio's I Quattro Libri dell'Architettura (The Four Books of Architecture)*

Cathedral, Torre Civica and Piazza Grande, Modena (19)

The magnificent 12th-century cathedral at Modena, located on the south side of the Po valley, is a supreme example of early Romanesque art. The Modena complex bears exceptional witness to the cultural traditions of the 12th century and is one of the best examples of an architectural complex where religious and civic values are combined in a medieval Christian town.

Historic Centre of Naples   (20)

From the Neapolis founded by Greek settlers in 470 BC to the city of today, Naples has retained the imprint of the successive cultures that emerged in Europe and the Mediterranean basin. This makes it a unique site, with a wealth of outstanding monuments such as the Church of Santa Chiara and the Castel Nuovo.

"See Naples and die. Well, I do not know that one would necessarily die after merely seeing it, but to attempt to live there might turn out a little differently. To see Naples as we saw it in the early dawn from far up on the side of Vesuvius, is to see a picture of wonderful beauty."

American writer
Mark Twain
(1835 – 1910)

Historic Centre of Siena   (21)

Siena is the embodiment of a medieval city of Tuscany. Its inhabitants pursued their rivalry with Florence right into the area of urban planning. Throughout the centuries, they preserved their city's Gothic appearance, acquired between the 12th and 15th centuries.

Costiera Amalfitana (22)

The Amalfi coast, a stretch of coastline on the southern side of the Sorrentine Peninsula (Province of Salerno), is an area of great physical beauty and natural diversity. It has been intensively settled by human communities since the early Middle Ages. There are a number of towns, such as Amalfi and Ravello, with architectural and artistic works of great significance.

Strada Nuova and the Palazzi dei Rolli in Genoa (23)

Called today Via Garibaldi, Strada Nuova is a beautiful street built from 1551 to 1583. It preserves exceptional artefacts of the palaces of the city's greatest aristocratic families. These palaces were real architectural models for the renewal of noble residences located along the main street of the ancient city, representing the reference point for the construction of new palaces within the medieval urban structure. As a consequence, the Strada Nuova symbolized the political achievement of a new ruling elite and was completed by several buildings stretching towards the sea and mountain.

Archaeological Areas of Pompei, Herculaneum and Torre Annunziata (24)

When Vesuvius erupted on 24 August AD 79, it engulfed the two flourishing Roman towns of Pompeii and Herculaneum, as well as the many wealthy villas in the area. These have been progressively excavated and made accessible to the public since the mid-18th century. The impressive remains provide a complete and vivid picture of society and daily life at a specific moment in the past that is without parallel anywhere in the world.

Assisi, the Basilica of San Francesco and Other Franciscan Sites (25)

This medieval city on a hill is the birthplace of Saint Francis, closely associated with the work of the Franciscan Order. Its medieval art masterpieces, such as the Basilica of San Francesco and its paintings, have made Assisi a fundamental reference point for the development of Italian and European art and architecture. The town is dominated by the medieval castle, called "Rocca Maggiore", built by Cardinal Albornoz (1367) and added to by Popes Pius II and Paul III.

"It is essential that religious people and communities should, in the clearest and most radical way, repudiate violence. There is no religious goal which can possibly justify the use of violence by man against man."

Pope John Paul II condemning violence and the events of September 11, 2001 in the name of religion at a gathering of world religious leaders in Assisi

"...darker, and larger, and mightier, spread the cloud above them. It was a sudden and more ghastly Night rushing upon the realm of Noon!"

Excerpt of "The Last Days of Pompeii" by Edward Bulwer-Lytton, 1834

Historic Centre of Florence (26)

Heart of Tuscany and symbol of the Italian Renaissance, Florence rose to economic and cultural pre-eminence under the Medici in the 15th and 16th centuries. Its 600 years of extraordinary artistic activity can be admired above all in the 13th-century cathedral (Santa Maria del Fiore), the Church of Santa Croce, the Uffizi and the Pitti Palace, and the work of great masters such as Giotto, Brunelleschi, Botticelli and Michelangelo.

"When I returned to Florence, I found myself famous. The City Council asked me to carve a colossal David from a nineteen-foot block of marble – and damaged to boot! I locked myself away in a workshop behind the cathedral, hammered and chiselled at the towering block for three long years..."

Renaissance sculptor, architect, painter, and poet Michelangelo (1475 - 1564)

Villa Romana del Casale (27)

Roman exploitation of the countryside is symbolized by the Villa Romana del Casale in Sicily, the centre of the large estate upon which the rural economy of the Western Empire was based. The villa is one of the most luxurious of its kind. It is especially noteworthy for the richness and quality of the mosaics that decorate almost every room.

Val d'Orcia   (28)

The landscape of the Val d'Orcia was celebrated by painters from the Siennese School, which flourished during the Renaissance. It is part of the agricultural hinterland of Siena, re-drawn and developed when it was integrated in the territory of the city-state in the 14th and 15th centuries to reflect an idealized model of good governance and to create an aesthetically pleasing picture.

City of Verona   (29)

This ancient town in northern Italy was founded in the 1st century BC. It particularly flourished under the rule of the Scaliger family in the 13th and 14th centuries, and as part of the Republic of Venice from the 15th to 18th centuries. Verona has preserved a remarkable number of monuments from antiquity, as well as the medieval and Renaissance periods. It also represents an outstanding example of a military stronghold. Today, Verona remains famous for its Roman amphitheatre and as the setting of the story of Romeo and Juliet.

Venice and its Lagoon (31)

Venice, the city of canals, stretches across 118 small islands in a marshy lagoon along the Adriatic Sea, in northeast Italy. Founded in the 5th century, Venice became a major maritime power in the 10th century. The whole city is an extraordinary architectural masterpiece in which even the smallest building contains works by some of the world's greatest artists such as Giorgione, Titian, Tintoretto, Veronese and others.

"A realist, in Venice, would become a romantic by mere faithfulness to what he saw before him."

British poet
Arthur Symons
1865 - 1945)

Rock Drawings in Valcamonica (30)

Valcamonica, situated in the Lombardy plain, has one of the world's greatest collections of prehistoric petroglyphs, more than 140,000 symbols and figures carved in the rock over a period of 8,000 years and depicting themes related to agriculture, navigation, war and magic.

Historic Centre of Urbino (32)

The small hill town of Urbino, in the Marche, experienced a great cultural flourish in the 15th century, attracting artists and scholars from all over Italy and beyond, and influencing cultural developments elsewhere in Europe. Owing to its economic and cultural stagnation from the 16th century onwards, it has preserved its Renaissance appearance to a remarkable extent.

Isole Eolie - Aeolian Islands   (33)

The Aeolian Islands, north of Sicily, provide an outstanding record of volcanic island-building and destruction. Studied since at least the 18th century, the islands have provided the science of vulcanology with examples of two types of eruption (Vulcanian and Strombolian), and thus have featured prominently in the education of geologists for more than 200 years.

Syracuse and the Rocky Necropolis of Pantalica   (34)

Located on the eastern coast of Sicily, the site consists of two separate elements, containing outstanding vestiges dating back to Greek and Roman times. The Necropolis of Pantalica features over 5,000 tombs cut into the rock near open stone quarries, most of them dating from the 13th to 7th century BC. Vestiges of the Byzantine era also remain in the area, notably the foundations of the Anaktoron (Prince's Palace). The other part of the property, Ancient Syracuse, includes the nucleus of the city's foundation in the 8th century BC under the name Ortygia, by Greeks who had come from Corinth.

"Syracuse is the greatest Greek city and the most beautiful of all."

*Marcus Tullius Cicero
(106 – 43 BC),
orator and statesman of Ancient Rome*

Historic Centre of the City of Pienza (35)

It was in this Tuscan town that Renaissance town-planning concepts were first put into practice after Pope Pius II decided, in 1459, to transform the look of his birthplace. This new vision of urban space was realized in the superb square known as Piazza Pio II.

Church and Dominican Convent of Santa Maria delle Grazie (36)

The refectory of the Convent of Santa Maria delle Grazie forms an integral part of this architectural complex, begun in Milan in 1463 and reworked at the end of the 15th century by Bramante. On the north wall is The Last Supper, the unrivalled masterpiece painted between 1495 and 1497 by Leonardo da Vinci, whose work was to herald a new era in art history.

"The second essential (thing) in painting is appropriate action and a due variety in the figures, so that the men may not all look like brothers."

Excerpt from the notebooks of Leonardo Da Vinci

Residences of the Royal House of Savoy   (37)

When Emmanuel-Philibert, Duke of Savoy, moved his capital to Turin in 1562, he began a vast series of building projects to demonstrate the power of the ruling house. This outstanding complex, designed and embellished by the leading architects and artists of the time, radiates out into the surrounding countryside from the Royal Palace in the "Command Area of Turin to include many country residences and hunting lodges.

"FERT: Foedere Et Religione Tenemur (We will be kept together by the constitutio pact and by religion)."

Motto of the Real Casa di Savoja dynasty

Botanical Garden (Orto Botanico), Padua (38)

The world's first botanical garden was created in Padua in 1545. It still preserves its original layout, a circular central plot symbolizing the world, surrounded by a ring of water. It has made a profound contribution to the development of many modern scientific disciplines, including botany, medicine, chemistry, ecology, and pharmacy.

Sacri Monti of Piedmont and Lombardy (39)

The nine Sacri Monti (Sacred Mountains) of northern Italy are groups of chapels and other architectural features created in the late 16th and 17th centuries and dedicated to different aspects of the Christian faith. In addition to their symbolic spiritual meaning, they are of great beauty by virtue of the skill with which they have been integrated into the surrounding natural landscape of hills, forests and lakes.

Etruscan Necropolises of Cerveteri and Tarquinia (40)

These two large Etruscan cemeteries reflect different types of burial practices from the 9th to the 1st century BC. They bear witness to the achievements of Etruscan culture, which flourished in the northern part of what is now Italy, prior to the formation of the Roman Republic. The necropolis of Tarquinia contains 6,000 graves cut in the rock. It is famous for its 200 painted tombs.

Villa d'Este, Tivoli (41)

The Villa d'Este is a masterpiece of Italian architecture and garden design. The principles of Renaissance design and aesthetics are illustrated in an exceptional manner by the Villa's gardens, which had a profound influence on the development of this art throughout Europe.

"The precise location of heaven on earth has never been established, but it may very well be right here."

*American Pulitzer Prize-winning columnist
Herb Caen
(1916 – 1997),
speaking of the Villa*

Malta

Italy

Tunisia

1

2

3

*Mediterranean
Sea*

Hal Saflieni Hypogeum (1)

This Hypogeum is a labyrinth of underground chambers dating from 2500 BC, probably used as both a burial site and a temple, with cyclopean rigging to lift huge blocks of coralline limestone. Many statuettes, amulets, figurines and vases were recovered here. The most famous figurine is that of the so-called Sleeping Lady, a reclining figure perhaps meant as a representation of eternal sleep.

City of Valletta   (2)

Valletta is named after its founder, the respected Grand Master of the Order of St. John, Jean Parisot de la Valette. But the city really owes its birth to his archenemy, Grand Turk Suleiman the Magnificent. The city was ruled successively by the Phoenicians, Greeks, Carthaginians, Romans, Byzantines, Arabs and the Order of the Knights of St. John. Valletta's 320 monuments make it one of the most concentrated historic areas in the world.

"I've heard the anchor fall and knew that we were in the harbour of Malta ... Valletta and all those proud ships here under the world's strongest fortress were only the frame for it. The setting was beautiful, one of the most beautiful I have seen."

Danish author and poet Hans Christian Andersen, March 1841

Megalithic Temples of Malta   (3)

Seven megalithic temples are found on the islands of Malta and Gozo, each the result of an individual development. The two temples of Ggantija on the island of Gozo are notable for their gigantic Bronze Age structures. On the island of Malta, the temples of Hagar Qin, Mnajdra and Tarxien are unique architectural masterpieces, given the limited resources available to their builders.

Historic Centre of Warsaw　(1)

In August 1944, during the Warsaw Uprising – an urban guerrilla movement opposing the Polish underground army and the Nazis – over 85% of Warsaw's historic centre was destroyed. Acting on Hitler's orders, German forces burned down city block after city block. After the war, a five-year reconstruction campaign by its citizens resulted in today's meticulous restoration of the Old Town of the Polish capital, with its churches, palaces and marketplace. It is an outstanding example of a near-total reconstruction covering a huge span of history, from the 13th to the 20th century.

"The heroes of Poland's resistance movement made a significant contribution to our joint victory over Nazism. (...) It will remain in the memory of Russians forever."

*Russian President
Vladimir Putin*

Poland

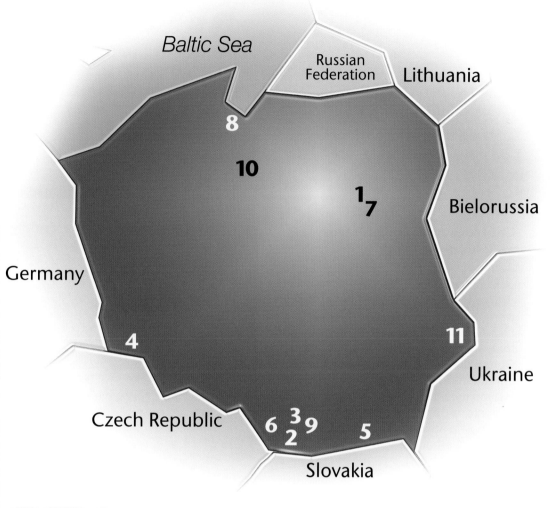

Baltic Sea

Russian Federation

Lithuania

8

10

1
7

Bielorussia

Germany

4

11

Ukraine

Czech Republic

6 3 9
2

5

Slovakia

Kalwaria Zebrzydowska (2)

Kalwaria Zebrzydowska is a breatht king cultural landscape of great spiritual significance. This southern city is the best-known sanctuary in Poland. Its natural setting, in which a series of symbolic places of worship relating to the Passion of Jesus Christ and the life of the Virgin Mary was laid out at the beginning of the 17th century, has remained virtually unchanged. It remains a place of pilgrimage to this day.

Crakow's Historic Centre (3)

The historic centre of Crakow, the former capital of Poland, is situated at the foot of the Royal Wawel Castle. The 13th-century merchants' town boasts Europe's largest market square and numerous historical houses, palaces and churches, with their magnificent interiors. The medieval urban layout of the Old Town has not changed for centuries. Thanks to a manoeuvre by advancing Soviet forces, Crakow escaped complete destruction during World War II.

Churches of Peace in Jawor and Swidnica (4)

The Churches of Peace, the largest timber-framed religious buildings in Europe, were built in the former Silesia in the mid-17th century, amid the religious strife that followed the Peace of Westphalia. Constrained by physical and political conditions, the Churches of Peace bear testimony to the quest for religious freedom and are a rare expression of Lutheran ideology in an idiom generally associated with the Catholic Church.

Wooden Churches of Southern Little Poland (5)

The wooden churches represent outstanding examples of the different aspects of medieval church-building traditions in Roman Catholic culture. Built using the horizontal log technique, common in Eastern and Northern Europe since the Middle Ages, these churches were sponsored by noble families and became status symbols.

Auschwitz Concentration Camp (6)

Situated about 60 km (37 miles) southwest of Crakow, the fortified walls, barbed wire, platforms, barracks, gallows, gas chambers and cremation ovens show the conditions within which the Nazi genocide took place in the former concentration and extermination camp of Auschwitz-Birkenau, the largest in the Third Reich. According to historical investigations, 1.5 million people, among them a great number of Jews, were systematically starved, tortured and murdered in this camp, the symbol of humanity's cruelty to its fellow human beings in the 20th century.

"Auschwitz.
What a sorrow. What a monstrosity.
And still a hope for mankind."

General Charles de Gaulle

Centennial Hall in Wroclaw (7)

This landmark in the history of reinforced concrete architecture was erected in 1911-1913 by Max Berg, at the time municipal architect in Breslau, as the Polish city of Wroc_aw was called at the time, when it was part of Germany. The structure of the Centennial Hall is a symmetrical quatrefoil form with a vast circular central space that can seat some 6,000 people.

Castle of the Teutonic Order in Malbork   (8)

Known as the biggest medieval castle in Europe, this 13th-century fortified monastery belonging to the Teutonic Order was substantially enlarged and embellished after 1309, when the seat of the Grand Master moved here from Venice. A particularly fine example of a medieval brick castle, it later fell into decay, but was meticulously restored in the 19th and early 20th centuries. Following severe damage in the Second World War, it was once again restored, using the detailed documentation prepared by earlier conservators.

"Next year we either conquer the Crossed Knights or we perish as a nation, and as individuals."

Wladislaus II Jagiello, Grand Prince of Lithuania and King of Poland, planning an attack against the Teutonic Knights in Malbork, in August 1401

Wieliczka Salt Mine   (9)

Beneath the town of Wieliczka lies one of the world's oldest operating salt mines. This deposit of rock salt has been mined since the 13th century. Spread over nine levels, it has 300 km (186 miles) of galleries with works of art, altars and statues sculpted in the salt, making it a fascinating pilgrimage into the past of a major industrial undertaking.

"The grimy workmen, the prodigious masses of salt, the colossal beams of timber, the gloomy caverns and wonderful labyrinth of passages. Earth and salt everywhere."

Writer and journalist J. Ross Browne, 1866

Medieval Town of Torun (10)

Birthplace of Nicolaus Copernicus, Torun owes its origins to the Teutonic Order, which built a castle there in northern Poland in the mid-13th century as a base for the conquest and evangelization of Prussia. It soon developed a commercial role as part of the Hanseatic League. In both the Old and New Town, many imposing public and private buildings from the 14th and 15th centuries are striking evidence of Torun's significance.

*"There is no one centre in the universe.
The Earth's centre is not the centre of the universe.
The centre of the universe is near the sun.
The rotation of the Earth accounts for the
apparent daily rotation of the stars."*

*Conclusions of Nicolaus Copernicus
in his book called the Little Commentary,
hand-written in 1514*

Old City of Zamoc (11)

Called the jewel of Polish Renaissance, Zamoc was founded in the 16th century in south-eastern Poland by chancellor Jan Zamoysky, on the trade route linking western and northern Europe with the Black Sea. Modelled on Italian theories of the "ideal city" and built by the architect Bernando Morando, Zamosc is a perfect example of a late-16th-century Renaissance town. It has retained its original layout and fortifications and a large number of buildings that combine Italian and central European architectural traditions.

Estonia

Historic Centre of Tallinn   (1)

Tallinn, located on the north coast of the Baltic Sea, is the capital city and main seaport of Estonia. The origins of Tallinn date back to the 13th century, when a castle was built there by the crusading knights of the Teutonic Order. It then developed as a major centre of the Hanseatic League. Historically, the city has been attacked, sacked, razed and pillaged on numerous occasions. Although extensively bombed during the latter stages of World War II, much of the mediaeval old town still retains its charm.

Latvia

Historic Centre of Riga (1)

Founded in 1201, Riga was a major centre of the Hanseatic League. The town's historic centre, while retaining its medieval and later urban fabric relatively intact, is of outstanding universal value by virtue of the quality and the quantity of its Art Nouveau/Jugendstil architecture (which is unparalleled anywhere in the world), and its 19th century wooden architecture.

"Riga is a jewel. The transformation since the Soviets left is absolutely incredible. It was a grey, dark depressing place in 1986. If you look at it now, Riga is a wonderful city on the Baltic Sea. It has beautiful architecture and a great downtown. It's like a little Paris."

Latvian-born American
Dr. Christopher Kristaps Zarins,
Chief of Stanford's Division
of Vascular Surgery

Lithuania

Historic Centre of Vilnius (1)

As the political centre of the Grand Duchy of Lithuania from the 13th to the late 18th century, Vilnius has had a profound influence on the cultural and architectural development of much of Eastern Europe. Despite invasions and partial destruction, it has preserved an impressive complex of Gothic, Renaissance, Baroque and classical buildings, as well as its medieval layout and natural setting.

Curonian Spit (2)
(Site shared with Russia Federation)

The Curonian Spit is a 100-km-long (62-mile) sandbank that stretches from the Sambian Peninsula to Klaipeda. Half of it is in Russia, the other in Lithuanian territory. Human habitation of these sand dunes, the highest in Europe, dates back to prehistoric times. The sandbank has been threatened by the natural forces of wind and waves, and its survival to the present day has been made possible only as a result of ceaseless human efforts to combat the erosion of the Spit, dramatically illustrated by continuing stabilisation and reforestation projects that began in 1825. Much of the Spit is now covered with forest.

"What is there left for the poor poet from these things that are materially tangible and poetic at the same time? I recall one piece of scenery that has grown deep into my heart over the past few years, and that is the Curonian Spit."

German novelist Paul Thomas Mann
(1875 – 1955)

Kernavé Archaeological Site (3)

The Kernavé Archaeological Site, in eastern Lithuania, about 35 km (22 miles) northwest of Vilnius, is an exceptional testimony to some 10 millennia of human settlements in the Baltic region. Situated in the valley of the River Neris, the site is a complex ensemble of archaeological properties, encompassing the town of Kernavé, several forts, some unfortified settlements, burial sites, and other archaeological, historical and cultural monuments from the late Palaeolithic period to the Middle Ages.

"Life, sometimes booming, in decline at other times, has lasted here for millennia from the Late Palaeolithic (9000 BC) to this day."

Archaeology professor Dr. A. Luchtanas

Slovakia

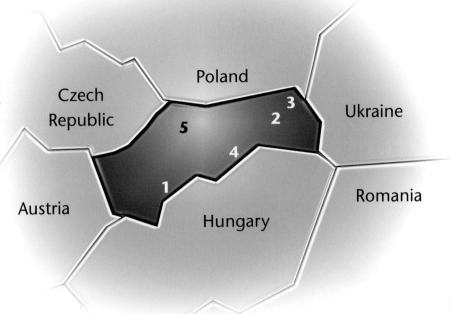

Banská Stiavnica   (1)

Over the centuries, the town of Banska Stiavnica in central Slovakia was visited by many outstanding engineers and scientists, many of whom contributed to its fame. The old medieval mining centre grew into a town with Renaissance palaces, 16th-century churches, elegant squares and castles. The urban centre blends into the surrounding landscape, which contains vital relics of the mining and metallurgical activities of the past.

"In 1627, gunpowder was used for the first time in the world in local mines for breaking the stone."

City of Banská Stiavnica

Spissky Hrad and its Associated Cultural Monuments   (2)

Spissky Hrad has one of the largest ensembles of 13th- and 14th-century military, political and religious buildings in Eastern Europe, and its Romanesque and Gothic architecture has remained remarkably intact.

"Climbing stairwells so low and narrow that only one hunched body at a time can pass, you emerge on the observation deck high above the beautiful Spi_ region. Yellow fields of rape weed checker the otherwise green landscape rolling up to the base of the High Tatras, creating an image that is typically Spi_."

Journalist Chris Togneri of The Slovak Spectator

Bardejov Town Conservation Reserve (3)

This site is a small but exceptionally complete and well-preserved example of a fortified medieval town from the 14th century. Among other remarkable features, it contains a small Jewish quarter around a fine 18th-century synagogue.

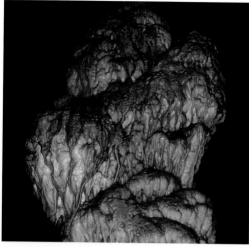

Caves of Aggtelek Karst and Slovak Karst (4)

(Site shared with Hungary)

Located on the border between Hungary and Slovakia, this network of 712 caves is a typical temperate-zone karstic system. Because they display an extremely rare combination of tropical and glacial climatic effects, these caves make it possible to study geological history over tens of millions of years. All three types of caves are present is this region: ice, stalactite and aragonite.

Vlkolínec (5)

Vlkolínec is a remarkably intact settlement of 45 buildings with the traditional features of a central European village. This region represents the type of central Slovakian settlement with wooden architecture that is widespread in mountain and foothill regions in the northern part of central Slovakia.

Historic Centre of Prague (1)

Referred as "the Pearl of Europe" or "the Heart of Europe", Prague is a magical city of bridges, cathedrals, gold-tipped towers and church domes. Built between the 11th and 18th centuries, the Old Town, the Lesser Town and the New Town speak of the great architectural and cultural influence enjoyed by this city since the Middle Ages. Prague is also the home of the famous historical Charles Bridge.

"It was at the latest in 1934 that I decided that Prague was the most beautiful city in Central Europe. This has not changed..."

*Austrian-born philosopher of science
Sir Karl Raimund Popper, 1994*

Lednice-Valtice Cultural Landscape (2)

Between the 17th and 20th centuries, the ruling dukes of Liechtenstein transformed their domains in southern Moravia into a striking landscape. It married Baroque architecture and the classical and neo-Gothic style of the castles of Lednice and Valtice, with countryside fashioned according to English romantic principles of landscape architecture. At 200 sq. km (49,421 acres), it is one of the largest artificial landscapes in Europe.

Czech Republic

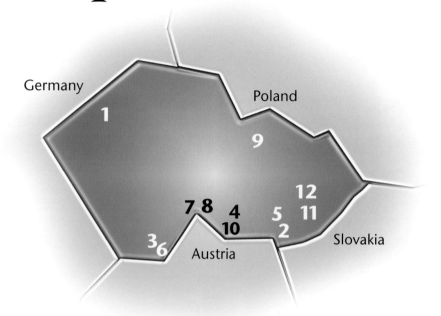

Holasovice Historical Village Reservation (3)

Holasovice is an exceptionally complete and well-preserved example of a traditional central European village. It has a large number of outstanding 18th- and 19th-century vernacular buildings in a style known as "South Bohemian Folk Baroque", and preserves a ground plan dating from the Middle Ages.

Jewish Quarter and Saint Procopius Basilica in Trebíc   (4)

The ensemble of the Jewish Quarter, the old Jewish cemetery and the Basilica of St. Procopius in Trebíc are reminders of the co-existence of Jewish and Christian cultures from the Middle Ages to the 20th century. St. Procopius Basilica, built as part of the Benedictine monastery in the early 13th century, is a remarkable example of the influence of Western European architectural heritage in this region.

Tugendhat Villa in Brno   (5)

The Tugendhat Villa, a masterpiece designed by the architect Mies van der Rohe, is an outstanding example of the international style in the modern movement of architecture as it developed in Europe in the 1920s. Its particular value lies in the application of innovative spatial and aesthetic concepts that aim to satisfy new lifestyle needs by taking advantage of the opportunities afforded by modern industrial production.

Historic Centre of Cesky Krumlov (6)

Situated on the banks of the Vltava River in the South Bohemia region, the town was built around a 13th-century castle with Gothic, Renaissance and Baroque elements. It is an outstanding example of a small central European medieval town whose architectural heritage has remained intact thanks to its peaceful evolution over more than five centuries.

Historic Centre of Telc (7)

The houses in Telc, which stands on a hilltop, were originally built of wood. After a fire in the late 14th century, the town was rebuilt in stone, surrounded by walls and further strengthened by a network of artificial ponds. The town's Gothic castle was rebuilt in High Gothic style in the late 15th century.

Kutná Hora (8)

Kutná Hora developed as a result of the exploitation of the silver mines. In the 14th century, it became a royal city endowed with monuments that symbolized its prosperity. The Church of St. Barbara, a jewel of the late Gothic period, and the Cathedral of Our Lady at Sedlec, which was restored in line with early-18th-century Baroque tastes, were to influence the architecture of central Europe.

"In 1870, a Czech woodcarver named Frantisek Rint decorated the church with the bones from the cemetery to make room for those who wanted to be buried there. The bones of 40,000 people were used to create this fascinating chapel."

California Academy of Sciences, about one of the most famous attractions of Kutná Hora, the Ossuary In Sedlec

Litomysl Castle (9)

The East Bohemian town of Litomysl emerged in the 13th century on the site of an older fortified settlement on the Trstenice path, an important trading route linking Bohemia and Moravia. Its castle is an outstanding and immaculately preserved example of the arcade castle, a type of building first developed in Italy and modified in the Czech lands to create an evolved form of special architectural quality. It preserves intact the range of ancillary buildings associated with an aristocratic residence of this type.

"The father of Bedrich Smetana rented a brewery in front of the castle. Bedrich Smetana was born here in 1824. They left Litomysl when he was nearly seven years old. But when he was six years old he played the piano at the theatre here for citizens and for the Duke of the Litomysl Castle."

Castellan Josef Holub, speaking of the famous Czech composer

Pilgrimage Church of Saint John of Nepomuk at Zelená Hora (10)

This pilgrimage church, built in honour of St. John of Nepomuk, stands at Zelena Hora, not far from Zdar nad Sazavou in Moravia. Constructed at the beginning of the 18th century on a star-shaped plan, it is the most unusual work by the great architect Jan Blazej Santini, whose highly original style falls between neo-Gothic and Baroque.

Gardens and Castle at Kromemeríz   (11)

Kromemeriz stands on the site of an earlier ford across the River Morava, at the foot of the Chriby mountain range, which dominates the central part of Moravia. The ensemble at Kromemeriz, and in particular the Pleasure Garden, played a significant role in the development of Baroque garden and palace design in central Europe.

Holy Trinity Column in Olomouc (12)

This memorial column, 35-metres (115-feet) high and erected in 1740, is the most outstanding example of a type of monument specific to central Europe. In the characteristic regional style known as Olomouc Baroque, it is decorated with many fine religious sculptures, the work of the distinguished Moravian artist Ondrej Zahner.

"... I shall raise a column so high and splendid it shall not have an equal in any other town..."

*Václav Render,
Olomouc master stonemason,
commenting on his project
for building an honorary column,
submitted to the City Council
on October 29, 1715*

Hungary

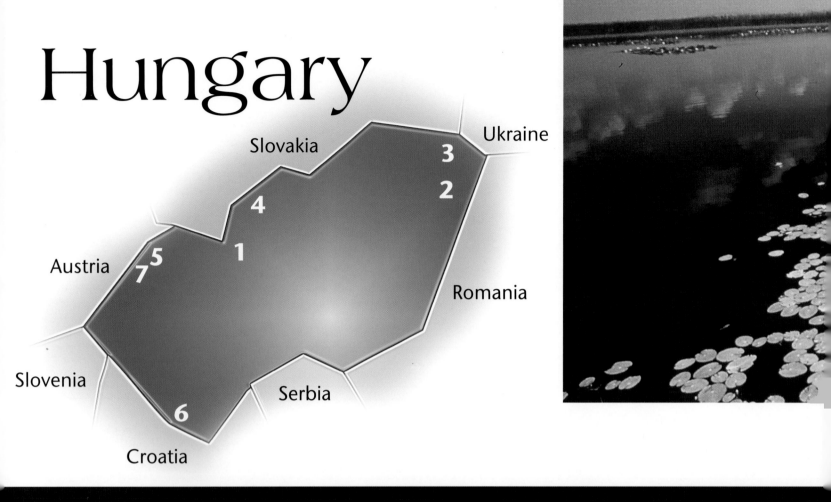

Slovakia

Ukraine

3

2

4

1

5

7

Austria

Romania

Slovenia

Serbia

6

Croatia

Budapest (1)

Various periods in the history of the Hungarian capital can be traced in the buildings on the banks of the Danube. This site boasts the remains of monuments such as the Roman city of Aquincum and the Gothic castle of Buda, which have had a considerable influence on the architecture of several eras. It is one of the world's outstanding urban landscapes, including buildings such as the magnificent Hungarian Parliament, the Buda Castle and Andrassy Street.

"The architectural heritage of Budapest is breathtaking, and no architect should miss visiting this fantastic city."

Lewis Gilbert Koerner,
President of the American Institute of
Architects (AIA) – Europe Division, 2001

Hortobágy National Park - The Puszta (2)

Near Debrecen, in eastern Hungary, the cultural landscape of the Hortobágy Puszta consists of a vast area of plains and wetlands. It is the largest continuous natural grassland in Europe. Traditional forms of land use, such as the grazing of domestic animals, have been present in this pastoral society for more than two millennia.

*"We are said to be an equestrian nation
and we also believe in it. (…)
The traditions, equipment, tools and buildings
of nomadic pastoral life are preserved
and fostered in many places in Hortobágy
and Bugacpuszta – in possibly the most
magnificent plains of Europe."*

Hungarian Equestrian Federation

Historic Cultural Landscape of the Tokaj Wine Region (3)

Tokaj, known around the world for its wine, is a small town in north-eastern Hungary, near the Slovakian border. The Tokaji wine region represents a distinct viticultural tradition that has existed for at least a thousand years, and which has survived intact up to the present. With its unique geological and geographical features, the area has enjoyed protection since 1737 when, by royal decree, it was declared a closed wine region, the first in the world.

*"… his kingdom of Hungary was one of
the finest countries in the world; it was most
fertile, producing in great abundance wines
of various sorts, all excellent, though Tokaj
was the best."*

*John Adams,
2nd President of the United States*

Old Village of Hollókö and its Surroundings   (4)

A few miles northeast of Budapest, Hollókö is an outstanding example of a deliberately preserved traditional settlement. This village, which developed mainly during the 17th and 18th centuries, is a living example of rural life before the agricultural revolution of the 20th century. The residents of the village are the Paloc people. In addition to their unique dialect, they retain their traditions and their colourful, richly decorated folk costumes.

Millenary Benedictine Abbey of Pannonhalma and its Natural Environment   (5)

The history of the abbey, built on the holy mount in the Roman province of Pannonia, near Gyor, is as old as the history of Hungary itself. The first Benedictine monks settled here in 996. They went on to convert the Hungarians, establish the country's first school and, in 1055, write the first document in the Hungarian language. From the time of its founding, this monastic community has promoted culture throughout central Europe.

Early Christian Necropolis of Pécs (6)

This city was once a Roman provincial town called Sopianae. In the 4th century, a remarkable series of decorated tombs were constructed in its cemetery. These are important both structurally and architecturally, since they were built as underground burial chambers with memorial chapels above the ground. The Sopianae cemetery bears outstanding testimony to the strength and faith of the Christian communities of Late Roman Europe.

Fertö/Neusiedlersee Cultural Landscape   (7)
(Site shared with Austria)

Located on the border between Austria and Hungary, the Fertö/Neusiedler Lake area has been the meeting place of different cultures for eight millennia. This is graphically demonstrated by its varied landscape, the result of an evolutionary symbiosis between human activity and the physical environment. The remarkable rural architecture of the villages surrounding the lake and of several 18th- and 19th-century palaces adds to the area's considerable cultural interest.

Romania

Slovakia
Ukraine
6 Moldova
5
Hungary
1
3
2
Black Sea
4 7
Serbia
Bulgaria

Historic Centre of Sighisoara   (1)

Founded by German craftsmen and merchants known as the Saxons of Transylvania, Sighisoara is a fine example of a small, fortified medieval town. It played an important strategic and commercial role on the fringes of central Europe for several centuries, and it is the birthplace of prince Vlad Tepes, better known as the mythical Dracula.

"He was not very tall, but very stocky and strong, with a cruel and terrible appearance, a long straight nose, distended nostrils, a thin and reddish face in which the large wide-open green eyes were framed by bushy black eyebrows, which made them appear threatening…"

Vatican Ambassador Nicholas of Modrussa, reporting in a letter to Pope Pio II the horrible acts of Vlad Tepes in 1464

Danube Delta   (2)

The waters of the Danube, which flow into the Black Sea, form the largest and best preserved of Europe's deltas. The Danube delta hosts over 300 species of birds as well as 45 freshwater fish species in its numerous lakes and marshes. This is the place where millions of birds from different places on Earth come to lay their eggs. There are currently some tensions between Romania and Ukraine regarding the management of the delta.

"The last worthy deed of the Danube, so rich in marvels, is the Delta."

Romanian geographer
Simion Mehedinti
(1869-1962)

Villages with Fortified Churches in Transylvania   (3)

With their fortified churches, these villages provide a vivid picture of the cultural landscape of southern Transylvania. The seven villages inscribed, founded by the Transylvanian Saxons, are characterized by a specific land-use system, settlement pattern and organization of the family farmstead that have been preserved since the late Middle Ages. They are dominated by their fortified churches, which illustrate building styles from the 13th to the 16th century.

"The beauty of the Saxon villages is not simply a matter of their evocative architecture and magnificent churches... The beauty of this – as perhaps of all landscapes – is that it is the outcome of successful settlement."

Jessica Douglas-Home, founder of the Mihai Eminescu Trust, which plays an important role in the region's academic and cultural revival

Dacian Fortresses of the Orastie Mountains　(4)

The extensive and well-preserved remains of these fortresses present a picture of a vigorous and innovative Iron Age civilisation. Built in the 1st centuries BC and AD under Dacian rule, the fortresses show an unusual fusion of military and religious architectural techniques and concepts from the classical world and the late European Iron Age.

Wooden Churches of Maramure (5)

These eight churches from northern Transylvania are outstanding examples of a range of architectural solutions from different periods and areas. They show the variety of designs and craftsmanship adopted for these narrow, high, timber constructions with their characteristic tall, slim clock towers at the western end of the building, either single- or double-roofed and covered with shingles. As such, they are a particular vernacular expression of the cultural landscape of this mountainous area of northern Romania.

Churches of Moldavia   (6)

With their painted exterior walls, decorated with 15th- and 16th-century frescoes that are considered masterpieces of Byzantine art, these seven churches in northern Moldavia are unique in Europe. Far from being merely wall decorations, the paintings represent complete cycles of religious murals on all facades. Their outstanding composition, elegant outline and harmonious colours blend perfectly with the surrounding landscape.

Monastery of Horezu   (7)

Founded in 1690 by Prince Constantine Brancovan, the monastery of Horezu, in Walachia, is a masterpiece of the "Brancovan" style. It is known for its architectural purity and balance, the richness of its sculptural detail, the treatment of its religious compositions, its votive portraits and its painted decorative works.

Croatia

The Cathedral of Saint James in Sibenik (1)

This cathedral, on the Dalmatian coast, bears witness to the considerable exchanges in the field of monumental arts between northern Italy, Dalmatia and Tuscany in the 15th and 16th centuries. The form and the decorative elements of the cathedral, such as a remarkable frieze decorated with 71 sculptured faces of men, women, and children, illustrate the successful fusion of Gothic and Renaissance art.

Plitvice Lakes National Park (2)

The waters flowing over the limestone and chalk have, over thousands of years, deposited travertine barriers, creating natural dams which, in turn, have created a series of beautiful lakes, caves and waterfalls. These geological processes continue today. The forests in the park are home to bears, wolves and many rare bird species.

"The lakes were formed by the Black Queen, answering people's prayers by making the rain pour and pour in the valley after a sultry oppression sat over the fields and mountains for months, drying up the Crna Rijeka (Black River)."

Legend of the foundation of the Plitvice Lakes

Historic City of Trogir   (3)

Trogir, a historic town and harbour at the Adriatic coast, has 2,300 years of fascinating, continuous urban traditions. The island settlement's orthogonal street plan dates back to the Hellenistic period, and successive rulers embellished it with many fine public and domestic buildings and fortifications. Trogir's medieval core, surrounded by walls, comprises a preserved castle and tower and a series of dwellings and palaces from the Romanesque, Gothic, Renaissance and Baroque periods.

Old City of Dubrovnik (4)

The "Pearl of the Adriatic", on the Dalmatian coast, became an important Mediterranean Sea power from the 13th century onwards. Although severely damaged by an earthquake in 1667, Dubrovnik managed to preserve its beautiful Gothic, Renaissance and Baroque churches, monasteries, palaces and fountains. Damaged again in the 1990s by armed conflict, it is now the focus of a major restoration program co-ordinated by UNESCO.

"You walk around the inner city, and there's nothing that reminds you of the war."

Dutch NATO official Bert Tiemes, speaking of the great recovery of the city after the war with Serbia

Historical Complex of Split with the Palace of Diocletian   (5)

On a small peninsula of the Adriatic Sea the ruins of Diocletian's Palace can be found throughout the city of Split. The palace was built between the late 3rd and the early 4th centuries AD. With the passage of time, its original architecture has been altered, but the people of the city were able to use the structure, damaging it as little as possible. Thus, a harmonious city came into being within the Roman walls.

Episcopal Complex of the Euphrasian Basilica in the Historic Centre of Porec   (6)

Located on the western coast of the Istria peninsula, the 6th-century group of religious monuments in Porec constitutes the most complete surviving complex of its kind. The basilica, atrium, baptistery and Episcopal palace are outstanding examples of religious architecture, while the basilica itself combines classical and Byzantine elements in an exceptional way.

Slovenia

Austria

Hungary

Italy

Croatia

Adriatic Sea

Skocjan Caves   (1)

This exceptional system of limestone caves includes collapsed dolines, some 6 km of underground passages with a total depth of more than 200 m (656 feet), many waterfalls and one of the largest known underground chambers. The site, located in the Kras region (literally meaning Karst), is one of the most famous in the world for the study of karstic phenomena.

Old Bridge Area of the Old City of Mostar (1)

The historic town of Mostar, spanning a deep valley of the Neretva River, developed in the 15th and 16th centuries as an Ottoman frontier town, and then during the Austro-Hungarian period in the 19th and 20th centuries. Mostar has long been known for its old Turkish houses and Old Bridge, Stari Most, after which it is named. In the 1990 conflict, however, most of the historic town and the Old Bridge, designed by renowned architect Sinan, were destroyed. The Old Bridge was recently rebuilt with the contribution of an international scientific committee established by UNESCO.

"Many people were killed during the war, but it was when the bridge was destroyed that Mostarians spontaneously declared a day of mourning."

Emir Balic,
Muslim resident of Mostar

Bosnia & Herzegovina

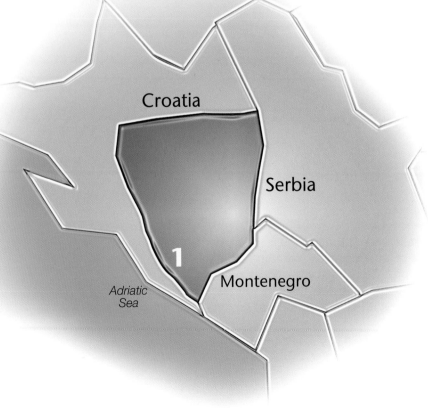

Croatia

Serbia

Montenegro

Adriatic Sea

1

Butrint (1)

Inhabited since prehistoric times, Butrint has been the site of a Greek colony, a Roman city and a bishopric. Originally an Illyrian town, it was taken by the Romans in 167 BC, and later occupied by the Byzantine Empire and the Republic of Venice, before being abandoned in the late Middle Ages. The present archaeological site is a repository of ruins representing each period in the city's development. The civil disturbances in the country in early 1997 did not cause irreversible damage to the archaeological site itself, but the showcases of the museum were opened and looted. No inventory of the stolen objects has yet been made, but fortunately the site's most famous treasure, the marble head of the 2nd-century BC "Goddess of Butrint", had been moved to Tirana before the event.

Albania

Museum-City of Gjirokastra (2)

Gjirokastra, in the Drinos River valley in southern Albania, is a rare example of a well-preserved Ottoman town, built by farmers of large estates. The 13th-century citadel provides the town's focal point, with its typical tower houses (Turkish kule). Characteristic of the Balkan region, Gjirokastra contains a series of outstanding examples of kule, a type of building which crystallized in the 17th century.

Republic of Macedonia

Montenegro Serbia

Bulgaria

Adriatic Sea

Albania **1**

Greece

Mirtoan Sea

Ohrid Region   (1)

Situated on the shores of Lake Ohrid, the town of Ohrid is one of the oldest human settlements in Europe. Built mainly between the 7th and 19th centuries, it has the oldest Slav monastery (St. Pantelejmon) and more than 800 Byzantine-style icons dating from the 11th to the end of the 14th century. After those of the Tretiakov Gallery in Moscow, this is considered to be the most important collection of icons in the world.

Serbia

Hungary

Croatia

Bosnia
and
Herzegovina

Romania

2 1
3

Bulgaria

Montenegro

Macedonia

Stari Ras and Sopocani   (1)

On the outskirts of Stari Ras, the first capital of Serbia, stands an impressive group of medieval monuments consisting of fortresses, churches and monasteries. The monastery at Sopocani is a reminder of the contacts between Western civilization and the Byzantine world.

Decani Monastery (2)

The Decani Monastery, at the foot of the Prokletije Mountains, in the western part of the province of Kosovo and Metohija, was built in the mid-14th century for the Serbian King Stefan Decanski. It is also his mausoleum. The monastery represents the last important phase of Byzantine-Romanesque architecture in the region and is the largest of all medieval Balkan churches. It contains exceptional, well-preserved Byzantine paintings.

"One of the jewels of the Serbian medieval civilization … The painting works took fifteen years to complete and were carried out by several groups of the best Serbian artists."

Serbian Unity Congress

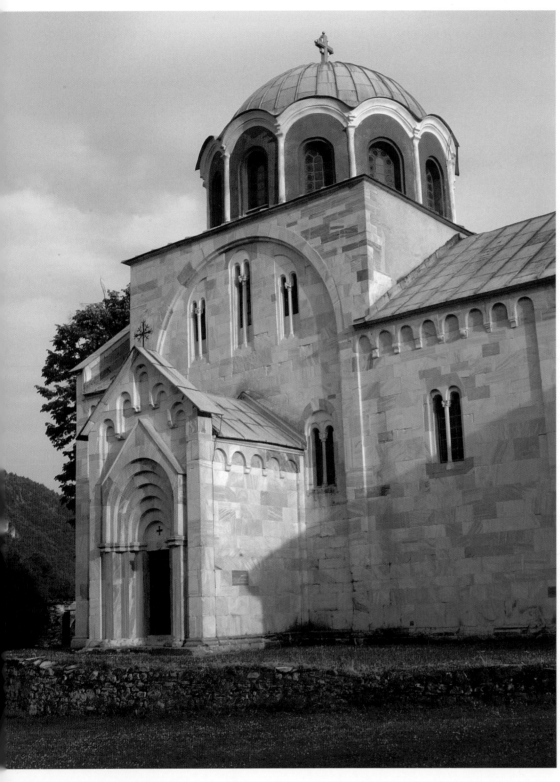

Studenica Monastery   (3)

The Studenica Monastery is the largest and richest Serbian Orthodox monastery. Located in south-eastern Serbia, it was founded in 1190 CE by Stevan Nemanja, founder of the medieval Serb state. Its two principal monuments, the Church of the Virgin and the Church of the King, both built of white marble, enshrine priceless collections of 13th- and 14th-century Byzantine paintings.

Durmitor National Park (1)

Resting in the northeast of the Republic of Montenegro, this breathtaking national park was formed by glaciers and is traversed by rivers and underground streams. Along the Tara River canyon, which has the deepest gorges in Europe, the dense pine forests are interspersed with clear lakes and harbour a wide range of endemic flora.

Montenegro

Croatia

Bosnia and Herzegovina

Serbia

Macedonia

Albania

Adriatic Sea

Natural and Culturo-Historical Region of Kotor (2)

In the Middle Ages, this natural harbour on the Adriatic coast in Montenegro was an important artistic and commercial centre, with its own famous schools of masonry and iconography. The old town of Kotor, surrounded by an impressive city wall, was very well preserved, but a large number of the monuments were seriously damaged by the 1979 earthquake. The town has been restored, largely with UNESCO's help.

"What can be said about Kotor, the town which has existed for almost 2,000 years? That, during that time, it has changed about 20 administrations, that it has been struc by 4 big earthquakes, that it has been under siege many times..."

Stevan Kordic, photographer and associate of the Centre for the Preservation and Presentation of Kotor's Documentary Heritage - "Notar"

Bulgaria

Ancient City of Nessebar   (1)

Situated on a rocky peninsula on the Black Sea, the more than 3,000-year-old site of Nessebar was originally a Thracian settlement. At the beginning of the 6th century BC, the city became a Greek colony. Its remains, which date mostly from the Hellenistic period, include the acropolis, a temple of Apollo, an agora and a wall from the Thracian fortifications.

Thracian Tomb of Kazanlak   (2)

Discovered in 1944, this tomb dates from the Hellenistic period, around the end of the 4th century BC. It is located near Seutopolis, the capital city of the Thracian King Seutes III, and is part of a large Thracian necropolis. The paintings are Bulgaria's best-preserved artistic masterpieces from the Hellenistic period.

"This is probably the richest tomb of a Thracian king ever discovered in Bulgaria. Its style and its making are entirely new to us as experts."

Georgi Kitov,
Bulgarian archaeologist
and head of the research team

Srebarna Nature Reserve   (3)

The Srebarna Nature Reserve is a freshwater lake adjacent to the Danube and extending over 600 ha (1,482 acres). It serves as a breeding ground for almost 100 species of birds, many of which are rare or endangered. Some 80 other bird species migrate and seek refuge there every winter. Among the most interesting birds are the Dalmatian pelican, great egret, night heron, purple heron, glossy ibis and white spoonbill.

Rila Monastery   (4)

The Rila Monastery was founded in the 10th century by St. John of Rila, a hermit canonized by the Orthodox Church. It is situated in the Rila Mountains, in western Bulgaria, in a spectacular setting in the deep valley of the Rilski River. St. John's ascetic dwelling and tomb became a holy site and were transformed into a monastic complex, which subsequently played an important role in the spiritual and social life of medieval Bulgaria.

"Those able to pass through the hole in the roof of the cave where Saint John of Rila is buried, in the forest near the monastery, are those who have not sinned."

Legend of the Rila Monastery cave

Rock-hewn Churches of Ivanovo (5)

In the valley of the Roussenski Lom River, in northeast Bulgaria, a complex of rock-hewn churches, chapels, monasteries and cells developed in the vicinity of the village of Ivanovo. This is where the first hermits had dug out their cells and churches during the 12th century. The 14th-century murals testify to the exceptional skill of the artists belonging to the Tarnovo School of painting.

Madara Rider (6)

The Madara Rider, representing the figure of a knight triumphing over a lion, is carved into a 100-m-high cliff (328 feet) near the village of Madara in northeast Bulgaria. Madara was the principal sacred place of the First Bulgarian Empire before its conversion to Christianity in the 9th century. The inscriptions beside the sculpture tell of events that occurred between AD 705 and 801.

"...There are also three sets of writings in the Greek language, two below the horse and one to the front. The relief is entirely unique; no similar work has been created in Europe before or since its construction."

Conservation scientist Dr. Valentin Todorov, from the Department of Conservation and Restoration at the National Academy of Arts of Bulgaria

Pirin National Park (7)

Pirin presents a limestone Balkan landscape, with lakes, waterfalls, caves and pine forests. The Pirin is noted for its rich flora and fauna. Much of the area is forested, with the best conifer woods in Bulgaria. They hold important populations of the Balkan-endemic species Macedonian pine, Bosnian pine and Bulgarian fir.

Boyana Church (8)

On the outskirts of Sofia, Boyana Church consists of three buildings. The eastern church was built in the 10th century, then enlarged at the beginning of the 13th century by Sebastocrator Kaloyan. The church owes its world fame to its frescoes from 1259. They form a second layer over the paintings from earlier periods and represent one of the most complete and perfectly preserved monuments of eastern European medieval art. A total of 89 scenes, with 240 human images, are depicted on the walls of the church

"The expressive, realistic portraits of the donors Sebastocrator Kaloyan and his wife Dessislava, and of the Bulgarian Tsar Constantine Asen Tikh and Tsaritsa Irina are among the oldest portraits of figures from Bulgarian history."

Boyana Church National Museum

Thracian Tomb of Sveshtari (9)

Discovered in 1982 near the village of Sveshtari, in northeast Bulgaria, this 3rd-century BC Thracian tomb reflects the fundamental structural principles of Thracian cult buildings. The tomb has a unique architectural decor, with polychrome half-human, half-plant caryatids and painted murals. The 10 female figures carved in high relief on the walls of the central chamber and the decoration of the lunette in its vault are the only examples of this type found so far in the Thracian lands.

Greece

Meteora (1)

In a region of almost inaccessible sandstone peaks, monks settled on these "columns of the sky" from the 11th century onwards. The Meteora (Greek: "levitating") are monasteries located in northeast Greece, on the edge of the Pindus Mountains, built on spectacular natural rock pillars. They were places of refuge in troubled times and access to them was extremely difficult.

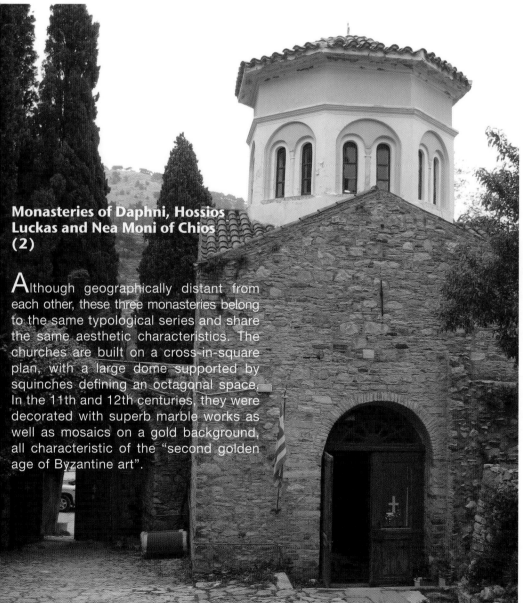

Monasteries of Daphni, Hossios Luckas and Nea Moni of Chios (2)

Although geographically distant from each other, these three monasteries belong to the same typological series and share the same aesthetic characteristics. The churches are built on a cross-in-square plan, with a large dome supported by squinches defining an octagonal space. In the 11th and 12th centuries, they were decorated with superb marble works as well as mosaics on a gold background, all characteristic of the "second golden age of Byzantine art".

Delos (3)

A small island near Mykonos, Delos was considered a holy sanctuary for a millennium before Olympian Greek mythology made it the birthplace of Apollo and Artemis. Apollo's sanctuary attracted pilgrims from all over Greece, which made Delos a prosperous trading port. The island also bears traces of succeeding civilizations in the Aegean world, from the 3rd millennium BC to the Palaeochristian era. The archaeological site is exceptionally extensive and conveys the image of a great cosmopolitan Mediterranean port.

Mount Athos (4)

Athos is a mountain and a peninsula in Macedonia, in northern Greece, called Agio Oros or "Holy Mountain" in the Modern Greek language. An Orthodox spiritual centre since 1054, Mount Athos has enjoyed autonomous status since Byzantine times. The mountain, which is forbidden to women and children, is also a recognized artistic site. The layout of the monasteries (about 20 of which are presently inhabited by some 1,400 monks) had an influence as far afield as Russia, and its school of painting influenced the history of Orthodox art.

"People say it is wrong to banish women. The European Union tells us we must change. We will never change. When man does not see woman, he sees inside himself."

A Macedonian monk, 2002

Archaeological Sites of Mycenae and Tiryns (5)

Theses archaeological sites, located about 90 km (56 miles) south-west of Athens, are the imposing ruins of the two greatest cities of the Mycenaean civilization, which dominated the eastern Mediterranean world from the 15th to the 12th century BC. These two cities are indissolubly linked to the Homeric epics, the Iliad and the Odyssey, which have influenced European art and literature for more than three millennia.

Acropolis, Athens (6)

The "Sacred Rock" is the most important site in Athens. It was also known as Cecropia, in honour of the legendary serpent-man Cecrops, the first Athenian king. It illustrates the civilizations, myths and religions that flourished in Greece over a period of more than 1,000 years. Also the site of four of the greatest masterpieces of classical Greek art – the Parthenon, the Propylaea, the Erechtheum and the Temple of Athena Nike – the Acropolis can be seen as symbolizing the idea of world heritage.

"Pausanias wrote that the day after the Persians burned the Acropolis in 480 BC, this tree sprouted a new branch four feet long. The present olive tree can be traced back to the one originally planted by Athena, goddess of wisdom and daughter of Zeus. Every invader cut it down and every time, someone saved a sprig to be planted later."

Myth of the Sacred Olive Tree

Historic Centre (Chorá) on the Island of Pátmos (7)

The small island of Pátmos, in the Dodecanese, is reputed to be where St. John the Theologian wrote both his Gospel and the Apocalypse. A monastery dedicated to the "beloved disciple" was founded there in the late 10th century and it has been a place of pilgrimage and Greek Orthodox learning ever since. Several monasteries on the island are dedicated to St. John.

Archaeological Site of Delphi   (8)

The pan-Hellenic sanctuary of Delphi, where the oracle of Apollo spoke, was the site of the omphalos, the "navel of the world". Located in a plateau on the side of Mount Parnassus and blending harmoniously with the superb landscape, Delphi is charged with sacred meaning. In the 6th century BC, it was the religious centre and symbol of unity of the ancient Greek world.

"Everything fits with the ancient writers being correct.
It shows again that many legends have some truth in them."

Geophysicist Jelle de Boer from Wesleyan University,
commenting recent scientific discoveries proving the Oracle at Delphi
inhaled strange vapours during divinatory ceremonies, 2003

Archaeological Site of Olympia (9)

The site of Olympia, in a valley in the Peloponnesus, has been inhabited since prehistoric times. In the 10th century BC, Olympia became a centre for the worship of Zeus. The Altis – the sanctuary to the gods – has one of the highest concentrations of masterpieces from the ancient Greek world. In addition to temples, the site features the remains of all sports structures erected for the Olympic Games, which were held in Olympia every four years beginning in 776 BC.

"People used to gather in Olympia both
to make a pilgrimage to the past and to
demonstrate faith in the future. This should
also be the case with modern Olympiads."

Pierre Frédy, Baron de Coubertin,
founder of the modern Olympic Games

Mystras (10)

Mystras, the "wonder of the Morea", was built as an amphitheatre around the fortress erected in 1249 by the prince of Achaia, William of Villehardouin. Re-conquered by the Byzantines, then occupied by the Turks and the Venetians, the city was abandoned in 1832, leaving only the breathtaking medieval ruins standing in a beautiful landscape.

Paleochristian and Byzantine Monuments of Thessalonika (11)

Founded in 315 BC, the provincial capital and seaport of Thessalonika was one of the first bases for the spread of Christianity. Among its Christian monuments are fine churches, some built on the Greek cross plan and others on the three-nave basilica plan. Constructed over a long period, from the 4th to the 15th century, they constitute a diachronic typological series, which had considerable influence in the Byzantine world.

Medieval City of Rhodes (12)

The Order of St. John of Jerusalem occupied Rhodes, the easternmost island of Greece in the Aegean Sea, from 1309 to 1523 and set about transforming the city into a stronghold. It subsequently came under Turkish and Italian rule. With the Palace of the Grand Masters, the Great Hospital and the Street of the Knights, the Upper Town is one of the most beautiful urban ensembles of the Gothic period. Historically, the city was known for its Colossus of Rhodes, a huge statue of the god Helios, erected by Chares of Lindos in the 3rd century BC. It was roughly the same size as the Statue of Liberty in New York.

"... even lying on the ground it is a marvel. Few people can make their arms meet round its thumbs, and its fingers are larger than most statues."

Ancient author Pliny the Elder (AD 23 – AD 79),
speaking of the Colossus of Rhodes

267

Temple of Apollo Epicurius at Bassae (13)

This famous temple to the god of healing and the sun was built towards the middle of the 5th century BC in the lonely heights of the Arcadian mountains. The temple, which has the oldest Corinthian capital yet found, combines the Archaic style and the serenity of the Doric style, with some daring architectural features.

Pythagoreion and Heraion of Samos (14)

Many civilizations have inhabited this small Aegean island, near the coast of Turkey, since the 3rd millennium BC. Still visible are the remains of Pythagoreion, an ancient fortified port with Greek and Roman monuments and a spectacular tunnel-aqueduct, as well as the Heraion, a temple from the Samian Hera.

"... he tried to use his symbolic method of teaching, which was similar in all respects to the lessons he had learnt in Egypt. The Samians were not very keen on this method and treated him in a rude and improper manner."

Neoplatonist Syrian philosopher Iamblichus, speaking of Pythagoras, father of the Pythagorean Theorem

Archaeological Site of Epidaurus (15)

In a small valley in the Peloponnesus, the site of Epidaurus sprawls out over several levels. Reputed to be the birthplace of Apollo's son, Asklepios the Healer, Epidaurus was known for its sanctuary situated about five miles from the town, as well as its theatre dating from the 4th century, which is once again in use today. The vast site is a tribute to the healing cults of Greek and Roman times, with temples and hospital buildings devoted to its gods.

Archaeological Site of Vergina (16)

The city of Aigai, the ancient first capital of the Kingdom of Macedonia, was discovered in the 19th century near Vergina, in northern Greece. The most important remains are the monumental palace, lavishly decorated with mosaics and painted stuccoes, and the burial ground with more than 300 tumuli, some of which date from the 11th century BC. The site is home to a remarkable series of royal tombs and their rich contents.

Cyprus

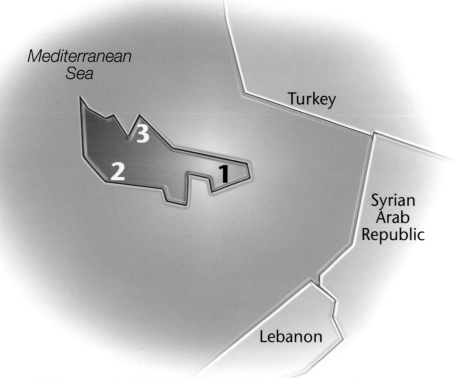

Mediterranean
Sea

Turkey

Syrian
Arab
Republic

Lebanon

Choirokoitia   (1)

The Neolithic settlement of Choirokoitia, occupied from the 7th to the 4th millennium BC, is one of the most important prehistoric sites in the eastern Mediterranean. Its remains and the finds from the excavations there have shed much light on the evolution of human society in this key region.

Paphos (2)

Pafos, usually written Paphos in English, is a coastal town in the southwest of Cyprus. The city has been inhabited since the Neolithic period. It is the mythical birthplace of Aphrodite, the Greek goddess of love, sex and beauty. A temple was erected by the Myceneans in the 12th century BC in honour of her birthday. The remains of villas, palaces, theatres, fortresses and tombs give the site its exceptional architectural and historic value.

"Not only did Aphrodite start the war by offering Helen of Troy to Paris, but the abduction was accomplished when Paris, seeing Helen for the first time, was inflamed with desire to have her."

Myth of Aphrodite
being the original cause
of the Trojan War

Painted Churches in the Troodos Region (3)

This region, located in the Troodos Mountains, is characterized by one of the largest groups of churches and monasteries of the former Byzantine Empire. The complex of 10 monuments included on the World Heritage List, all richly decorated with murals, provides an overview of Byzantine and post-Byzantine painting in Cyprus.

Turkey

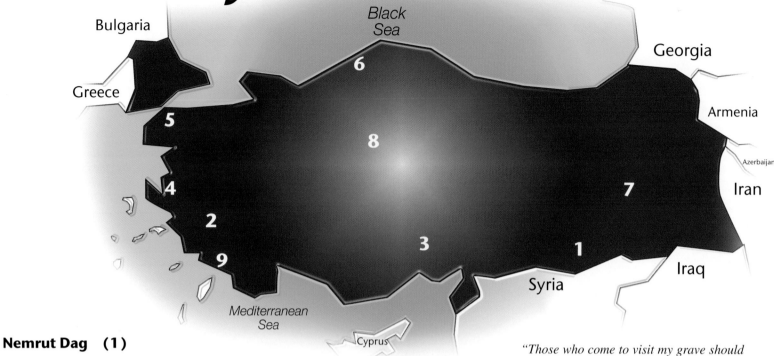

Nemrut Dag (1)

Nemrud Dag is a 2,150-metre-high mountain (7,053 feet) near the Ankar Mountains in Anatolia, in south-eastern Turkey. At its peak, King Antiochus Theos of Commagene built his tomb-sanctuary along with huge statues (8-9 meters high) of himself and various Greek and Persian gods in 62 BC.

"Those who come to visit my grave should wear their most beautiful clothes and the most fragrant perfumes. I will give them happiness and prosperity for generations on these lands."

King Antiochus, 50 BC.

Hierapolis-Pamukkale (2)

Deriving from springs in a cliff almost 200 m (656 feet) high overlooking the plain, calcite-laden waters have created at Pamukkale (Cotton Palace) an unreal landscape, made up of mineral forests, petrified waterfalls and a series of terraced basins. At the end of the 2nd century BC, the dynasty of the Attalids, the kings of Pergamon, established the thermal spa of Hierapolis. The ruins of the baths, temples and other Greek monuments can be seen at the site.

Göreme National Park and the Rock Sites of Cappadocia (3)

In a spectacular landscape, entirely sculpted by erosion, the Göreme valley and its surroundings contain rock-hewn sanctuaries that provide unique evidence of Byzantine art in the post-Iconoclastic period. Dwellings, troglodyte villages and underground towns – the remains of a traditional human habitat dating back to the 4th century – can also be seen there.

Archaeological Site of Troy (4)

With its 4,000 years of history, Troy is a legendary city, scene of the Trojan War. The siege of Troy by Spartan and Achaean warriors from Greece, in the 13th or 12th century BC, was immortalized by Homer in the Iliad, and it has inspired great creative artists throughout the world ever since. The first excavations at the site were undertaken by the famous archaeologist Heinrich Schliemann in 1870. The site is located in Anatolia, close to the seacoast in what is now northwest Turkey, southwest of the Dardanelles, under Mount Ida.

"Blood ran in torrents, church was all the earth, as Trojans and their alien helpers died. Here were men lying quelled by bitter death. All up down the city in their blood "

Greek poet Quintus Smyrnoeus, Posthomerica

273

Historic Areas of Istanbul   (5)

Originally founded by Greek colonists as Byzantium, this city was made the seat of government in 324 CE by the Roman Emperor Constantin. Byzantium was renamed Nova Roma (New Rome), and then soon became known as Constantinople, the City of Constantine. Constantinople became part of the Ottoman Empire and soon its capital. On March 28, 1930, it was officially renamed Istanbul. With its strategic location on the Bosphorus peninsula between the Balkans and Anatolia, the Black Sea and the Mediterranean, the city has been associated with major political, religious and artistic events for more than 2,000 years. Today, Istanbul's vestiges are under threat from population pressure, industrial pollution and uncontrolled urbanization.

"This is a modern city, in which people have to live and get to work each day. The challenge for Istanbul is developing a modern city while protecting its ancient heritage."

UNESCO official Minja Yang, in 2005, commenting potential damage of the construction of a new subway tunnel

City of Safranbolu   (6)

Located in the Karabuk province, the old town of Safranbolu is about 200 kilometres north of Ankara and about 100 kilometres (62 miles) south of the Black Sea coast. From the 13th century to the advent of the railway in the early 20th century, Safranbolu was an important caravan station on the main east-west trade route. The Old Mosque, Old Bath and Süleyman Pasha Medrese were built in 1322.

Great Mosque and Hospital of Divrigi   (7)

This region of Anatolia was conquered by the Turks at the beginning of the 11th century. In 1228–29, Emir Ahmet Shah founded a mosque, with its adjoining hospital, at Divrigi. The mosque has a single prayer room and is crowned by two cupolas. The highly sophisticated technique of vault construction and a creative, exuberant type of decorative sculpture are the unique features of this masterpiece of Islamic architecture.

Hattusha (8)

The former capital of the Hittite Empire, is notable for its urban organization, the types of construction that have been preserved (temples, royal residences, fortifications), the rich ornamentation of the Lions' Gate and the Royal Gate, and the ensemble of rock art at Yazilikaya. The city enjoyed considerable influence in Anatolia and northern Syria in the 2nd millennium BC.

"At night I took the city by force; I have sown weeds in its place. Should any king after me attempt to resettle Hattush, may the Weathergod of Heaven strike him down."

Anitta, King of the Hittites, around 1700 BC

Xanthos-Letoon (9)

This site, which was the capital of Lycia, illustrates the blending of Lycian traditions and Hellenic influence, especially in its funerary art. The epigraphic inscriptions are crucial for our understanding of the history of the Lycian people and their Indo-European language.

Azerbaijan

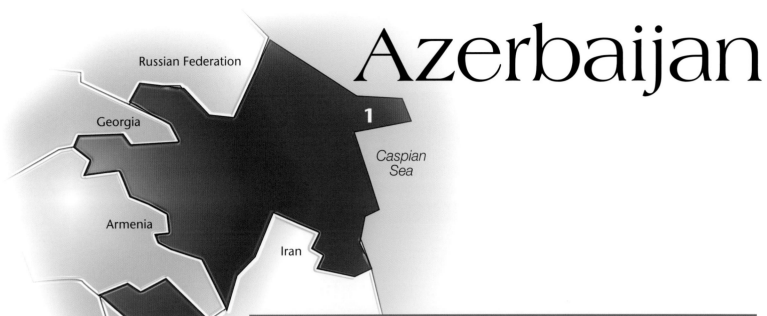

Russian Federation

Georgia

Armenia

Iran

Caspian Sea

1

Walled City of Baku   (1)

Capital of Azerbaijan, the Walled City of Baku is located on the southern shore of the Apsheron Peninsula. Its history dates back to the 1st millennium BC. The city reveals evidence of Zoroastrian, Sasanian, Arabic, Persian, Shirvani, Ottoman, and Russian presence in cultural continuity. The Inner City (Icheri Sheher) has preserved much of its 12th-century defensive walls. The site sustained significant damage during the earthquake of November 2000 and is increasingly affected by the pressure of urban development.

"Baku is a beautiful city. It is a pleasure to live and work in this city!"

Leonid Ilyich Brezhnev
(1906 – 1982), General Secretary of the
Communist Party of the Soviet Union

Georgia

Russian Federation

Black
Sea

2

3

1

Turkey

Armenia

Azerbaija

**City-Museum Reserve of Mtskheta
(1)**

The historic churches of Mtskheta, former capital of Georgia, are outstanding examples of medieval religious architecture in the Caucasus. They show the high artistic and cultural level attained by this ancient kingdom.

Upper Svaneti   (2)

Preserved by its long isolation, the Upper Svaneti region of the Caucasus is an exceptional example of mountain scenery with medieval-type villages and tower-houses. The village of Chazhashi still has more than 200 of these very unusual houses, which were used both as dwellings and as defence posts against the invaders who plagued the region.

279

Bagrati Cathedral and Gelati Monastery (3)

The construction of Bagrati Cathedral, named after Bagrat III, the first king of united Georgia, started at the end of the 10th century and was completed in the early years of the 11th century. The Gelati Monastery was erected between the 12th and 17th centuries. The cathedral and monastery represent the flourish of medieval architecture in Georgia. In Gelati is buried one of the greatest Georgian kings, David the Builder.

"At the grave of King David we must all say: Georgia will be united, strong, will restore its wholeness and become a united, strong state."

Mikheil Saakashvili,
President of Georgia, 2004

Ukraine

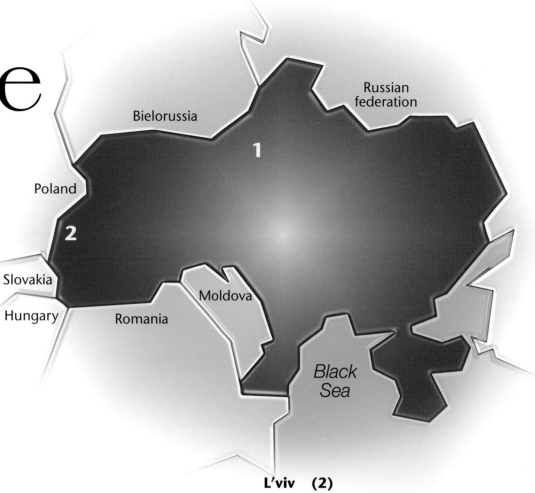

Bielorussia

Russian federation

1

Poland

2

Slovakia

Hungary

Romania

Moldova

Black Sea

L'viv (2)

L'viv is a jewel of Eastern Europe. The city resembles an open-air museum, housing 2,000 historic and cultural monuments. It was founded in the mid-13th century (1256) by Prince Danylo Halytskyi and was named after his son Lev. It was a flourishing administrative, religious and commercial centre for several centuries. The medieval urban topography has been preserved virtually intact, along with many fine Baroque and later buildings.

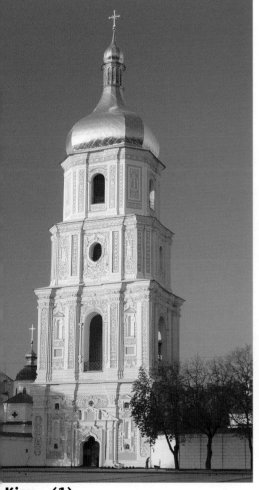

Kiev (1)

Designed to rival Hagia Sophia in Constantinople, Kiev's Saint Sophia Cathedral symbolizes the "new Constantinople", capital of the Christian principality of Kiev, which was created in the 11th century in a region evangelized after the baptism of St. Vladimir in 988.

*"A church of wonder and glory,
the envy of all countries far and wide."*

Writer of Old Rus llarion

Armenia

**Monasteries of Haghpat
and Sanahin   (1)**

These two Byzantine monasteries in the Tumanian region originate from the period of prosperity during the Kiurikian dynasty (10th to 13th century). They were important centres of learning, and Sanahin in particular was renowned for its school of illuminators and calligraphers. The two monastic complexes represent the highest flowering of Armenian religious architecture.

Monastery of Geghard
and the Upper Azat Valley   (2)

This monastery contains a number of churches and tombs, most of them cut into the rock, which illustrate the very peak of Armenian medieval architecture. While the main chapel was built in 1215, the monastery complex was founded in the 4th century by Gregory the Illuminator at the site of a sacred spring inside a cave.

Cathedral and Churches
of Echmiatsin and Zvartnots   (3)

Located in the Armavir province, west of Yerevan, the cathedral and churches of Echmiatsin and the archaeological remains at Zvartnots graphically illustrate the evolution and development of the Armenian central-domed cross-hall type of church, which exerted a profound influence on architectural and artistic development in the region.

"In the seventh century, while Byzantium and the Latin West slept, medieval Armenia enjoyed a veritable architectural building boom."

Dr. Christina Maranci, expert scholar of Medieval Armenian Architecture

Belarus

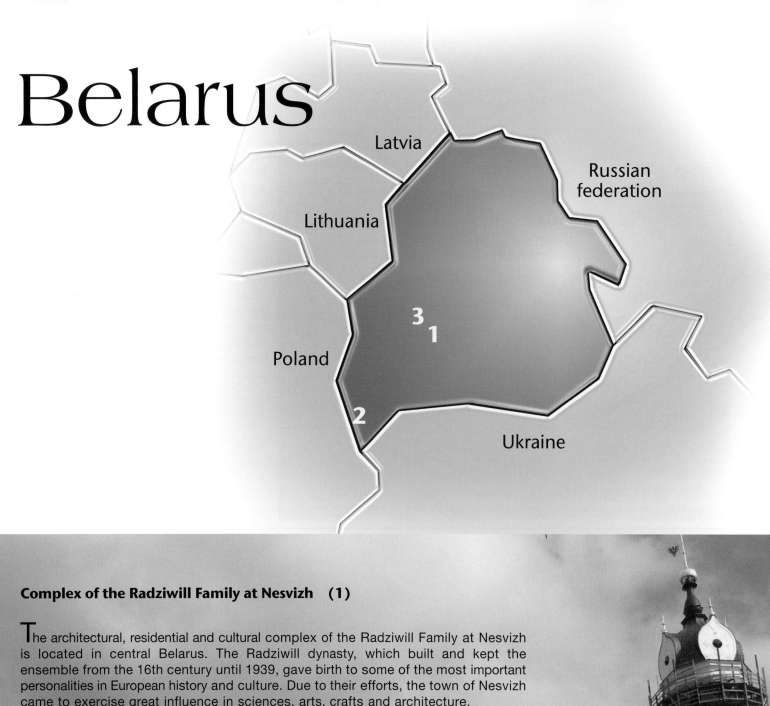

Complex of the Radziwill Family at Nesvizh   (1)

The architectural, residential and cultural complex of the Radziwill Family at Nesvizh is located in central Belarus. The Radziwill dynasty, which built and kept the ensemble from the 16th century until 1939, gave birth to some of the most important personalities in European history and culture. Due to their efforts, the town of Nesvizh came to exercise great influence in sciences, arts, crafts and architecture.

Belovezhskaya Pushcha / Bialowieza Forest   (2)
(site shared with Poland)

Situated on the watershed of the Baltic Sea and the Black Sea, this immense forest range, consisting of evergreens and broad-leaved trees, is home to some remarkable animal life, including rare mammals such as the wolf, the lynx and the otter, as well as some 300 European bison, a species which has been reintroduced into the park.

"Belovezhskaya Pushcha: a quiet, untouched wood in the Polish part, a wood disturbed by honking timber Lorries on the Belarusian side."

Belarusian Radio Liberty Life,
February 6, 2005

Mir Castle Complex   (3)

The construction of this castle began at the end of the 15th century, in Gothic style. It was subsequently extended and recons-tructed, first in the Renaissance and then in the Baroque style. After being abandoned for nearly a century and suffering severe damage during the Napoleonic period, the castle was restored at the end of the 19th century. Its present form is graphic testimony to an often turbu-lent history.

Russian Federation

15

Bering Sea

Artic Ocean

Barents Sea

Laptev Sea

Sweden

Finland

10

Estonia

Latvia

16

3

17

18

11

2

Sea
of Okhotsk

Belarus

14

13

1

12

9

5

8

Ukraine

China

20

7

Sea
of Japan

Black
Sea

6

Caspian
Sea

Kazakhstan

Mongolia

4

19

Georgia

Azerbaijan

Architectural Ensemble
of the Trinity Sergius Lavra in Sergiev Posad   (1)

This is a fine example of a working Orthodox monastery, with military features that are typical of the 15th to the 18th century, the period during which it developed. The main church of the Lavra, the Cathedral of the Assumption (echoing the Kremlin Cathedral of the same name), contains the tomb of Boris Godunov. Among the treasures of the Lavra is the famous icon, The Trinity, by Andrei Rublev.

Volcanoes of Kamchatka (2)

This is one of the most outstanding volcanic regions in the world, with a high density of active volcanoes, a variety of types, and a wide range of related features. Together, the six sites included in the serial designation represent the majority of volcanic features of the Kamchatka peninsula. The interplay of active volcanoes and glaciers forms a dynamic landscape of great beauty.

Kizhi Pogost (3)

The pogost of Kizhi is located on one of the many islands in Lake Onega, in Karelia. Two 18th-century wooden churches, and an octagonal clock tower, also in wood and built in 1862, can be seen there. These unusual constructions, in which carpenters created a bold, visionary architecture, perpetuate an ancient model of parish space.

"The existing ensemble was gradually formed during a 250-year period (from 1694 to 1959). Every new century made its contribution in its development and its present appearance was formed when the log wall was reconstructed."

Kizhi Museum

Golden Mountains of Altai (4)

The Altai Mountains, in southern Siberia, form the major mountain range in the Western Siberia biogeographic region and provide the source of its greatest rivers, the Ob and the Irtysh. The total area covers 1,611,457 ha (3,982,000 acres). The region represents the most complete sequence of altitudinal vegetation zones in central Siberia: steppe, forest-steppe, mixed forest, subalpine, and alpine vegetation. The site is also an important habitat for endangered animal species such as the snow leopard.

Church of the Ascension, Kolomenskoye (5)

The Church of the Ascension was built in 1532 on the imperial estate of Kolomenskoye, near Moscow, to celebrate the birth of the prince who was to become Tsar Ivan IV, known as Ivan the Terrible. One of the earliest examples of a traditional wooden tent-roofed church on a stone and brick substructure, it had a great influence on the development of Russian ecclesiastical architecture.

Western Caucasus (6)

The Western Caucasus, extending over 275,000 ha (679,540 acres) at the extreme western end of the Caucasus Mountains and located 50 km (31 miles) north-east of the Black Sea, is one of the few large mountain areas in Europe that has not experienced significant human impact. Its subalpine and alpine pastures have only been grazed by wild animals, and its extensive tracts of undisturbed mountain forests, extending from the lowlands to the subalpine zone, are unique in Europe.

Lake Baikal (7)

Situated in south-east Siberia, the 3.15-million-ha (7,800,000-acre) Lake Baikal is the oldest (25 million years) and deepest (1,700 m or 5,577 feet) lake in the world. It contains 20% of the world's total unfrozen freshwater reserve. Known as the "Galapagos of Russia", its age and isolation have produced one of the world's richest and most unusual freshwater faunas, which is of exceptional value to evolutionary science. Today, the site is threatened by illegal oil transportation, pipeline projects and forest cuttings.

"We appeal to the international community to avoid making investments into the pipeline that threaten the unique lake."

Greenpeace Russia

Historic and Architectural Complex of the Kazan Kremlin (8)

Built on an ancient site, the Kazan Kremlin dates from the Muslim period of the Golden Horde and the Kazan Khanate. It was conquered by Ivan the Terrible in 1552 and became the Christian See of the Volga Land. The only surviving Tatar fortress in Russia and an important place of pilgrimage, the Kazan Kremlin consists of an outstanding group of historic buildings dating from the 16th to the 19th century, integrating remains of earlier structures of the 10th to 16th century.

White Monuments of Vladimir and Suzdal   (9)

These two artistic centres in central Russia hold an important place in the country's architectural history. There are a number of magnificent 12th- and 13th-century public and religious buildings, above all the masterpieces of the Collegiate Church of St. Demetrios and the Cathedral of the Assumption of the Virgin.

Cultural and Historic Ensemble of the Solovetsky Islands (10)

The Solovetsky archipelago comprises six islands in the western part of the White Sea, covering 300 sq. km (74,130 acres). They have been inhabited since the 5th century BC and important traces of a human presence from as far back as the 5th millennium BC can be found there. The archipelago has been the site of fervent monastic activity since the 15th century, and there are several churches dating from the 16th to the 19th century.

"Every place has its soul. Here it's defined by the faith of the monks and the humanity of the prisoners who survived the gulag. How we preserve that soul will determine the future of the Solovetsky Islands."

Mikhail Lopatkin, Director of the Solovetsky Islands Museum, 2003

Virgin Komi Forests   (11)

These forests cover 3.28 million ha (8,100,000 acres) of tundra and mountain tundra in the Urals, as well as one of the most extensive areas of virgin boreal forest remaining in Europe. It is vast area of conifers, aspens, birches, peat bogs, rivers and natural lakes that has been monitored and studied for over 50 years. It provides valuable evidence of the natural processes affecting biodiversity in the taiga.

"This decision by UNESCO will mean safe haven for the rich natural heritage that the people of Komi have depended on for hundreds of years."

Volodya Chuprov, member of the Komi indigenous people, speaking about Komi Forests being named as a World Heritage Site

Kremlin and Red Square, Moscow (12)

Inextricably linked to all the most important historical and political events in Russia since the 13th century, the Kremlin was both the residence of the Great Prince and a religious centre. The irregular triangle of the Kremlin walls encloses an area of 275,000 square metres (68 acres). Cathedral Square is the heart of the Kremlin. At the foot of its ramparts, on Red Square, St. Basil's Basilica is one of the most beautiful Russian Orthodox monuments.

"Ilyich liked to stroll about the Kremlin which commanded a sweeping view of the city. He liked best of all to walk along the pavement facing the Grand Palace, where there was plenty to fill the eye."

Nadezhda Konstantinovna Krupskaya,
wife of the first Premier of the Soviet Union,
Vladimir Ilyich Lenin,
speaking of his affection for the city

Ensemble of the Novodevichy Convent   (13)

The Novodevichy Convent, in south-western Moscow, was built in the 16th and 17th centuries as part of a chain of monastic ensembles that were integrated into the defence system of the city. The Convent was directly associated with the political, cultural and religious history of Russia, and closely linked to the Moscow Kremlin. It was used by women of the Tsar's family and of the aristocracy. The Convent provides an example of the highest accomplishments of Russian architecture, with rich interiors and an important collection of paintings and artefacts.

Historical Centre of the City of Yaroslavl   (14)

At the confluence of the Volga and Kotorosl rivers, some 250 km (155 miles) northeast of Moscow, the historic city of Yaroslavl developed into a major commercial centre starting in the 11th century. It is renowned for its numerous 17th-century churches and as an outstanding example of the urban planning reforms that Empress Catherine the Great ordered for the whole of Russia in 1763.

Natural System of Wrangel Island Reserve (15)

Located well above the Arctic Circle, the site includes the mountainous Wrangel Island (7,608 km2), Herald Island (11 km2) and surrounding waters. Wrangel was not glaciated during the Quaternary Ice Age, resulting in exceptionally high levels of biodiversity for this region. The island boasts the world's largest population of Pacific walrus and the highest density of ancestral polar bear dens. It is a major feeding ground for the grey whale migrating from Mexico and the northernmost nesting ground for 100 migratory bird species, many endangered.

"I have named this northern land Wrangell Land as an appropriate tribute to the memory of a man who spent three consecutive years north of latitude 68°, and demonstrated the problem of this open polar sea forty-five years ago."

Captain Thomas Long,
1867

Historic Centre of Saint Petersburg (16)

Founded by Tsar Peter the Great in 1703 as a "window to Europe", the city served thenceforth as the capital of the country during the imperial period of its history, until 1918. Later known as Leningrad (in the former USSR), the city is closely associated with the October Revolution. Its architectural heritage reconciles the very different Baroque and pure neoclassical styles. Because of its numerous canals and bridges, Saint Petersburg is sometimes referred as the "Venice of the North".

"The most purposeful city in the world."

*Fyodor Mikhailovich Dostoevsky,
one of Russia's greatest writers*

Historic Monuments of Novgorod and Surroundings (17)

Velikiy Novgorod is the foremost historic city in north-western Russia, situated on the highway and railway connecting Moscow and St. Petersburg. Novgorod was Russia's first capital in the 9th century. Surrounded by churches and monasteries, it was a centre for Orthodox spirituality as well as Russian architecture. Its medieval monuments and the 14th-century frescoes of Theophanes the Greek (Andrei Rublev's teacher) illustrate the development of its remarkable architecture and cultural creativity.

The Ensemble of Ferrapontov Monastery (18)

The Ferrapontov Monastery, in the Vologda region in northern Russia, is an exceptionally well-preserved and complete example of a Russian Orthodox monastic complex of the 15th-17th century, a period of great significance in the development of the unified Russian state and its culture. The architecture of the monastery is outstanding in its inventiveness and purity. The interior is graced by the magnificent wall paintings of Dionisy, the greatest Russian artist of the late 15th century.

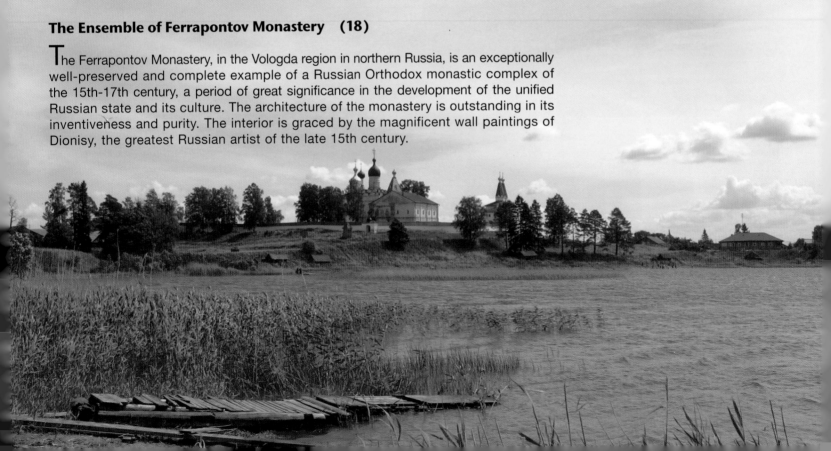

Citadel, Ancient City and Fortress Buildings of Derbent (19)

These three monuments of Derbent were part of the northern lines of the Sasanian Persian Empire, which extended east and west of the Caspian Sea. The fortification was built in stone. It consisted of two parallel walls that formed a barrier from the seashore up to the mountain. The town of Derbent was built between these two walls, and has retained part of its medieval fabric.

"There was significant settlement in the area of Derbent from the extreme Antiquity. The famous Derbent fortress and the walls constructed from the sea up to the mountains, closing pass at the seaside lowland, were constructed by Sassanids-era Persians (V-VI century)."

Excerpt of Dobrinin B.F., Geography of the Dagestan Socialist Republic, 1926

Central Sikhote-Alin (20)

Bordering China and North Korea at the southern extreme of the Russian Far East, the Sikhote-Alin mountain range contains one the richest and most unusual temperate forests of the world. In this mixed zone between taiga and subtropics, southern species such as the Amur tiger and Himalayan bear cohabit with northern species such as the brown bear and lynx.

Africa

Africa is home to the oldest inhabited territory on earth, with the human race originating from this continent. The name Africa came into Western use through the Romans, who used the name Africa terra — "land of the Afri" — for the northern part of the continent. That ancient province of Africa, which had Carthage as its capital, now corresponds to modern-day Tunisia, and many regions there still bear witness to this long-ago era.

Africa has been the birthplace of mankind's first great civilisations such as Egypt, Ethiopia, the Nubian Kingdom, the kingdoms of the Sahel (Ghana, Mali and Songhai) and Great Zimbabwe. Colonization dramatically changed the history of this generous land, and Africa bears the scars of a tragic period marked by the slavery market, controlled by northern colonial empires to feed New World demand.

Despite its troubled history and current tensions, many still consider Africa to be paradise on earth, with some of the most magical wilderness in the world. Through the ages, the continent has attracted travellers from all around the globe, all touched by its beauty, its rawness, its powerful animal kingdom and most of all, the kindness of its people. Certainly, there is also devastation and, at times, a feeling of hopelessness here. But because of its extraordinary natural heritage, Africa remains a land of riches.

How long can this paradise be preserved? Only we have the answer. We will decide. It is up to us, Africans, Westerners, Asians, Australians, to save and protect the "Magical World" of Africa.

Morocco

Historic City of Meknes   (1)

Founded in the 11th century by the Almoravids as a military settlement, Meknes became a capital under Sultan Moulay Ismaïl (1672–1727), the founder of the Alawite dynasty. The sultan turned it into an impressive city in Spanish-Moorish style, surrounded by high walls with great doors, where the harmonious blending of the Islamic and European styles of 17th-century Maghreb is still evident today.

Ksar of Ait-Ben-Haddou (2)

The ksar, a group of earthen buildings surrounded by high walls, is a traditional pre-Saharan habitat. The houses crowd together within the defensive walls, which are reinforced by corner towers. Ait-Ben-Haddou, in Ouarzazate province, is a striking example of the architecture of southern Morocco.

Medina of Fez (3)

Founded in the 9th century and home to the oldest university in the world, Fez reached its peak in the 13th and 14th centuries under the Marinids, when it replaced Marrakesh as the capital of the kingdom. Although the political capital of Morocco was transferred to Rabat in 1912, Fez has retained its status as the country's cultural and spiritual centre.

"Marrakesh, Rabat and Casablanca live in the present, but Fez lives in the past."

*Moroccan saying
about the historic city of Fez*

Medina of Essaouira
-formerly Mogador   (4)

This site is an exceptional example of a late-18th-century fortified town, built according to the principles of contemporary European military architecture in a North African context. Since its foundation, it has been a major international trading seaport, linking Morocco and its Saharan hinterland with Europe and the rest of the world.

Archaeological Site of Volubilis
(5)

Founded in the 3rd century BC, became an important outpost of the Roman Empire and was graced with many fine buildings. Extensive remains of these survive in the archaeological site, located in a fertile agricultural area near Meknes. Volubilis was later briefly to become the capital of Idris I, founder of the Idrisid dynasty, who is buried at nearby Moulay Idris.

"Volubilis takes its name from the ancient Latin name for the Oleander flower."

Institute of Archaeology, UCL

Medina of Marrakesh (6)

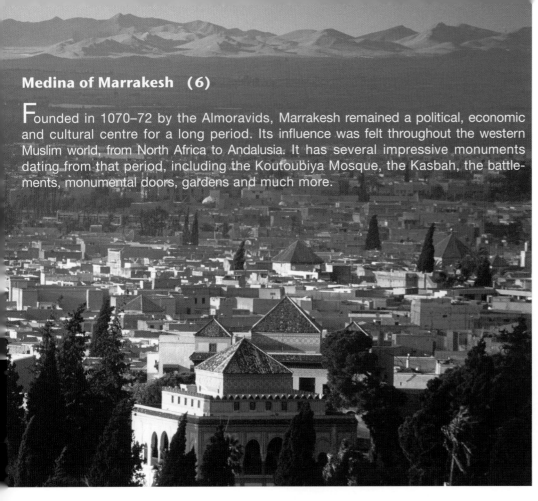

Founded in 1070–72 by the Almoravids, Marrakesh remained a political, economic and cultural centre for a long period. Its influence was felt throughout the western Muslim world, from North Africa to Andalusia. It has several impressive monuments dating from that period, including the Koutoubiya Mosque, the Kasbah, the battlements, monumental doors, gardens and much more.

"You cannot come all this way to North Africa without seeing Marrakesh. Let us spend two days there. I must be with you when you see the sun set on the Atlas Mountains."

U.K. Prime Minister Winston Churchill, inviting U.S. President Franklin Roosevelt to visit Marrakesh in December 1935

Medina of Tétouan
- formerly known as Titawin (7)

Tétouan was of particular importance in the Islamic period, from the 8th century onwards, since it served as the main point of contact between Morocco and Andalusia. After the Reconquest, the town was rebuilt by Andalusian refugees who had been expelled by the Spanish. Although one of the smallest of the Moroccan medinas, Tétouan is unquestionably the most complete and it has been largely untouched by subsequent outside influences.

Portuguese City of Mazagan
- El Jadida (8)

The Portuguese fortification of Mazagan, now part of the city of El Jadida, 90 km (56 miles) southwest of Casablanca, was built as a fortified colony on the Atlantic coast in the early 16th century. It was taken over by the Moroccans in 1769. The fortification, with its bastions and ramparts, is an early example of Renaissance military design. The Portuguese City of Mazagan is an outstanding testament to the interchange of influences between European and Moroccan cultures, well reflected in architecture, technology, and town planning.

Algeria

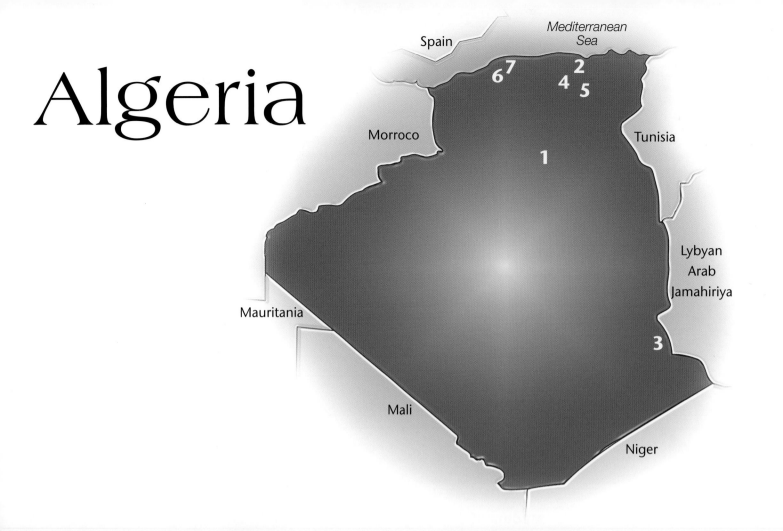

M'Zab Valley (1)

A traditional human habitat, created in the 10th century by the Ibadites around their five ksour (fortified cities), has been preserved intact in the M'Zab valley. Simple, functional and perfectly adapted to the environment, the architecture of M'Zab was designed for community living, while respecting the structure of the family. It is a source of inspiration for today's urban planners.

"The cities of the M'zab are a perfect example of how architecture can shape nature without defacing it."

Italian architect and professor Pietro Laureano

Djémila (2)

Situated 900 m (2,952 feet) above sea level, Djémila, or Cuicul, with its forum, temples, basilicas, triumphal arches and houses, is an interesting example of Roman town planning adapted to a mountain location.

Tassili n'Ajjer (3)

Located in a strange lunar landscape of great geological interest, this site has one of the most important groupings of prehistoric cave art in the world. More than 15,000 drawings and engravings record the climatic changes, animal migrations and evolution of human life on the edge of the Sahara from 6000 BC to the first centuries of the present era. The geological formations are of outstanding scenic interest, with eroded sandstones forming "forests of rock".

Al Qal'a of Beni Hammad (4)

In a mountainous site of extraordinary beauty, the ruins of the first capital of the Hammadid emirs, founded in 1007 and demolished in 1152, provide an authentic picture of a fortified Muslim city. The mosque, whose prayer room has 13 aisles with eight bays, is one of the largest in Algeria.

Timgad (5)

Timgad lies on the northern slopes of the Aurès Mountains and was created ex nihilo as a military colony by the Emperor Trajan in AD 100. With its square enclosure and orthogonal design based on the cardo and decumanus (the two perpendicular routes running through the city), it is an excellent example of Roman town planning. In the 5th century, the city was sacked by the Vandals before falling into decline. In the 7th century, it was briefly repopulated as a primarily Christian centre before being sacked by Berbers and abandoned. The city disappeared from history until its excavation in 1881.

Tipasa (6)

On the shores of the Mediterranean, Tipasa was an ancient Punic trading post conquered by Rome and turned into a strategic base for the conquest of the kingdoms of Mauritania. It comprises a unique group of Phoenician, Roman, palaeochristian and Byzantine ruins, alongside indigenous monuments such as the Kbor er Roumia, the great royal mausoleum of Mauritania.

"At springtime, Tipaza is inhabited by the Gods."
French writer Albert Camus, Noces, 1939

Kasbah of Algiers (7)

The Kasbah is a unique kind of medina, or Islamic city. It stands in one of the finest coastal sites on the Mediterranean, over-looking the islands where a Carthaginian trading post was established in the 4th century BC. The Kasbah contains the remains of the citadel, old mosques and Ottoman-style palaces, as well as the vestiges of a traditional urban structure associated with a deep-rooted sense of community.

"By order of the prophet, we ban that boogie sound. Degenerate the faithful with that crazy Kasbah sound. The shareef don't like it – rock the Kasbah, rock the Kasbah"
Lyrics of The Clash's hit "Rock the Kasbah", released in 1982

Mauritania

Algeria

Morocco

Atlantic
Ocean

Mali

Senegal

Ancient Ksour of Ouadane, Chinguetti, Tichitt and Oualata (1)

Founded in the 11th and 12th centuries to serve the caravans crossing the Sahara, these trading and religious centres became focal points of Islamic culture. They have managed to preserve an urban fabric that evolved between the 12th and 16th centuries. They illustrate a traditional way of life centred on the nomadic culture of the people of the Western Sahara.

Banc d'Arguin National Park (2)

On the fringe of the Atlantic coast, the park includes sand dunes, coastal swamps, small islands and shallow coastal waters. The contrast between the harsh desert environment and the biodiversity of the marine zone has resulted in a land and seascape of outstanding natural significance. A wide variety of migrating birds spend winter in this region.

"There is no place like it in Africa."

Jean Worms, chief scientist of Banc d'Arguin National Park, referring in 2001 to the region's unique and abundant marine life

Tunisia

Algeria

Mediterranean Sea

Lybyan Arab Jamahiriya

Site of Carthage (1)

Carthage was founded in the 9th century BC on the Gulf of Tunis. From the 6th century onwards, it developed into a great trading empire covering much of the Mediterranean and was home to a brilliant civilization. In the course of the long Punic wars, Carthage occupied territories belonging to Rome, which finally destroyed its rival in 146 BC. A second, Roman, Carthage was then established on the ruins of the first. Louis IX of France (St. Louis) died there while on crusade. A chapel in his honour stands on the hill that is traditionally identified as Byrsa Hill, site of the ancient citadel.

"The catastrophe should be regarded not just with curiosity, or with a love for archaeology, but ... with the eyes of those who wish for and ... work for peace today."

Former mayor of Rome Ugo Vetere, visiting Carthage in 1985

Dougga / Thugga (2)

Before the Roman annexation of Numidia, the town of Thugga, built on an elevated site overlooking a fertile plain, was the capital of an important Libyco-Punic state. It flourished under Roman and Byzantine rule, but declined in the Islamic period. The impressive ruins that are visible today give some idea of the resources of a small Roman town on the fringes of the empire.

Amphitheatre of El Jem   (3)

The impressive ruins of the largest coliseum in North Africa, a huge amphitheatre which could hold up to 35,000 spectators, are found in the small village of El Jem.

This 3rd-century monument illustrates the grandeur and extent of Imperial Rome. At a tense moment during struggles with the Ottomans, the Turks used cannons to flush rebels out of the amphitheatre.

Punic Town of Kerkuane and its Necropolis   (4)

Located in north-eastern Tunisia, near Cape Bon, this Phoenician city was probably abandoned during the First Punic War (c. 250 BC) and, as a result, was not rebuilt by the Romans. The remains constitute the only surviving example of a Phoenicio-Punic city. The houses were built to a standard plan in accordance with a sophisticated notion of town planning.

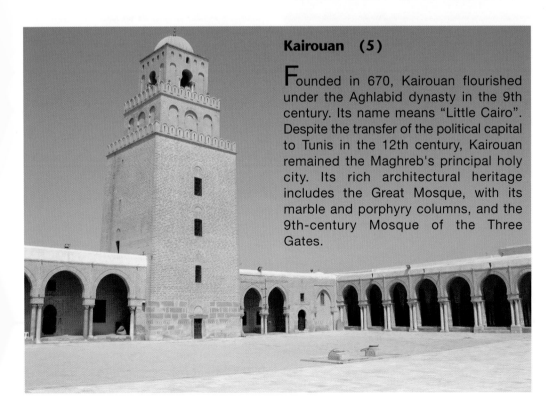

Kairouan   (5)

Founded in 670, Kairouan flourished under the Aghlabid dynasty in the 9th century. Its name means "Little Cairo". Despite the transfer of the political capital to Tunis in the 12th century, Kairouan remained the Maghreb's principal holy city. Its rich architectural heritage includes the Great Mosque, with its marble and porphyry columns, and the 9th-century Mosque of the Three Gates.

Ichkeul National Park   (6)

The Ichkeul lake and wetland are a major stopover point for hundreds of thousands of migrating birds such as ducks, geese, storks and pink flamingos, who come to feed and nest there. Ichkeul is the last remaining lake in a chain that once extended across North Africa. The Park was inscribed on the List of World Heritage in Danger in 1996 as a result of significant deterioration. The construction of three dams on rivers supplying Lake Ichkeul and its marshes has cut off almost all inflow of fresh water, causing a destructive increase in the salinity of the lake and marshes.

Medina of Sousse   (7)

Situated on the east coast of Tunisia, Sousse was an important commercial and military port during the Aghlabid period (800–909) and is a typical example of a town dating from the first centuries of Islam. With its kasbah, ramparts, medina, Bu Ftata Mosque and typical ribat, Sousse was part of a coastal defence system.

Medina of Tunis   (8)

The city is located on the Lake of Tunis and is connected to the Gulf of Tunis, an arm of the Mediterranean Sea. Under the Almohads and the Hafsids, from the 12th to the 16th century, Tunis was considered one of the greatest and wealthiest cities in the Islamic world. Some 700 monuments, including palaces, mosques, mausoleums, madrasas and fountains, testify to this remarkable past.

"First, we passed down a long canal.
On shore, very close, our first Arabs.
The sun has a dark power. The colourful
clarity on shore full of promise..."

Swiss painter Paul Klee,
when he fist saw Tunis in 1914

Air and Ténéré Natural Reserves   (1)

This is the largest protected site in Africa, covering some 7.7 million ha (19 million acres), though the area considered a protected sanctuary constitutes only one-sixth of the total space. It includes the volcanic rock mass of the Aïr, a small Sahelian pocket isolated with regard to its climate, flora and fauna, situated in the Saharan desert of Ténéré. The reserves boast an outstanding variety of landscapes, plant species and wild animals. The region has recently suffered from military conflict and civil disturbance, leading the Government of Niger to ask the Director General of UNESCO to launch an appeal for the protection of the site.

Niger

Lybian Arab Jamahiriya

Algeria

Mali

1

Chad

Burkina Faso

2

Benin

Nigeria

W National Park of Niger   (2)

The part of "W" National Park that lies in Niger is situated in a transition zone between savannah and forest lands. It represents important ecosystem characteristics of the West African Woodlands/Savannah Biogeo-graphical Province. The site reflects the interaction between natural resources and humans since Neolithic times, and it illustrates the evolution of biodiversity in this zone.

Libyan Arab Jamahiriya

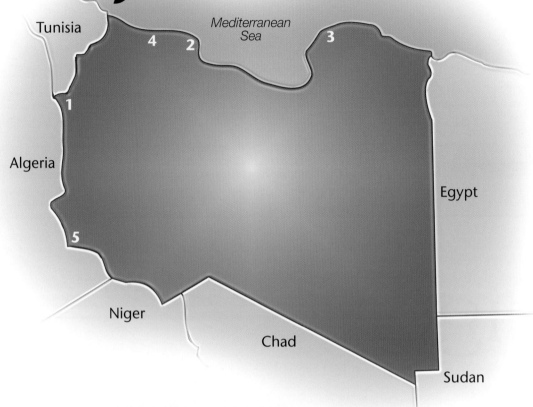

Tunisia
Mediterranean Sea
4 2
3
Algeria
Egypt
1
5
Niger
Chad
Sudan

Old Town of Ghadamès   (1)

Ghadamès, known as "the pearl of the desert", stands in an oasis. It is one of the oldest pre-Saharan cities and an outstanding example of a traditional settlement. Its domestic architecture is characterized by a vertical division of functions: the ground floor, used to store supplies; then another floor for the family; overhanging covered alleys that create what is almost an underground network of passageways; and, at the top, open-air terraces reserved for the women.

"With its large, organic labyrinth of covered, burrowing passages and whitewashed mud-brick houses, Ghadames could have come from another planet rather than another time."

"All roads lead to Libya"
by Anthony Sattin, The Sunday Times,
October 24, 2004

Archaeological Site of Leptis Magna (2)

Near Tripoli, Leptis Magna was enlarged and embellished by Septimius Severus, who was born there and later became emperor. It was one of the most beautiful cities of the Roman Empire, with its imposing public monuments, harbour, marketplace, storehouses, shops and residential districts.

"Since the first excavation in the 1920s, the incredible remains of this city have attracted less attention than they deserve."

Dr. Hafed Walda,
Kings College, London

Archaeological Site of Cyrene (3)

Cyrene was the oldest and most important of the five ancient Greek cities in the region. It gave eastern Libya the classical name "Cyrenaica", which it retained to modern times. The city was Romanized and remained a great capital until the earthquake of 365. A thousand years of history is written into its ruins, which have been famous since the 18th century.

"Passing by, the god Apollo saw Cyrene wrestling a lion which was attacking her father's sheep. He immediately fell in love with her. He carried her off to Africa, where he built her a city."

Greek mythology

Archaeological Site of Sabratha (4)

A Phoenician trading post that served as an outlet for the products of the African hinterland, Sabratha was part of the short-lived Numidian Kingdom of Massinissa before being Romanized and rebuilt in the 2nd and 3rd centuries AD. The city was badly damaged by earthquakes during the 4th century.

Rock-Art Sites of Tadrart Acacus (5)

On the border of Tassili N'Ajjer in Algeria, this rocky massif has thousands of cave paintings in very different styles, dating from 12,000 BC to AD 100. They reflect marked changes in the fauna and flora, and also the different ways of life of the populations that succeeded one another in this region of the Sahara.

Sudan

Gebel Barkal and the Sites of the Napatan Region (1)

North of Khartoum, on a large bend of the Nile River, these five archaeological sites are testimony to the Napatan (900 to 270 BC) and Meroitic (270 BC to AD 350) cultures of the second kingdom of Kush. Tombs (with and without pyramids), temples, living complexes and palaces, are to be found on the site. Since Antiquity, the hill of Gebel Barkal has been strongly associated with religious traditions and folklore.

Egypt

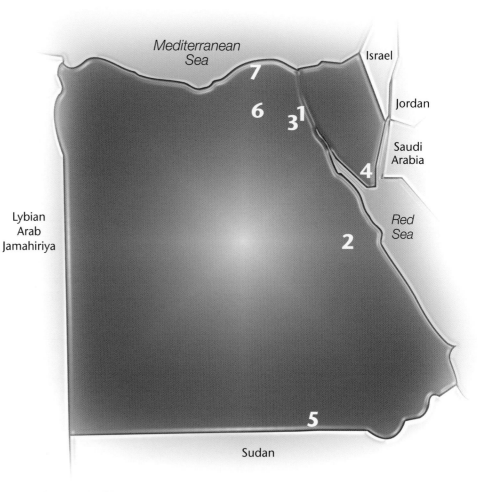

Mediterranean
Sea

Israel

Jordan

Saudi
Arabia

Lybian
Arab
Jamahiriya

Red
Sea

Sudan

7
6 **3** **1**
4
2
5

Islamic Cairo   (1)

Tucked away amid the modern urban area of Cairo lies one of the world's oldest Islamic cities, with its famous mosques, madrasas, hammams and fountains. Founded in the 10th century, it became the new centre of the Islamic world, reaching its golden age in the 14th century.

Ancient Thebes with its Necropolis (2)

Located about 700 km (435 miles) south of the Mediterranean, on the east bank of the Nile, Thebes, the city of the god Amon, was the capital of Egypt during the period of the Middle and New Kingdoms. With the temples and palaces at Karnak and Luxor, and the necropolises of the Valley of the Kings and the Valley of the Queens, Thebes is a striking testimony to Egyptian civilization at its height.

"I found it near the remains of its body (Ramesses II) and chair, with its face upwards, and apparently smiling on me, at the thought of being taken to England."

Italian explorer
Giovanni Battista Belzoni, 1815

Memphis and its Necropolis - the Pyramid Fields from Giza to Dahshur (3)

Located 19 km (12 miles) south of Cairo on the West Bank of the Nile, the capital of the Old Kingdom of Egypt has some extraordinary funerary monuments, including rock tombs, ornate mastabas, temples, pyramids and the Great Sphinx. In ancient times, the site was considered one of the Seven Wonders of the World.

"From the heights of these pyramids, forty centuries look down on us."

Napoleon Bonaparte

Saint Catherine Area   (4)

The Orthodox Monastery of St. Catherine stands at the foot of Mount Horeb where, the Old Testament records, Moses received the Tablets of the Law. The mountain is known and revered by Muslims as Jebel Musa. The entire area is sacred to three world religions: Christianity, Islam, and Judaism. The Monastery, founded in the 6th century, is the oldest Christian monastery still in use for its initial function. Its walls and buildings, of great significance to studies of Byzantine architecture, house outstanding collections of early Christian manuscripts and icons.

"God came down on Mount Sinai, to the peak of the mountain.
He summoned Moses to the mountain peak, and Moses climbed up."

The Holy Bible

Nubian Monuments from Abu Simbel to Philae   (5)

Built on the western bank of the River Nile (presently Lake Nasser), this outstanding archaeological area contains such magnificent monuments as the Temples of Ramses II at Abu Simbel and the Sanctuary of Isis at Philae, which were saved from the rising waters of the Nile thanks to the International Campaign launched by UNESCO, in 1960 to 1980.

"Every morning I waked in time to witness that daily miracle. Every morning I saw those awful brethren pass from death to life, from life to sculptured stone."

Novelist Amelia B. Edwards,
A Thousand Miles Up the Nile (1877)

Wadi Al-Hitan (Whale Valley) (6)

Located in the Western Desert of Egypt, Wadi Al-Hitan contains invaluable fossil remains of the earliest, and now extinct, suborder of whales, the archaeoceti. These fossils represent one of the major stories of evolution: the emergence of the whale as an ocean-going mammal from a previous life as a land-based animal. This is the most important site in the world for the demonstration of this stage of evolution.

Abu Mena   (7)

The church, baptistery, basilicas, public buildings, streets, monasteries, houses and workshops in this early Christian holy city were built over   the tomb of the martyr Menas of Alexandria, who died in AD 296. A land-reclamation program for the agricultural development of the region, funded by the World Bank, has caused a dramatic raise of the water table in the past ten years. Huge underground cavities have opened in the town's north-western region. The risk of collapse is so high that the authorities were forced to fill with sand the bases of some of the most endangered buildings, including the crypt of Abu Mena with the tomb of the Saint, and close them to the public.

Ethiopia

Tiya (1)

Tiya is among the most important of the roughly 160 archaeological sites discovered so far in the Soddo region, south of Addis Ababa. The site contains 36 monuments, including 32 carved stelae covered with symbols, most of which are difficult to decipher. They are the remains of an ancient Ethiopian culture whose age has not yet been precisely determined.

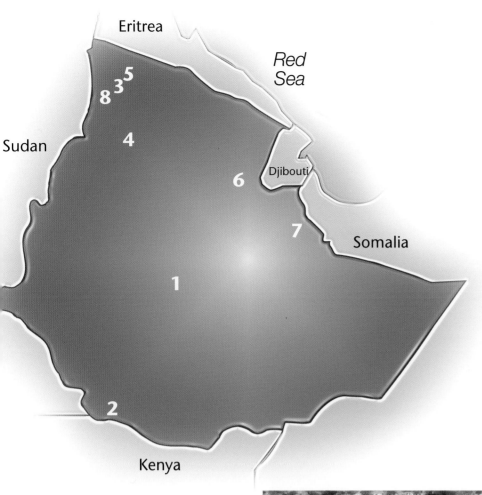

Lower Valley of the Omo   (2)

A prehistoric site near Lake Turkana, the lower valley of the Omo is renowned the world over. The discovery of many fossils there, especially Homo gracilis, has been of fundamental importance in the study of human evolution.

"These are the oldest well-dated fossils of modern humans (Homo sapiens) currently known anywhere in the world."

Geologist and Professor Frank Brown, University of Utah

Simien National Park   (3)

Massive erosion over the years on the Ethiopian plateau has created one of the most spectacular landscapes in the world, with jagged mountain peaks, deep valleys and sharp precipices dropping some 1,500 m (4,921 feet). The park is home to some extremely rare animals such as the Gelada baboon, the Simien fox and the Walia ibex, a goat found nowhere else in the world. The World Heritage Committee decided to inscribe Simien National Park on the List of World Heritage in Danger due to evidence of recent deterioration of the Walia ibex population.

Rock-hewn Churches, Lalibela   (4)

The 11 medieval monolithic cave churches of this 13th-century "New Jerusalem" are situated in a mountainous region in the heart of Ethiopia, near a traditional village with circular-shaped dwellings. Lalibela is a high place of Ethiopian Christianity, still today a site of pilgrimage and devotion.

"I weary of writing more about these buildings, because it seems to me that I shall not be believed if I write more ... I swear by God, in Whose power I am, that all I have written is the truth."

Portuguese priest Francisco Alvarez, first European to see the churches, 1520

Aksum   (5)

The ruins of the ancient city of Aksum are found close to Ethiopia's northern border. They mark the location of the heart of ancient Ethiopia, when the Kingdom of Aksum was the most powerful state between the Eastern Roman Empire and Persia. The massive ruins, dating from between the 1st and the 13th century AD, include monolithic obelisks, giant stelae, royal tombs and the ruins of ancient castles.

"This is a historic moment. After 68 years in exile, the Aksum obelisk returns to the heart of ancient Ethiopia, to the Tigrai region. It will once again be erected in the former kingdom."

Koïchiro Matsuura, Director-General of UNESCO, on the occasion of the Aksum obelisk's return to Ethiopia from Italy in March 2005

Lower Valley of the Awash (6)

The Awash Valley contains one of the most important groupings of palaeontological sites on the African continent. The remains found at the site, the oldest of which date back at least 4 million years, provide evidence of human evolution which has modified our conception of the history of humankind. The most spectacular discovery came in 1974, when 52 fragments of a skeleton enabled the famous Lucy to be reconstructed.

"Johanson suggested taking an alternate route back to the Land Rover, through a nearby gully. Within moments, he spotted a right proximal ulna (forearm bone) and quickly identified it as a hominid."

Discovery of the skeleton Lucy,
November 24, 1974
Institute of Human Origins

Harar Walled Town (7)

The walls surrounding this sacred Muslim city were built between the 13th and 16th centuries. It became the capital of a powerful Islamic state exerting its spiritual, economic and cultural influence at a worldwide level. Harar Jugol, said to be the fourth holiest city of Islam, numbers 82 mosques, three of which date from the 10th century, and 102 shrines.

"The company has founded an agency in Harar, a region that you'll find on the map in the south-east of Abyssinia. We'll export coffee, hides, gum, and so on ... The country is very healthy and cool due to its elevation."

French poet Arthur Rimbaud,
writing to his family about Harar,
November 1880

Fasil Ghebbi, Gondar Region (8)

In the 16th and 17th centuries, the fortress-city of Fasil Ghebbi was the residence of the Ethiopian emperor Fasilides and his successors. Surrounded by a 900-m-long wall (2,952 feet), the city contains palaces, churches, monasteries and unique public and private buildings marked by Hindu and Arab influences, subsequently transformed by the Baroque style brought to Gondar by the Jesuit missionaries.

Senegal

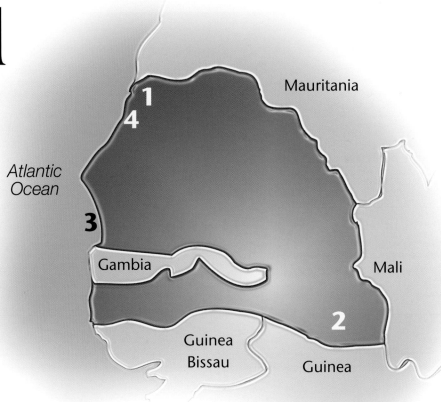

Mauritania

Atlantic Ocean

Mali

Gambia

Guinea Bissau

Guinea

Djoudj National Bird Sanctuary (1)

Situated in the Senegal River delta, the Djoudj Sanctuary is a wetland of 16,000 ha (3,953,686 acres), comprising a large lake surrounded by streams, ponds and backwaters. It forms a living, but fragile sanctuary for some 1.5 million birds, such as the white pelican, the purple heron, the African spoonbill, the great egret and the cormorant.

"In view of the imminent danger facing the site, the Director of Senegal National Parks had requested that the site be inscribed in the List of World Heritage in Danger."

24th Session of the World Heritage Committee, November 2000

Niokolo-Koba National Park (2)

Located in a well-watered area along the banks of the Gambia River, the gallery forests and savannahs of Niokolo-Koba National Park boast a very rich fauna, among them Derby elands, chimpanzees, lions, leopards and a large population of elephants, as well as many birds, reptiles and amphibians. The park covers an area of over 8,000 km_ (1,976,843 acres).

Island of Gorée   (3)

The island lies off the coast of Senegal, opposite Dakar. From the 15th to the 19th century, it was the largest slave-trading centre on the African coast. Ruled in succession by the Portuguese, Dutch, English and French, its architecture is characterized by the contrast between the grim slave quarters and the elegant houses of the slave traders. Today it continues to serve as a reminder of human exploitation and as a sanctuary for reconciliation.

"My hope is that this site contributes to making more people visit our museum and that the pilgrimage to the Island of Gorée provides an impetus to an enhanced brotherhood able to exorcise the demons of the past."

Abdoulaye Wade,
President of the Republic of Senegal,
2005

Island of Saint-Louis   (4)

Founded as a French colonial settlement in the 17th century, Saint-Louis was urbanised in the mid-19th century. It was the capital of Senegal from 1872 to 1957 and played an important cultural and economic role in the whole of West Africa. The location of the town (on an island at the mouth of the Senegal River), its regular town plan, its system of quays and its characteristic colonial architecture give Saint-Louis its distinctive appearance and identity.

Mali

Old Towns of Djenné (1)

Inhabited since 250 BC, Djenné became a market centre and an important link in the trans-Saharan gold trade. In the 15th and 16th centuries, it was one of the centres for the propagation of Islam. Its traditional houses, of which nearly 2,000 have survived, are built on hillocks (toguere) as protection from the seasonal floods. The Great Mosque of Djenné is the largest mud brick building in the world and is considered by many architects to be the greatest achievement of the Sudano-Sahelian architectural style.

Timbuktu (2)

It was established as a seasonal camp by the nomadic Tuareg, perhaps as early as the 10th century, and grew to great wealth because of its key role in trans-Saharan trade in gold, ivory, slaves and salt. Home of the prestigious Koranic Sankore University and other madrasas, Timbuktu was an intellectual and spiritual capital and a centre for the propagation of Islam throughout Africa in the 15th and 16th centuries. Its three great mosques, Djingareyber, Sankore and Sidi Yahia, recall Timbuktu's golden age. In 1990, the World Heritage Committee inscribed the city on the List of the World Heritage in Danger due to the threat of encroachment by desert sands. A program was set up to safeguard the site.

"On the east side of the city of Timbuktu, there is a large forest, in which are a great many elephants. The timber here is very large. The trees on the outside of the forest are remarkable."

Shabeni, a merchant from Tetuan
when he was 14, around 1787

Cliff of Bandiagara - Land of the Dogons (3)

The Bandiagara site is an outstanding landscape of cliffs and sandy plateaux with some beautiful architecture. Several age-old social traditions live on in the region. The geological, archaeological and ethnological interest, together with the landscape, makes the Bandiagara plateau one of West Africa's most impressive sites.

Tomb of Askia (4)

The dramatic 17-metre (56-foot) pyramidal structure of the Tomb of Askia was built by Askia Mohamed, the Emperor of Songhai, in 1495 in his capital Gao. It bears testimony to the power and riches of the empire that flourished in the 15th and 16th centuries through its control of the trans-Saharan trade, notably in salt and gold. It is also a fine example of the monumental mud-building traditions of the West African Sahel.

"Somehow the Tomb of Askia manages to look unkempt, like a man waking up on a sofa after a night on the vodka."

Travel writer Mark Moxon, 2002

Senegal

1 2

Senegal

Gambia

James Island and Related Sites (1)

The first European settlers on the island were the Courlanders, who called it St. Elizabeth Island and used it as a trade base from 1651 until its capture by the English in 1661. As Britain withdrew from the slave trade, the fort was largely abandoned in 1779. James Island and its related sites present a testimony to the main periods and facets of the encounter between Africa and Europe along the River Gambia, a continuum stretching from pre-colonial and pre-slavery times to independence. The site is particularly significant for its relation to the beginning of the slave trade and its abolition.

"Whenever I hear anyone arguing for slavery, I feel a strong impulse to see it tried on him personally."

Abraham Lincoln,
16th President of the United States

Prehistoric Stone Circle Sites (2)

Over one hundred prehistoric stone circles survive in Gambia, built over a period of some fifteen hundred years, from the 3rd century BC to the 13th century AD, in at least 34 sites. The circles are composed of standing stones between 10 and 24 in number, in one or two concentric rings. All the circles appear to enclose a burial area, with a grave under a slightly raised mound in the centre of the circle.

Côte d'Ivoire

Taï National Park   (1)

This park is one of the last major remnants of the primary tropical forest of West Africa. Its rich natural flora, and threatened mammal species such as the pygmy hippopotamus and 11 species of monkeys, are of great scientific interest.

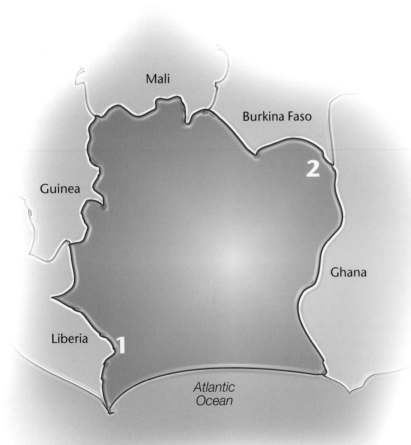

Comoé National Park   (2)

One of the largest protected areas in West Africa, this park is characterized by its great plant diversity. Due to the presence of the Comoé River, it contains plants which are normally only found much farther south, such as shrub savannahs and patches of thick rainforest. The present unrest in Côte d'Ivoire is having an adverse effect on the site, as is poaching of wildlife, fires caused by poachers, over-grazing by large cattle herds, and the absence of effective management.

Guinea

Mount Nimba Strict Nature Reserve
(1) (*Site shared with Cote d'Ivoire*)

Bordering Guinea, Liberia and Côte d'Ivoire, Mount Nimba rises above the surrounding savannah. Its slopes are covered by dense forest at the foot of grassy mountain pastures. They harbour an especially rich flora and fauna, with endemic species such as the viviparous toad and chimpanzees that use stones as tools. The reserve was inscribed on the List of the World Heritage in Danger in 1992 as a result of two factors: a proposed iron-ore mining concession to an international consortium, and the arrival of a large number of refugees to areas in and around the Guinean part of the site.

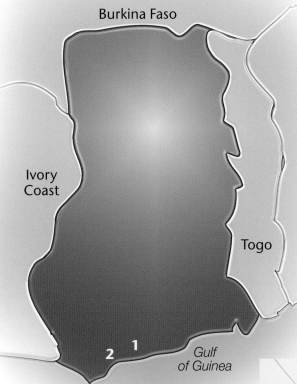

Burkina Faso

Ivory Coast

Togo

2 1

Gulf of Guinea

Ghana

Forts and Castles, Volta Greater Accra, Central and Western Regions   (1)

The remains of fortified trading posts, erected between 1482 and 1786, can still be seen along the coast of Ghana between Keta and Beyin. They were links in the trade routes established by the Portuguese in many areas of the world during their era of great maritime exploration.

Asante Traditional Buildings   (2)

To the north-east of Kumasi, these are the last material remains of the great Ashanti civilization, which reached its peak in the 18th century. Ashanti wealth was based on the region's substantial deposits of gold. Since the dwellings are made of earth, wood and straw, they are vulnerable to the onslaught of time and weather.

"We are Ashantis within Ghana. We stand for our traditional values, values of fairness, respect, honesty, integrity and of each being our brother's keeper."

Prince Akyempe-hene

Koutammakou, the Land of the Batammariba (1)

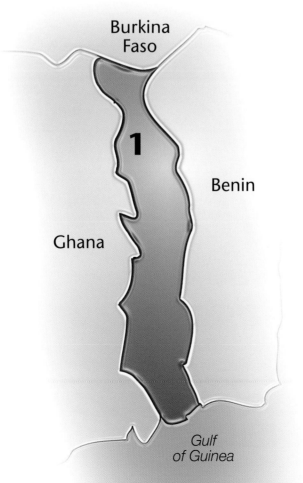

The Koutammakou landscape in north-eastern Togo, which extends into neighbouring Benin, is home to the Batammariba, whose remarkable mud Takienta tower-houses have come to be seen as a symbol of the country. In this landscape, nature is strongly associated with social rituals and beliefs. Many of the buildings are two stories high and those with granaries feature an almost spherical form above a cylindrical base.

Togo

Burkina Faso

1

Benin

Ghana

Gulf of Guinea

Benin

Royal Palaces of Abomey (1)

From 1625 to 1900, 12 kings succeeded one another at the head of the powerful Kingdom of Abomey. With the exception of King Akaba, who had his own separate enclosure, they all had their palaces built within the same cob-wall area, in keeping with previous palaces with regard to the use of space and materials. The royal palaces of Abomey are a unique reminder of this vanished kingdom. The site was inscribed on the List of the World Heritage in Danger in 1985 after a tornado struck Abomey on March 15, 1984. According to a report at the time, the royal enclosure and museums had suffered extensive damage. Since 1984, several conservation programs have led to remarkable work on the site.

"In spite of King Gbêhanzin's (1889-1894) strong resistance to European penetration atthe end of the 19th century, the kingdom lost its independence and became part of the French colony of Dahomey."

The Abomey Historical Museum

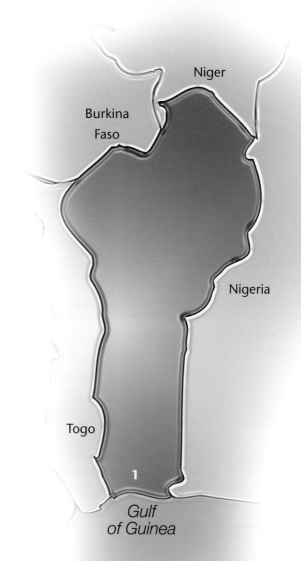

Sukur Cultural Landscape (1)

The Sukur Cultural Landscape, with the Palace of the Hidi (Chief) on a hill dominating the villages below, the terraced fields with their sacred symbols, and the extensive remains of a former flourishing iron industry, is a remarkably intact physical expression of a society and its spiritual and material culture.

"Thursday, June 5, 1851. Billama (Barth's Kanuri companion) gave me much interesting information about the country before us, chiefly with reference to Sugur, a powerful and entirely independent pagan chief in the mountains south from Mandara."
Great African explorer
Heinrich Barth

Nigeria

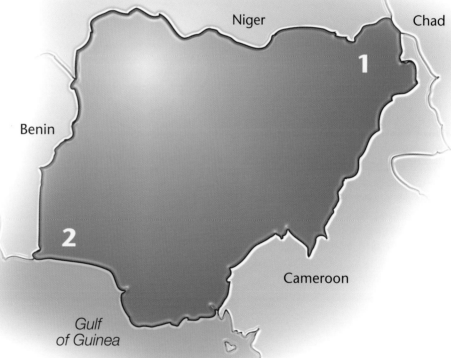

Osun-Osogbo Sacred Grove (2)

The dense forest of the Osun Sacred Grove, on the outskirts of the city of Osogbo, is one of the last remnants of primary high forest in southern Nigeria. Regarded as the abode of the goddess of fertility Osun, one of the pantheons of Yoruba gods, the landscape of the grove and its meandering river is dotted with sanctuaries, shrines, sculptures and artworks in honour of Osun and other Yoruba deities.

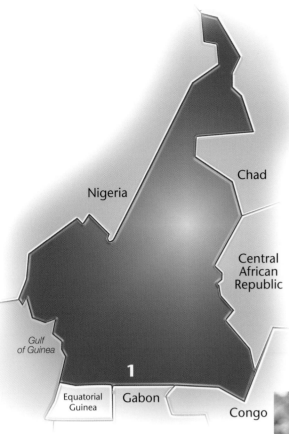

Cameroon

Dja Faunal Reserve   (1)

This is one of the largest and best-protected rainforests in Africa, with 90% of its area left undisturbed. Almost completely surrounded by the Dja River, which forms a natural boundary, the reserve is especially noted for its biodiversity and a wide variety of primates. It contains 107 mammal species, five of which are threatened.

Central African Republic

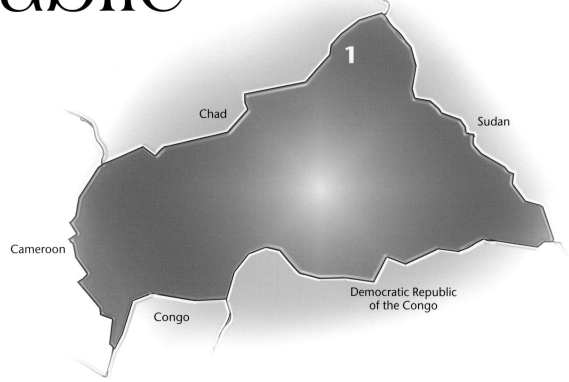

Manovo -Gounda St. Floris National Park   (1)

The importance of this park derives from its wealth of flora and fauna. Its vast savannahs are home to a wide variety of species – black rhinoceroses, elephants, cheetahs, leopards, wild dogs, red-fronted gazelles and buffalo – while various types of waterfowl are to be found in the northern floodplains. The site was added to the List of World Heritage in Danger following reports of illegal grazing and poaching by heavily armed hunters, who, according to some reports, may have harvested as much as 80% of the park's wildlife.

"The Committee was seriously concerned that uncontrolled poaching by heavily armed groups, from within and outside of CAR, has resulted in security problems, leading to the deaths of four park staff in early 1997."

21st Session of the World Heritage Committee, December 1997

Uganda

Tombs of Buganda Kings at Kasubi (1)

These monuments constitute a site embracing almost 30 ha (74 acres) of hillside within Kampala district. Most of the site is agricultural, farmed by traditional methods. At its core on the hilltop is the former palace of the Kabakas of Buganda, built in 1882 and converted into the royal burial ground in 1884. Four royal tombs now lie within the Muzibu Azaala Mpanga, which is the main building, circular-shaped and surmounted by a dome. It is a major example of an architectural achievement in organic materials, principally wood, thatch, reed, wattle and daub.

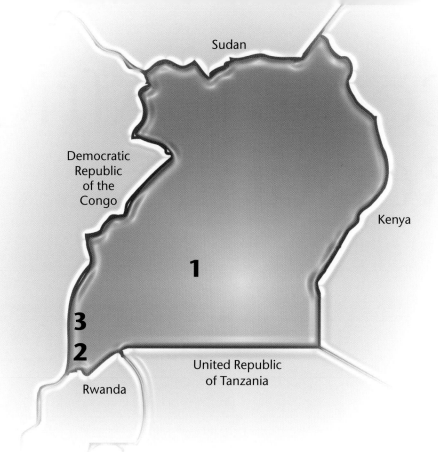

Bwindi Impenetrable National Park (2)

At the junction of the plain and mountain forests, Bwindi Park covers 32,000 ha (79,000 acres). The park is part of the Bwindi Impenetrable Forest. It is known for its exceptional biodiversity, with more than 160 species of trees and over 100 species of ferns. Many types of birds and butterflies can also be found there, as well as many endangered species, including the mountain gorilla.

"The Bwindi Impenetrable Forest is known as Place of Darkness."

Aliette Frank
or National Geographic News,
March 8, 2001

Rwenzori Mountains National Park (3)

The Rwenzori Mountains National Park covers nearly 100,000 ha (247,105 acres) in western Uganda and comprises the main part of the Rwenzori mountain chain, which includes Africa's third highest peak (Mount Margherita, at 5,109 m or 16,761 feet). The region's glaciers, waterfalls and lakes make it one of Africa's most beautiful alpine areas, often called "The Mountains of the Moon."

"There has been hidden to this day a giant amongst mountains, the melting snow of whose tops has been for some 50 centuries most vital to the people of Egypt."

Henry Morton Stanley,
first European sighting of
the Ruwenzori, 1889

Kenya

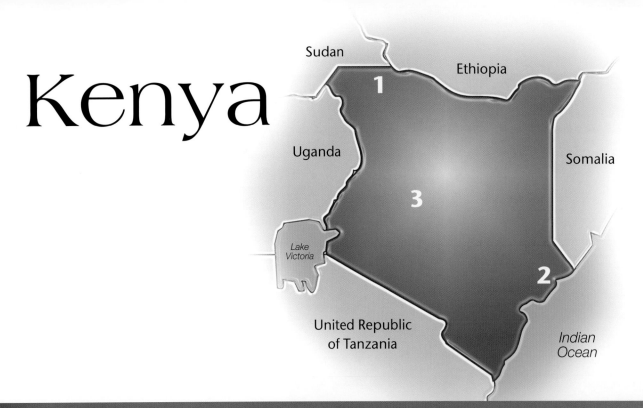

Sudan

Ethiopia

1

Uganda

Somalia

3

Lake
Victoria

2

United Republic
of Tanzania

Indian
Ocean

Lake Turkana National Parks   (1)

Also known as the Jade Sea, the most saline of Africa's large lakes, Turkana is an outstanding laboratory for the study of plant and animal communities. The three National Parks serve as a stopover for migrant waterfowl and are major breeding grounds for the Nile crocodile, hippopotamus and a variety of venomous snakes. The lake was featured in Fernando Meirelles's film The Constant Gardener.

Lamu Old Town   (2)

Cast into the Indian Ocean off the coast of Kenya, Lamu Old Town is the oldest and best-preserved Swahili settlement in East Africa, retaining its traditional functions. Built in coral stone and mangrove timber, the town is characterized by the simplicity of structural forms enriched by such features as inner courtyards, verandas, and elaborately carved wooden doors. Lamu has hosted major Muslim religious festivals since the 19th century.

"Many of the world's destinations loudly boast an opportunity for the traveller to enter another world. The island of Lamu offers this experience in its purest form."
Lamu Museum

Mount Kenya National Park / Natural Forest   (3)

At 5,199 m (17,057 feet), Mount Kenya is the second highest peak in Africa. It is an ancient extinct volcano, during whose period of activity it is thought to have risen to 6,500 m (21,325 feet). There are 12 remnant glaciers on the mountain, all receding rapidly, and four secondary peaks that sit at the head of the U-shaped glacial valleys. With its rugged glacier-clad summits and forested middle slopes, Mount Kenya is one of the most impressive landscapes in East Africa.

"Let each country have a mountain."

Queen of England,
at the time when the three snows of Africa, i.e.
Mount Kenya, Kilimanjaro and Ruwenzori,
were each given to Kenya, Tanzania and
Uganda when the border of the countries were
forged during colonial times.

339

United Republic of Tanzania

Selous Game Reserve (1)

Large numbers of elephants, black rhinoceroses, cheetahs, giraffes, hippopotamuses and crocodiles live in this immense sanctuary, which measures 50,000 sq. km (12 million acres) and is relatively undisturbed by human impact. The park has a variety of vegetation zones, ranging from dense thickets to open wooded grasslands.

Kilimanjaro National Park   (2)

At 5,895 m (19,340 feet), Kilimanjaro is the highest point in Africa. This volcanic massif stands in splendid isolation above the surrounding plains, with its snowy peak looming over the savannah. The mountain is encircled by mountain forest. Numerous mammals, many of them endangered species, live in the park.

"That mountain is the most mystical, magical draw to people's imagination. Once the ice disappears, it's going to be a very different place."

Douglas R. Hardy,
geologist at the University of Massachusetts,
about the effect of global warming,
February 2001

Ngorongoro Conservation Area (3)

A large permanent concentration of wild animals can be found in the huge and perfect crater of Ngorongoro. Excavations carried out in Olduvai Gorge, not far from there, have resulted in the discovery of one of our more distant ancestors, Homo habilis. Laitoli Site, which also lies within the area, is one of the main localities of early hominid footprints, dating back 3.6 million years.

"They look just like the prints of one of us or one of our children. Absolutely human, but when you think they're 3.6 million years old, I think it gives you a chill."

Archaeologist
Fiona Marshal

Stone Town of Zanzibar   (4)

Built on a triangular peninsular of land on the western coast of the island, the Stone Town of Zanzibar is a fine example of the Swahili coastal trading towns of East Africa. It retains its urban fabric and townscape virtually intact and contains many fine buildings that reflect its particular culture, which has brought together and homogenized disparate elements of the cultures of Africa, the Arab region, India, and Europe over more than a millennium.

Serengeti National Park　(5)

The vast plains of the Serengeti comprise 1.5 million ha (3,7 million acres) of savannah. The annual migration to permanent watering holes of vast herds of herbivores (wildebeest, gazelles and zebras), followed by their predators, is one of the most impressive natural events in the world.

"We walked for miles over burnt out country ... Then I saw the green trees of the river, walked two miles more and found myself in paradise."

Stewart Edward White, American hunter, 1913

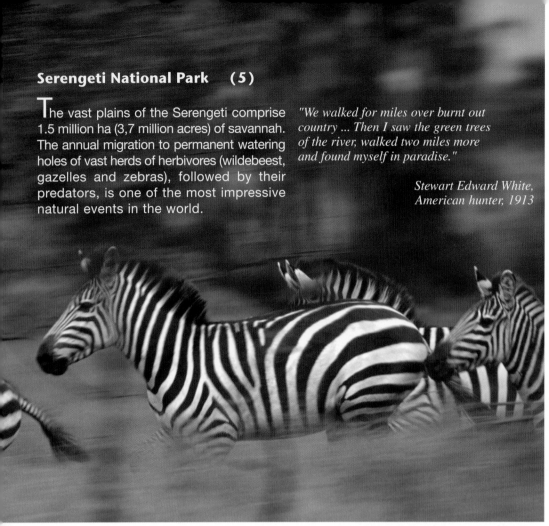

Kondoa Irangi Rock Paintings　(6)

The rock art found at these sites is the northernmost extension of the southern African hunter-gatherer rock art tradition. It comes primarily from the hunter-gatherer period with red pigment in the outline, streaky, and silhouette styles. Subject matter ranges from animals significant to the cosmology of the artists, to human figures in a variety of postures and non-figurative designs. Giraffe, elandand elephants predominate. Art can also be found from the more recent agriculturist period.

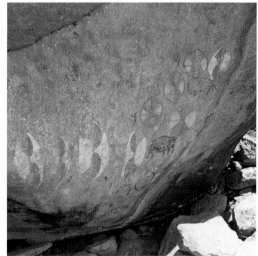

Ruins of Kilwa Kisiwani and Ruins of Songo Mnara　(7)

The remains of two great East African ports admired by early European explorers are situated on two small islands near the coast. From the 13th to the 16th century, the merchants of Kilwa dealt in gold, silver, pearls, perfumes, Arabian crockery, Persian earthenware and Chinese porcelain; much of the trade in the Indian Ocean thus passed through their hands. According to the World Heritage Centre, the site needs protection, otherwise it will slowly vanish.

"Some of the more formidable structures contained second and third stories, and many were embellished with cut-stone decorative borders framing the entranceway."

Abu Abdullah Ibn Battuta, famous Arabic traveller, 1331

Malawi

Lake Malawi National Park   (1)

Located at the southern end of the great expanse of Lake Malawi, with its deep, clear waters and mountain backdrop, the national park is home to the highest vertebrate diversity in the world, with an estimated 900 species of cichlid fish, nearly all endemic. Its importance for the study of evolution is comparable to that of the finches of the Galapagos Islands.

The Chongoni Rock Art Monument Area   (2)

The area is part of the Dedza Chongoni Highlands, which are dominated by the Chongoni Mountain, rising above the Central Malawi Plain. Much of the area is protected forest reserve. Over 200 rock-painted sites have been located here, most of which are shelters. Still, a number of paintings have also been found on isolated large and small rocks, and some of them depict figures of the "Gule Wamkulu" or Nyau secret society. Nyau traditions are still practiced today.

"Gule Wamkulu", literally meaning "big dance", have become a sort of title for secret societies of traditional Chewa religious practices. The Gule Wamkulu ceremonies consist of formally organized dances to admire the remarkable physical abilities of these individuals."

Amy Gough,
The Peoples of The World Foundation

Democratic Republic of the Congo

Garamba National Park (1)

The park's immense savannahs, grasslands and woodlands, interspersed with gallery forests along the riverbanks and the swampy depressions, are home to four large mammals: the elephant, giraffe, hippopotamus and above all the white rhinoceros. Though much larger than the black rhino, it is harmless and only some 30 individuals remain. The site was returned to the List of World Heritage in Danger in 1996.

"It is ironic that now as peace is supposed to be coming to the region, the exploitation of large mammals has escalated."

Kes Hillman Smith,
Garamba National Park Project, August 2004

Kahuzi-Biega National Park (2)

The park lies in a vast area of primary tropical forest dominated by two spectacular extinct volcanoes, Kahuzi and Biega. It features a diverse and abundant fauna, including one of the last groups of mountain gorillas (consisting of only some 250 individuals), which lives at between 2,100 and 2,400 m (6,890 to 7,874 feet) above sea level. Grave concern that portions of the park had been deforested and that hunting had been reported there, as well as war and civil strife ravaging the country, led the World Heritage Committee to inscribe the site on the List of World Heritage in Danger.

"When you realize the value of all life, you dwell less on what is past and concentrate on the preservation of the future.

The last entry of Dr. Dian Fossey's diary before her murder. She dedicated her life to the observation of mountain gorillas.

Okapi Wildlife Reserve (3)

Located in the north-east of the Democratic Republic of the Congo, near the borders with Sudan and Uganda, the Okapi Wildlife Reserve occupies about one-fifth of the Ituri forest. The Zaire River basin, of which the reserve and forest are a part, is one of the largest drainage systems in Africa. The reserve contains threatened species of primates and birds and about 5,000 of the estimated 30,000 okapi surviving in the wild. It also has some dramatic scenery, including waterfalls on the Ituri and Epulu rivers. The Okapi Wildlife Reserve was inscribed on the List of World Heritage in Danger in 1998, due to reports that the armed conflict had led to the looting of facilities and the killing of elephants in this site.

"The Okapi Wildlife Reserve is a model example of what great things can be achieved when local people and local government, in collaboration with a non-governmental organization, come together in a common cause."

Gilman International Conservation

Salonga National Park   (4)

Situated at the heart of the central basin of the Zaire River, Salonga National Park is Africa's largest tropical rainforest reserve. The park is very isolated and accessible only by water. It is the habitat of many endemic endangered species, such as the dwarf chimpanzee, the Zaire peacock, the forest elephant and the African slender-snouted or "false" crocodile. The Park was inscribed in 1999 on the List of the World Heritage in Danger for the first time since the period from 1984 to 1992, due to a serious decline in population of the white rhinoceros.

Virunga National Park   (5)

The park was established in 1925 as an animal reserve. In later years it has become known for its mountain gorillas. Virunga National comprises an outstanding diversity of habitats, ranging from swamps and steppes to the snowfields of Rwenzori at an altitude of over 5,000 m (16,404 feet), and from lava plains to the savannahs on the slopes of volcanoes. Virunga National Park was inscribed on the List of World Heritage in Danger in 1994 in the wake of the war in neighbouring Rwanda and the subsequent massive influx of refugees from that country, which led to massive deforestation and poaching at the site.

Mosi-oa-Tunya / Victoria Falls　(1)
(Site shared with Zimbabwe)

Zambia

United Republic
of Tanzania

Democratic Republic
of the Congo

Angola

Malawi

Mozambique

1

Namibia

Zimbabwe

Botswana

These are among the most spectacular waterfalls in the world. The Zambezi River, which is more than 2 km (1.2 miles) wide at this point, plunges noisily down a series of basalt gorges and raises an iridescent mist that can be seen more than 20 km away. The falls form a border between Zambia and Zimbabwe.

"... scenes so lovely that they must have been gazed upon by angels in their flight."

Scottish explorer Dr. David Livingstone, who visited the falls in 1855 and named them for Queen Victoria.

Mana Pools National Park, Sapi and Chewore Safari Areas (1)

On the banks of the Zambezi, great cliffs overhang the river and the floodplains. The area is home to a remarkable concentration of wild animals, including elephants, buffalo, leopards and cheetahs. It also has the country's biggest concentration of hippopotamuses and crocodiles.

Zimbabwe

Zambia

Namibia

1

Mozambique

2
3

Botswana

4

South africa

Khami Ruins National Monument (2)

Khami, which developed after the capital of Great Zimbabwe had been abandoned in the mid-16th century, is of great archaeological interest. The discovery of objects from Europe and China shows that Khami was a major centre for trade over a long period of time. Khami was the capital of the Torwa dynasty from 1450 until 1683.

Matobo Hills (3)

The area exhibits a profusion of distinctive rock landforms rising above the granite shield that covers much of Zimbabwe. The large boulders provide abundant natural shelters and have been associated with human occupation from the early Stone Age right through to early historical times, and intermittently since. They also feature an outstanding collection of rock paintings. The famous English businessman Cecil John Rhodes is buried in these hills.

"We will call them Matobo (the bald heads)."

Southern African King
Mzilikazi, 1840

Great Zimbabwe National Monument (4)

The ruins of Great Zimbabwe – the capital of the Queen of Sheba, according to an age-old legend – are a unique testimony to the Bantu civilization of the Shona between the 11th and 15th centuries. The city, which covers an area of nearly 80 ha (198 acres), was an important trading centre and was renowned from the Middle Ages onwards. At its peak, estimates are that Great Zimbabwe had as many as 18,000 inhabitants.

"Among the gold mines of the inland plains between the Limpopo and Zambezi rivers, there is a fortress built of stones of marvellous size."

Viçente Pegado,
Captain, Portuguese garrison of Sofala,
1531

Vredefort Dome   (1)

Vredefort Dome, near Johannesburg, is a representative part of a larger meteorite impact structure, or astrobleme. Dating back 2,023 million years, it is the oldest astrobleme found on earth so far. With a radius of 190 km, it is also the largest and the most deeply eroded. Vredefort Dome bears witness to the world's greatest known single energy release event, which caused devastating global change, including, according to some scientists, major evolutionary changes.

"Like a drop of water falling into a pond, the asteroid punched a hole in the earth's crust and caused a recoil of molten matter into the atmosphere."

Researcher and writer Graeme Addison,
specialist of the Vredefort Dome

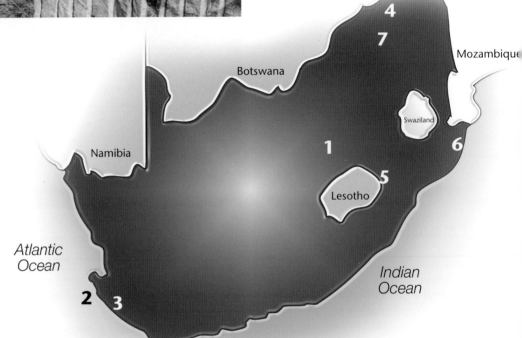

South Africa

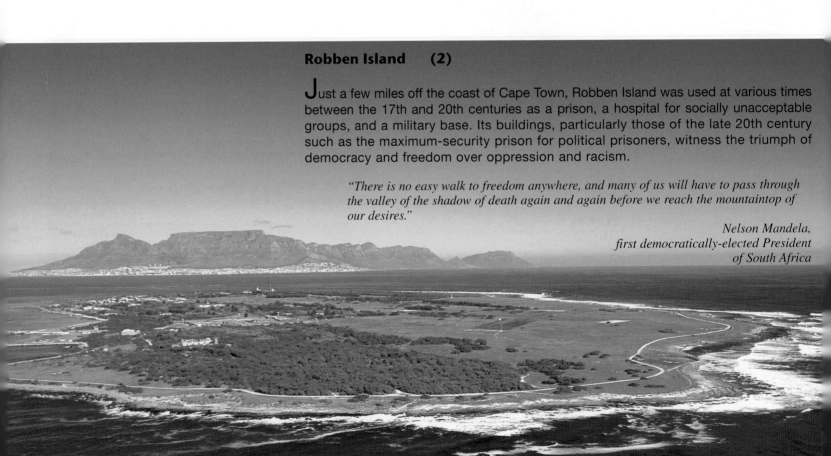

Robben Island   (2)

Just a few miles off the coast of Cape Town, Robben Island was used at various times between the 17th and 20th centuries as a prison, a hospital for socially unacceptable groups, and a military base. Its buildings, particularly those of the late 20th century such as the maximum-security prison for political prisoners, witness the triumph of democracy and freedom over oppression and racism.

"There is no easy walk to freedom anywhere, and many of us will have to pass through the valley of the shadow of death again and again before we reach the mountaintop of our desires."

Nelson Mandela,
first democratically-elected President
of South Africa

Cape Floral Region Protected Areas   (3)

This is a serial site, in Cape Province, South Africa, made up of eight protected areas, covering 553,000 ha (1.4 million acres). The Cape Floral region is one of the richest areas for plants in the world. It displays outstanding ecological and biological processes associated with the Fynbos vegetation, which is unique to the area. The outstanding diversity, density and endemism of the flora are among the highest worldwide.

Mapungubwe Cultural Landscape (4)

Mapungubwe is set hard against the northern border of South Africa, joining Zimbabwe and Botswana. It is an open, expansive savannah landscape at the confluence of the Limpopo and Shashe rivers. Mapungubwe developed into the largest kingdom in the sub-continent before it was abandoned in the 14th century. What survives are the almost untouched remains of the palace sites and also the entire settlement area dependent upon them, as well as two earlier capital sites, the whole presenting an unrivalled picture of the development of social and political structures over some 400 years.

"Today we reach back through the mists of more than 1000 years of African heritage and touch the essence of a people and a time too long forgotten."

Marthinus Van Schalkwyk,
South African Minister of Environmental
Affairs & Tourism, at the launch of
Mapungubwe National Park, September 2004

uKhahlamba / Drakensberg Park (5)

The uKhahlamba – Drakensberg Park has exceptional natural beauty in its soaring basaltic buttresses, incisive dramatic cutbacks, and golden sandstone ramparts. Rolling high altitude grasslands, the pristine steep-sided river valleys and rocky gorges also contribute to the beauty of the site. Its diversity of habitats protects a high level of endemic and globally threatened species, especially birds and plants. This spectacular natural site also contains many caves and rock shelters with the largest and most concentrated group of paintings in Africa south of the Sahara, made by the San people over a period of 4,000 years.

Greater Saint Lucia Wetland Park (6)

Situated on the east Coast of KwaZulu-Natal, about 275 km (170 miles) north of Durban, the park is made up of around 3,280 km_ of pristine natural ecosystems. The ongoing fluvial, marine and aeolian processes in the site have produced a variety of landforms, including coral reefs, long sandy beaches, coastal dunes, lake systems, swamps, and extensive reed and papyrus wetlands.

Fossil Hominid Sites of Sterkfontein, Swartkrans and Kromdraai   (7)

These sites have produced abundant scientific information on the evolution of human beings over the past 3.5 million years, including insight into their way of life and the animals with which they lived and on which they fed. The landscape also preserves many features of that prehistoric period. Sterkfontein is sometimes referred to as the cradle of humanity.

*"Evolution is fascinating to watch.
To me it is the most interesting when one can observe the evolution of a single man."*

*American columnist
Shana Alexander*

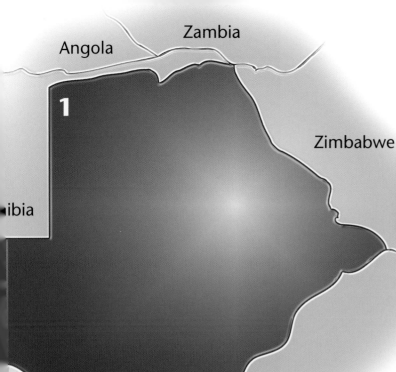

Botswana

Tsodilo (1)

With one of the highest concentrations of rock art in the world, Tsodilo has been called the "Louvre of the Desert". Over 4,500 paintings are preserved in an area of only 10 sq. km (2,471 acres) in the Kalahari Desert. The archaeological record of the area gives a chronological account of human activity and environmental changes over at least 100,000 years. Local communities in this hostile environment respect Tsodilo as a place of worship frequented by ancestral spirits.

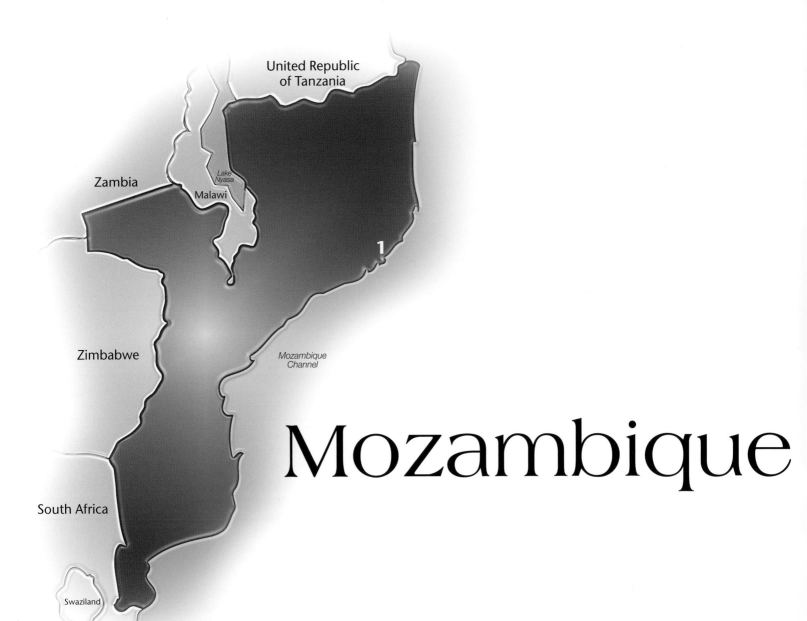

Mozambique

Island of Mozambique   (1)

The fortified city of Mozambique is located on this island, a former Portuguese trading post on the route to India. Its remarkable architectural unity is due to the consistent use, since the 16th century, of the same building techniques, building materials (stone or macuti) and decorative principles.

Royal Hill of Ambohimanga (1)

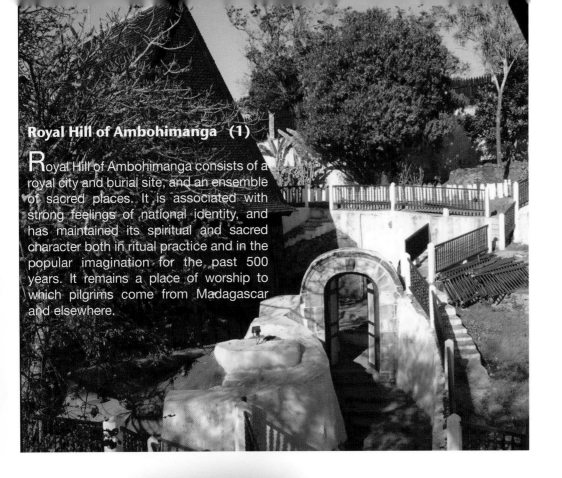

Royal Hill of Ambohimanga consists of a royal city and burial site, and an ensemble of sacred places. It is associated with strong feelings of national identity, and has maintained its spiritual and sacred character both in ritual practice and in the popular imagination for the past 500 years. It remains a place of worship to which pilgrims come from Madagascar and elsewhere.

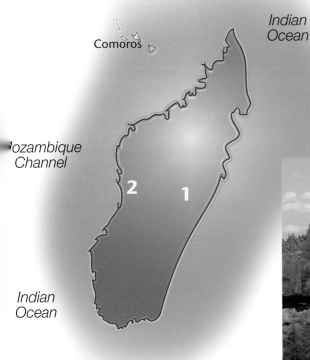

Comoros

Indian Ocean

Mozambique Channel

2 1

Indian Ocean

Madagascar

Tsingy de Bemaraha Strict Nature Reserve (2)

This reserve includes karstic landscapes and limestone uplands cut into impressive "tsingy" peaks and a "forest" of limestone needles, in addition to the spectacular canyon of the Manambolo River, rolling hills and high peaks. The undisturbed forests, lakes and mangrove swamps are the habitat for rare and endangered lemurs and birds.

Indian
Ocean

Comoros

Madagascar

Seychelles

Aldabra Atoll   (1)

The atoll is comprised of four large coral islands which enclose a shallow lagoon. The group of islands is itself surrounded by a coral reef. Due to difficulties of access and the atoll's isolation, Aldabra has been protected from human influence, and thus retains some 152,000 giant tortoises, the world's largest population of this reptile.

Vallée de Mai Nature Reserve   (2)

In the heart of the small island of Praslin, the reserve has the vestiges of a natural palm forest preserved almost in its original state. The famous coco de mer, from a palm tree once believed to grow in the depths of the sea, is the largest seed in the plant kingdom.

Mauritius (1)

In 1834, the British Government selected the island of Mauritius to be the first site for what it called "the great experiment" in the use of "free" labour to replace slaves. Between 1834 and 1920, almost half a million indentured labourers arrived from India at Aapravasi Ghat to work in the sugar plantations of Mauritius, or to be transferred either to Reunion Island, Australia, southern or eastern Africa, or the Caribbean.

" Indentured labour made the immigrant forget his home and his people. He came to Mauritius to settle for life and often re-indentured. He passed a life of great difficulty and he worked hard… and the system of morcellement helped him to acquire land in proprietary tenure In general, Indians have bettered their conditions in Mauritius…"

Kunwar Maharaj,
Officer of the United Province Civil Service
in India, Observing immigration
in Mauritania for the British Government
of India,
1925

Mauritius

Madagascar

Indian Ocean

1

Reunion

Asia

The largest and most populous continent in the world, Asia has a long and rich history marked by powerful empires and cultures. This can be seen as the distinct histories of several peripheral coastal regions: East Asia, South Asia, and the Middle East.

The Qing Dynasty ruled Chinese territories for centuries, leaving behind great marks of its legendary reign. Japan, the Land of the Rising Sun, has inspired the entire world with its stories of shoguns and samurais, and Shinto's monuments. Mongolia was the centre of the Mongol Empire in the 13th century, the largest contiguous land empire ever known. The Middle East, the cradle of humanity, was once Persia, an empire that emerged in the 6th century BC and that controlled lands from present-day Greece to Pakistan. Further east, the Mughal dynasties left an indelible architectural heritage in India. In the continent's south-eastern region, the Khmer Empire, a powerful kingdom from the 7th to the 15th centuries, left us a rich cultural legacy, which hopefully will not be affected by the booming economies of some parts of this area.

Because of its grandiose territory, Asia is also home to an impressive variety of natural world heritage sites, from coral reefs to arid deserts, from lush tropical forests to the highest peaks on earth. Southeast Asian coral reefs have the highest levels of biodiversity in the world's marine ecosystems. Although mainly a desert, the Arabian Peninsula has incredible wildlife, adapted to its rough living conditions. The Philippine archipelago is one of the world's great reservoirs of biodiversity and endemism. The Himalayas, one of the numerous mountain ranges in Asia, boast the planet's highest summit.

Clearly, Asia has an extraordinary variety of natural treasures… treasures that cannot be allowed to vanish from the face of the earth.

Israel

Masada (1)

Masada is the site of ancient palaces and fortifications on top of an isolated rock cliff on the eastern edge of the Judean desert, overlooking the Dead Sea. It is a symbol of the ancient kingdom of Israel, its violent destruction and the last stand of Jewish patriots in the face of the Roman army in AD 73. It was built as a palace complex, in the classic style of the early Roman Empire, by Herod the Great, King of Judaea, who reigned from the years 37 to 4 BC.

"We were the very first that revolted, and we are the last to fight against them (the Romans); and I cannot but esteem it as a favour that God has granted us, that it is still in our power to die bravely, and in a state of freedom."

Elazar ben Yair,
the Zealots' Leader, Masada's Fall

Incense Route - Desert Cities in the Negev   (2)

The four Nabatean towns of Haluza, Mamshit, Avdat and Shivta, along with associated fortresses and agricultural landscapes in the Negev Desert, are spread along routes linking them to the Mediterranean end of the Incense and Spice route. Together they reflect the hugely profitable trade in frankincense and myrrh from southern Arabia to the Mediterranean, which flourished from the 3rd century BC to 2nd century AD.

White City of Tel-Aviv   (3)

Founded in 1909, Tel Aviv was developed as a metropolitan city under the British Mandate in Palestine. The White City was constructed from the early 1930s until the 1950s, based on the urban plan by Sir Patrick Geddes, reflecting modern organic planning principles. The buildings were designed by architects who were trained in Europe, where they practised their profession before immigrating. They created an outstanding architectural ensemble of the Modern Movement in a new cultural context.

"The city hosts a dramatic array of architecture worth seeing for yourself."

Ruth Heiges, Jewish exponent

Biblical Tells – Megiddo, Hazor, Beer Sheba   (4)

Tells, or pre-historic settlement mounds, are characteristic of the flatter lands of the eastern Mediterranean, particularly Lebanon, Syria, Israel and Eastern Turkey. Of the more than 200 Israeli tells, Megiddo, Hazor and Beer Sheba are representative of ones that contain substantial remains of cities with biblical connections.

Jerusalem (5)
(Site proposed by Jordan)

As a holy city for Judaism, Christianity and Islam, Jerusalem has always been of great symbolic importance. Among its 220 historic monuments, the Dome of the Rock stands out: built in the 7th century, it is decorated with beautiful geometric and floral motifs. It is recognized by all three religions as the site of Abraham's sacrifice. The Wailing Wall delimits the quarters of the different religious communities, while the Resurrection rotunda in the Church of the Holy Sepulchre houses Christ's tomb. The old city is threatened with destruction due to urban development plans and deterioration of monuments resulting from lack of maintenance and responsible management.

"Jerusalem is like no other city on earth. In a special sense, Jerusalem belongs to the whole world."

Uri Lupolianski,
Mayor of Jerusalem,
2005

Old City of Acre (6)

Located in Western Galilee, Acre is a historic walled port-city with continuous settlement from the Phoenician period. The present city is characteristic of a fortified town dating from the Ottoman 18th and 19th centuries, with typical urban components such as the citadel, mosques, khans and baths. The remains of the Crusader town, dating from 1104 to 1291, lie almost intact, providing an exceptional picture of the layout and structures of the capital of the medieval Crusader kingdom of Jerusalem.

Lebanon

Mediterranean
Sea

Syrian
Arab
Republic

Israel

Anjar (1)

Formerly known as Gerrha, the city of Anjar was founded by Caliph Walid I at the beginning of the 8th century. The ruins reveal a very regular layout, reminiscent of the palace-cities of ancient times, and are a unique testimony to city planning under the Umayyads.

Byblos (2)

Nestled on the Mediterranean coast about 42 km (26 miles) north of Beirut, Byblos is one of the oldest Phoenician cities. It is attractive to archaeologists because of the successive layers of debris resulting from centuries of human habitation. Inhabited since Neolithic times, it has been closely linked to the legends and history of the Mediterranean region for thousands of years. Byblos is also directly associated with the history and dissemination of the Phoenician alphabet.

"Isis traveled to Byblos, where she used the magic taught to her by Thoth to bring her husband back to life long enough to conceive a child by him."

Legend of the Egyptian goddess Isis

Ouadi Qadisha and the Forest of the Cedars of God (3)

The Qadisha valley is one of the most important early Christian monastic settlements in the world. Its monasteries, many of which are very old, stand in dramatic positions in a rugged landscape. Nearby are the remains of the great forest of cedars of Lebanon, highly prized in antiquity for the construction of great religious buildings.

Baalbek (4)

This Phoenician city, where a triad of deities was worshipped, was known as Heliopolis during the Hellenistic period. It retained its religious function during Roman times, when the sanctuary of the Heliopolitan Jupiter attracted thousands of pilgrims. Baalbek, with its colossal structures, is one of the finest examples of Imperial Roman architecture at its peak.

"Built of stone blocks weighing up to a hundred tons, transported to the site by muscular force alone, the temples of Baalbek have survived majestically to the present day."

Journalist Joanne Farchakh,
Beirut, Lebanon

Tyre (5)

According to legend, Tyre was the birthplace of purple dye, which was known as Tyrian purple. The people of this great Phoenician city ruled the seas and founded prosperous colonies such as Cadiz and Carthage, but Tyre's historical role declined at the end of the Crusades. There are important archaeological remains, mainly from Roman times.

"And they shall destroy the walls of Tyrus, and break down her towers."

Ezekial 26:4, 12, 14,
The Holy Bible

Bahrain

Saudi Arabia

1

Persian Gulf

Qatar

United Arab Emirates

Qal'at al-Bahrain Archaeological Site   (1)

The strata of the 300 x 600-metre (984 x 1,968-foot) tell testify to continuous human presence from about 2300 BC to the 16th century AD. About 25% of the site has been excavated, revealing structures of different types: residential, public, commercial, religious and military. They testify to the importance of the site – a trading port – over the centuries. On the top of the 12-metre-high (39-foot) mound lies the impressive Portuguese fort, which gave the entire site its name, "qal'a", meaning fort.

Syrian Arab
Republic

Turkey

Mediterranean Sea

2

5

1

Lebanon

4　3

Israel

Jordan

Iraq

Site of Palmyra　(1)

An oasis in the Syrian desert, northeast of Damascus, Palmyra contains the monumental ruins of a great city that was one of the most important cultural centres of the ancient world. From the 1st to the 2nd century, the art and architecture of Palmyra, standing at the crossroads of several civilizations, married Greco-Roman techniques with local traditions and Persian influences.

"We are neither Jew nor Christian that we should fear his wrath, but free Palmyreans who bend the knee neither to Roman nor Persian masters."

Zenobia, Warrior Queen of Palmyra and descendant of Cleopatra, AD 270

Ancient City of Aleppo　(2)

Located at the crossroads of several trade routes from the 2nd millennium BC, Aleppo was ruled successively by the Hittites, Assyrians, Arabs, Mongols, Mamelukes and Ottomans. The 13th-century citadel, 12th-century Great Mosque and various 17th-century madrasas, palaces, caravanserais and hammams all form part of the city's cohesive, unique urban fabric, now threatened by overpopulation.

Ancient City of Bosra (3)

An incredible archaeological site, Bosra, once the capital of the Roman province of Arabia, was an important stopover on the ancient caravan route to Mecca. The city contains what is thought to be the best-preserved Roman amphitheatre in the world.

Ancient City of Damascus (4)

Founded in the 3rd millennium BC, Damascus is one of the oldest cities in the Middle East. In the Middle Ages, it was the centre of a flourishing craft industry, specializing in swords and lace. The city has some 125 monuments from different periods of its history – one of the most spectacular is the 8th-century Great Mosque of the Umayyads, built on the site of an Assyrian sanctuary.

"Whose like was never built before, nor will ever be built after."

Omayyad Caliph al-Walid ibn Abdul Malek, in AD 705, about the Great Mosque

Crac des Chevaliers and Qal'at Salah El-Din (5)

The two castles represent the most significant examples illustrating the exchange of influences and documenting the evolution of fortified architecture in the Near East during the time of the Crusades (11th to 13th century). Crac des Chevaliers was built by the Hospitaller Order of Saint John of Jerusalem from 1142 to 1271. Qal'at Salah El-Din (Fortress of Saladin) retains features from its Byzantine beginnings in the 10th century, the Frankish transformations in the late 12th century, and fortifications added by the Ayyubids dynasty (late 12th to mid-13th century).

"Crac des Chevaliers is the most wholly admirable castle in the world."

Lieutenant-Colonel Thomas Edward Lawrence, British liaison officer (1888 – 1935)

Jordan

Petra (1)

Inhabited since prehistoric times, this Nabataean caravan-city, situated between the Red Sea and the Dead Sea, was an important crossroads between Arabia, Egypt and Syria-Phoenicia. Petra is half-built, half-carved into the rock, and is surrounded by mountains riddled with passages and gorges. It is one of the world's most famous archaeological sites, where ancient Eastern traditions blend with Hellenistic architecture.

"Petra was a rose-red city half as old as time."

Famous numismatist
John William Burgon

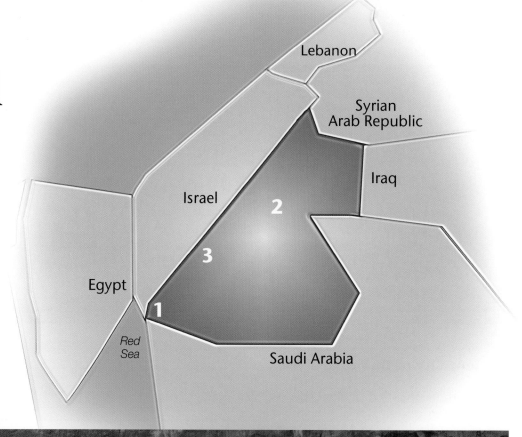

Quseir Amra (2)

Built in the early 8th century, this exceptionally well-preserved desert castle was both a fortress with a garrison and a residence of the Umayyad caliphs. The most outstanding features of this small pleasure palace are the reception hall and the hammam, both richly decorated with figurative murals that reflect the secular art of the time. The castle is one of the most important examples of early Islamic art and architecture.

"The bathhouse complex itself has such an intimate character that the frescoes also vividly reflect for us, 1,200 years later, the lifestyle of an eighth-century Arab prince."

Islamic art and architecture expert
Patricia Baker

Um er-Rasas (Kastrom Mefa'a) (3)

Most of the Um er-Rasas archaeological site has not been excavated. Containing remains from the Roman, Byzantine and Early Moslem periods (end of 3rd to 9th century AD), the site started as a Roman military camp and grew to become a town as of the 5th century. Um er-Rasas is surrounded by, and dotted with, remains of ancient agricultural cultivation.

Oman

Saudi
Arabia

*Gulf
of Oman*

1 **2** **4**

3

5

Yemen

*Arabian
Sea*

Gulf of Aden

Archaeological Sites of Bat, Al-Khutm and Al-Ayn   (1)

The protohistoric site of Bat lies near a palm grove in the interior of the Sultanate of Oman. Together with the neighbouring sites, it forms the world's most complete collection of settlements and necropolises from the 3rd millennium BC.

The Falaj System   (2)

The term "falaj" is used to describe any type of canal, either on the ground or subterranean. Underground falaj networks are of paramount importance in the agricultural settlements of Oman, and can certainly be considered masterpieces of technical work. Several of them are still active all around the country.

Arabian Oryx Sanctuary   (3)

This sanctuary is an area within the Central Desert and Coastal Hills biogeographical regions of Oman. Seasonal fogs and dews support a unique desert ecosystem whose diverse flora includes several endemic plants. Its rare fauna features the first free-ranging herd of Arabian oryx since the global extinction of the species in the wild in 1972 and its reintroduction here in 1982.

"In October 1972, a motorized hunting party from outside Oman killed or removed this last herd of oryx. The oryx no longer occurred in the wild."

The Arabian Oryx Project

Bahla Fort   (4)

The oasis of Bahla owes its prosperity to the Banu Nebhan, the dominant tribe in the area from the 12th to the end of the 15th century. The ruins of the immense fort, with its walls and towers of unbaked brick and its stone foundations, is a remarkable example of this type of fortification and attests to the power of the Banu Nebhan.

The Frankincense Trail   (5)

The frankincense trees of Wadi Dawkah and the remains of the caravan oasis of Shisr/Wubar and the affiliated ports of Khor Rori and Al-Balid vividly illustrate the trade in frankincense that flourished in this region for many centuries, as one of the most important trading activities of the ancient and medieval world.

"The three wise men who traveled to Bethlehem to worship the Christ Child brought gold, frankincense and myrrh as gifts."

Christian belief

373

Yemen

Old City of Sana'a   (2)

In a mountain valley at an altitude of 2,200 m (7,217 feet), Sana'a has been inhabited for more than 2,500 years. In the 7th and 8th centuries, the city became a major centre for the propagation of Islam. This religious and political heritage can be seen in its 103 mosques, 14 hammams and over 6,000 houses, all built before the 11th century.

"Sanaá must be seen."

*Imam Mu_ammad ibn Idris al-Shafi'i
(768-820)*

Historic Town of Zabid   (1)

Capital of Yemen from the 13th to the 15th century, Zabid played an important role in the Arab and Muslim world for many centuries because of its Islamic university. The city's domestic and military architecture, along with its urban plan, make it an out-standing archaeological and historical site.

Old Walled City of Shibam   (3)

Surrounded by a fortified wall, the 16th-century city of Shibam is one of the oldest and best examples of urban planning based on the principle of vertical construction. Houses of Shibam are all made out of mud bricks, but still there are about 500 tower houses, rising 5 to 9 storeys high. The city's impressive, tower-like structures rise out of the cliff and have earned it the nickname "the Manhattan of the desert".

"Their shape may call to mind the modern skyscraper but they are in fact five-hundred years old and only one family lives in each one of them."

Professor Pietro Laureano, architect

Ashur (1)

The ancient city of Ashur is located on the Tigris River in northern Mesopotamia in a specific geo-ecological zone, at the borderline between rain-fed and irrigation agriculture. The city dates back to the 3rd millennium BC. From the 14th to the 9th centuries BC, it was the first capital of the Assyrian Empire, a city-state and trading platform of international importance. It also served as the religious capital of the Assyrians, associated with the god Ashur. The site was inscribed on the List of World Heritage in Danger simultaneously with its inscription on the World Heritage List. When the property was nominated before the conflict, a large dam project threatened the site, which would have been partially flooded by a reservoir.

"Losing it would be like, I guess you could say, losing the Vatican."

Mark Altaweel,
Baghdad-born doctoral student at
the University of Chicago, 2003

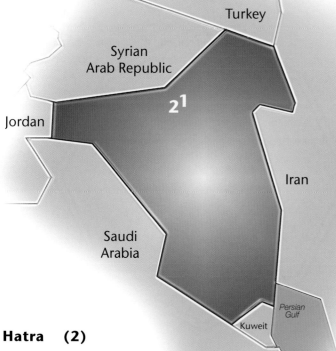

Turkey

Syrian
Arab Republic

Jordan

2¹

Iran

Saudi
Arabia

Persian
Gulf

Kuweit

Iraq

Hatra (2)

A large fortified city under the influence of the Parthian Empire and capital of the first Arab Kingdom, Hatra withstood invasions by the Romans in AD 116 and 198. The remains of the city, especially the temples where Hellenistic and Roman architecture blend with Eastern decorative features, attest to the greatness of its civilization. Hatra is also one of the 10 Legendary Lost Cities of Tayyab.

"It was the brute effectiveness of Hatra's defensive biological and chemical weapons that overcame Roman morale, manpower and siege machines."

Classical folklorist Adrienne Mayor
about Scorpion Bombs, clay pots filled
with scorpions, used to defend Hatra

Iran

Turkey

Armenia | Azerbaijan

Caspian
Sea

8 7

Turkmenistan

4

Iraq

1 **2**

Kuweit

3⁶

Afghanistan

5

Barhaim

Persian
Gulf

Qatar

Pakistan

United Arab
Emirates

Gulf
of Oman

Tchogha Zanbil   (1)

The ruins of the holy city of the Kingdom of Elam, surrounded by three huge concentric walls, are found at Tchogha Zanbil. Established c. 1250 BC, the city remained unfinished after it was invaded by Ashurbanipal, as shown by the thousands of unused bricks left at the site.

Meidan Emam, Esfahan (2)

Located about 340 km (211 miles) south of Tehran, Esfahan contains a wide variety of Islamic architectural sites ranging from the 11th to the 19th century. Built by Shah Abbas I the Great at the beginning of the 17th century, and bordered on all sides by monumental buildings linked by a series of two-storey arcades, the site is known for the Royal Mosque, the Mosque of Sheykh Lotfollah, the magnificent Portico of Qaysariyyeh, and the 15th-century Timurid palace.

"Who can claim to have seen the most beautiful city of the world without having seen Esfahan?"

French author Andre Malraux (1901 - 1976)

Persepolis (3)

Founded by Darius I in 518 BC, Persepolis was the capital of the Achaemenid Empire. Situated some 70 km (44 miles) northeast of Shiraz, it was built on an immense half-artificial, half-natural terrace, where the king of kings created an impressive palace complex inspired by Mesopotamian models.

"Is it not passing brave to be a King and ride in triumph through Persepolis?"

English dramatist and poet Christopher Marlowe (1564 – 1593)

Bistun Bas-Relief and Inscription (4)

The bas-relief and inscription date back to the beginning of the reign of the Achaemenian King of Kings Darius I (523 -483 BC). It represents, in alphabetical order, Darius I and several pretenders to the throne. The inscription is written in cuneiform script, in Old Persian, Elamite and Babylonian. These relics bear indications to an important historical event, namely the subjugation of the Magian Gaumat and other pretenders to the throne.

"The Oil Ministry constructed the factory without asking the Cultural Heritage and Tourism Organization for permission, so the factory is in violation of the regulations of the organization."

Mohammad-Hassan Mohebali, Iranian Cultural Heritage and Tourism Organization official, explaining, in July 2005, why a new oil factory could jeopardize the chances of the site being listed by UNESCO

Bam and its Cultural Landscape (5)

The origins of Bam can be traced back to the Achaemenid period (6th-4th century BC). Its heyday was from the 7th to 11th century, being at the crossroads of important trade routes and known for the production of silk and cotton garments. The existence of life in the oasis was based on the underground irrigation canals, the qan_ts, of which Bam has preserved some of the earliest evidence in Iran. Most of the city was devastated by an earthquake in December 2003. Since then, Bam has been inscribed on the List of World Heritage in Danger.

Pasargadae (6)

Built by Cyrus II of Persia (Cyrus the Great), Pasargadae was the first dynastic capital of the Achaemenid Empire, homeland of the Persians, in the 6th century BC. Its palaces, gardens, and the mausoleum of Cyrus are outstanding examples of the first phase of royal Achaemenid art and architecture and exceptional testimonies of Persian civilization.

"Passer-by, I am Cyrus the Great, I have given the Persians an empire and I have ruled over Asia, so do not envy me for this tomb."

Inscription on Cyrus the Great's tomb

Soltaniyeh   (7)

The mausoleum of Oljaytu was constructed from 1302 to 1312 in the city of Soltaniyeh, the capital of the Ilkhanid dynasty, which was founded by the Mongols. Situated in the province of Zanjan, Soltaniyeh is one of the outstanding examples of the achievements of Persian architecture and a key monument in the development of Islamic architecture. The octagonal building is crowned with a 50-m-tall (164-foot) dome covered in turquoise blue faience and surrounded by eight slender minarets.

"The supreme Iranian art, in the proper meaning of the word, has always been its architecture. The supremacy of architecture applies to both pre- and post-Islamic periods."

Professor Arthur Upham Pope (1881-1969), archaeologist and historian of Persian art

Takht-e Soleyman   (8)

The archaeological site of Takht-e Soleyman, in north-western Iran, is situated in a valley set in a volcanic mountain region. The site includes the principal Zoroastrian sanctuary, partly rebuilt in the Ilkhanid (Mongol) period (13th century), as well as a temple of the Sasanian period (6th and 7th centuries) dedicated to Anahita. This site has strongly influenced the development of Islamic architecture. The name "Takht e Soleiman" means The Throne of Solomon in Persian.

Pakistan

Buddhist Ruins of Takht-i-Bahi (1)

The Buddhist monastic complex of Takht-i-Bahi (Throne of Origins) was founded in the early 1st century. Owing to its location on the crest of a high hill, it escaped successive invasions and is still exceptionally well preserved. Nearby are the ruins of Sahr-i-Bahlol, a small fortified city dating from the same period.

"It stands 500 feet above the plain and is approached by a steep and winding path, but the visitor is repaid for his climb by the architectural diversity of the ruins and by their romantic mountain setting."

Sir Mortimer Wheeler,
archaeological adviser to the Government
of Pakistan, in 1949

Fort and Shalamar Gardens in Lahore   (2)

These are two masterpieces from the time of the brilliant Mughal civilization, which reached its peak during the reign of the Emperor Shah Jahan. The fort contains marble palaces and mosques decorated with mosaics and gilt. The elegance of the splendid gardens, built near the city of Lahore on three terraces with lodges, waterfalls and large ornamental ponds, is unequalled. Tanks built 375 years ago to supply water to the Garden's fountains were destroyed in June 1999 to widen the road. As a result, the site has been inscribed in 2000 on the List of World Heritage in Danger.

Archaeological Ruins at Moenjodaro   (3)

The ruins of the huge city of Moenjodaro – built entirely of unbaked brick in the 3rd millennium BC – lie in the Indus valley. The city is a remarkable construction, considering its antiquity. It has a planned layout based on a grid of streets, with structures constructed of bricks of baked mud, sun dried bricks and burned wood. It had an advanced drainage system, a variety of buildings up to two storeys high, and an elaborate bath area.

"A highly advanced urban civilization of Mohenjo Daro has been discovered on the Indus, 'between Attock and Sind', exactly the location mentioned in The Secret Doctrine as the abode of the Aethiopians."

American author and Theosophist Gottfried von Purucker (1874 - 1942), after the discovery of the Indus Valley civilisation in 1920

Taxila (4)

From the ancient Neolithic tumulus of Saraikala to the ramparts of Sirkap (2nd century BC) and the city of Sirsukh (1st century AD), Taxila illustrates the different stages in the development of a city on the Indus that was alternately influenced by Persia, Greece and Central Asia and which, from the 5th century BC to the 2nd century AD, was an important Buddhist centre of learning.

Rohtas Fort (5)

Following his defeat of the Mughal emperor Humayun in 1541, Sher Shah Suri built a strong fortified complex at Rohtas, a strategic site in the north of what is now Pakistan. The fort was never taken by storm and has survived intact to the present day. The main fortifications consist of the massive walls, which extend for more than 4 km, lined with bastions and pierced by monumental gateways.

Historical Monuments of Thatta (6)

The capital of three successive dynasties, later ruled by the Mughal emperors of Delhi, Thatta was constantly embellished from the 14th to the 18th century. The remains of the city and its necropolis provide a unique view of civilization in Sind.

Afghanistan

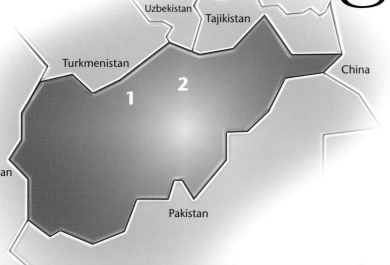

Minaret and Archaeological Remains of Jam   (1)

Located in western Afghanistan, by the Hari Rud River, the 65-m-tall Minaret of Jam is a graceful, soaring structure, dating back to the 12th century. Covered in elaborate brickwork with a blue tile inscription at the top, it is noteworthy for the quality of its architecture and decoration, which represent the culmination of an architectural and artistic tradition in this region. The minaret of Jam is currently threatened by erosion, water infiltration and floods, which is why it is inscribed on the List of World Heritage in Danger.

"The sight of this giant decorated tower is just magical."

French archaeologist André Maricq, who rediscovered the site in 1957 after it had been forgotten for centuries

Cultural Landscape and Archaeological Remains of the Bamiyan Valley   (2)

In the centre of Afghanistan, the Bamiyan Valley represents the artistic and religious developments which, from the 1st to the 13th centuries, characterized ancient Bakhtria. The area contains numerous Buddhist monastic ensembles and sanctuaries, as well as fortified edifices from the Islamic period. The site was also the scene of the tragic destruction by the Taliban of the two standing Buddha statues, an event which shook the world in March 2001. The property is in a fragile state of conservation considering that it has suffered from abandonment, military action and dynamite explosions. The site is inscribed on the List of World Heritage in Danger.

"Based on the verdict of the clergymen and the decision of the supreme court of the Islamic Emirate (Taliban), all the statues around Afghanistan must be destroyed."

Afghanistan's Taliban Militia Supreme Leader Mulla Mohammad Omar, February 26, 2001

383

Uzbekistan

Kazakhstan

Aral Sea

Kazakhstan

Turkmenistan

2

1

4 **3**

Kyrzyzstan

Tajikistan

Afghanistan

Historic Centre of Bukhara (1)

Situated on the Silk Route, Bukhara is more than 2,000 years old. It is the most complete example of a medieval city in Central Asia, with an urban fabric that has remained largely intact. Monuments of particular interest include the famous tomb of Ismail Samani, a masterpiece of 10th-century Muslim architecture, and a large number of 17th-century madrasas.

"My heart is with Bukhara and the idols of Taraz."

Persian poet Abu Abdullo Rudaki,
founder of Persian-Tajik literature
(860 – 941)

Itchan Kala   (2)

Itchan Kala is the inner town (protected by brick walls some 10 metres high) of the old Khiva oasis, which was the last resting place of caravans before crossing the desert to Iran. Although few very old monuments still remain, it is a coherent and well-preserved example of the Muslim architecture of Central Asia. The old town retains more than 50 historic monuments and 250 old houses, dating primarily from the 18th and 19th centuries.

Samarkand
- Crossroads of Cultures   (3)

The historic town of Samarkand is a crossroads and melting pot of world cultures. Founded in the 7th century BC as ancient Afrasiab, Samarkand had its most significant development in the Timurid period from the 14th to the 15th century. The major monuments include the Registan Mosque and madrasas, Bibi-Khanum Mosque, the Shakhi-Zinda compound and the Gur-Emir ensemble, as well as Ulugh-Beg's Observatory.

Historic Centre of Shakhrisyabz (4)

Birthplace of the famous conqueror Timur the Lame, Shakhrisyabz contains a collection of exceptional monuments and ancient quarters which bear witness to the city's secular development, and particularly to the period of its apogee, under the rule of the Timurids Empire, in the 15th-16th century.

Timur's skeleton was exhumed on the night of June 19-20, 1941 by a team of Soviet scientists. There was a local tradition at the time that said that "the War God's sleep must not be disturbed." If it was, then Tamerlane would return from the dead bringing war. Three days after the sarcophagus was opened, on June 22, Hitler launched Operation Barbarossa against the USSR

Kazakhstan

Mausoleum of Khoja Ahmed Yasawi   (1)

This mausoleum was built in southern Kazakhstan at the time of Timur (Tamerlane), from 1389 to 1405. In this partly unfinished building, Persian master builders experimented with architectural and structural solutions later used in the construction of Samarkand, the capital of the Timurid Empire. Today, it is one of the largest and best-preserved constructions of the Timurid period.

Petroglyphs within the Archaeological Landscape of Tamgaly   (2)

Set around the comparatively lush Tamgaly Gorge, amidst the vast, arid Chu-Ili Mountains, is a remarkable concentration of some 5,000 petroglyphs (rock carvings) dating from the second half of the second millennium BC to the beginning of the 20th century. Distributed among 48 complexes with associated settlements and burial grounds, they bear witness to the husbandry, social organization and rituals of pastoral peoples.

State Historical and Cultural Park - site of Ancient Merv (1)

Situated on the southern edge of the Kara-kum desert, Merv is the oldest and best-preserved of the oasis-cities along the Silk Route in Central Asia. The remains in this vast oasis span 4,000 years of human history. A number of monuments are still visible, particularly from the last two millennia.

"Nowhere else in all Central Asia are ruins so abundant or so vast."

American geologist Raphael Pumpelly,
1904 expedition to Merv

Turkmenistan

Kazakhstan

Aral Sea

Caspian Sea

2

Uzbekistan

Iran

1

Afghanistan

Kunya-Urgench (2)

Formerly situated on the Amu-Darya River, Old Urgench was one of the greatest cities on the Silk Route. The town contains a series of monuments mainly from the 11th to 16th centuries, including a mosque, the gates of a caravanserai, fortresses and mausoleums. The most striking landmark of Old Urgench is the early 11th-century Kutlug-Timur Minaret, which used to be the tallest brick minaret prior to the construction of the Minaret of Jam in Afghanistan.

India

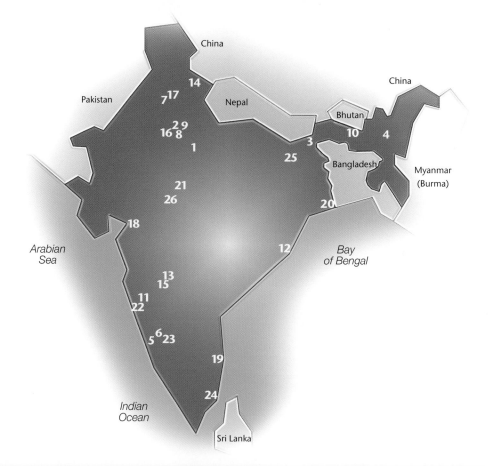

Khajuraho Group of Monuments (1)

About 620 kilometres (385 miles) southeast of Delhi, the temples at Khajuraho were built during the Chandella dynasty, which reached its peak between 950 and 1050. Only about 20 temples remain. They fall into three distinct groups and belong to two different religions – Hinduism and Jainism – striking a perfect balance between architecture and sculpture.

Taj Mahal   (2)

This immense mausoleum of white marble was built in Agra between 1631 and 1648 by order of the Mughal emperor Shah Jahan, in memory of his favourite wife, Arjumand Banu Begum. The Taj Mahal is the jewel of Muslim art in India and one of the universally admired masterpieces of world heritage.

"A tear on the face of eternity."

Bengali poet Rabindranath Tagore,
describing the Taj Mahal

Darjeeling Himalayan Railway   (3)

Ticknamed "Toy Train", this site is the first and still the most outstanding example of a hill passenger railway. Opened in 1881, it applied bold, ingenious engineering solutions to the problem of establishing an effective rail link across a mountainous terrain of great beauty. It is still fully operational and retains most of its original features.

"The most enjoyable day I've spent
on earthis a mixed ecstasy of deadly fright
and unimaginable joy."

Mark Twain,
after his ride on the "Toy Train",
1895

Kaziranga National Park (4)

In the heart of Assam, this park is one of the last areas in eastern India undisturbed by human presence. It is inhabited by the world's largest population of one-horned rhinoceroses, as well as many mammals, including tigers, elephants, panthers and bears, and thousands of birds. Kaziranga was declared a reserve forest in 1908 by the British. In 1950, the area was declared a wildlife sanctuary and in 1954, the rhinoceros was given legal protection.

"The only way to save a rhinoceros is to save the environment in which it lives, because there's a mutual dependency between it and millions of other species of both animals and plants."

Anthropologist and BBC presenter
Sir David Attenborough

Churches and Convents of Goa (5)

Located in south-western India, Goa was under Portuguese rule from 1510 and became the capital of Portuguese India until its incorporation in the Republic of India, in 1961. Its churches and convents, particularly the Church of Bom Jesus, which contains the tomb of St. Francis-Xavier, illustrate the evangelization of Asia. These monuments were influential in spreading forms of Manueline, Mannerist and Baroque art in all the Asian countries where missions were established.

Group of Monuments at Pattadakal (6)

This site represents the high point of an eclectic art which, in the 7th and 8th centuries under the Chalukya dynasty, achieved a harmonious blend of architectural forms from northern and southern India. An impressive series of nine Hindu temples, as well as a Jain sanctuary, can be seen there. One masterpiece from the group stands out – the Temple of Virupaksha, built c. 740 by Queen Lokamahadevi to commemorate her husband's victory over the kings from the south.

Qutb Minar and its Monuments, Delhi (7)

Built in the early 13th century a few kilometres south of Delhi, the red sandstone tower of Qutb Minar is 72.5 m (238 feet) high, tapering from 2.75 m (9 feet) in diameter at its peak to 14.32 m (xx feet) at its base, and alternating angular and rounded flutings. The surrounding archaeological area contains funerary buildings, notably the magnificent Alai-Darwaza Gate, a masterpiece of Indo-Muslim art built in 1311, and two mosques.

Fatehpur Sikri (8)

Built on a rocky outcrop near the city of Agra during the second half of the 16th century by the Emperor Akbar, Fatehpur Sikri (the City of Victory) was the capital of the Mughal Empire for only about 10 years. The complex of monuments and temples, all in a uniform architectural style, includes one of the largest mosques in India, the Jama Masjid.

"My revered father, regarding the village of Sikri, my birthplace, as fortunate to himself, made it his capital, and in the course of fourteen or fifteen years the hills and deserts, which abounded in beasts of prey, became converted into a magnificent city."

Emperor Jahangir,
about his father Akbar, who built the city

Agra Fort   (9)

In Agra, near the gardens of the Taj Mahal, stands the important 16th-century Mughal monument known as the Red Fort of Agra. This powerful fortress of red sandstone encompasses, within its 2.5-km -long (1.6-mile) enclosure walls, the imperial city of the Mughal rulers. It comprises many fairytale palaces, such as the Jahangir Palace and the Khas Mahal, built by Shah Jahan; audience halls, such as the Diwan-i-Khas; and two very beautiful mosques.

"In that charmless Hind, plots of garden were laid out with order and symmetry, with suitable borders and parterres in every corner, and in every border, rose and narcissus in perfect arrangement."

Emperor Barbur,
about the gardens and grounds around Agra

Manas Wildlife Sanctuary   (10)

On a gentle slope in the foothills of the Himalayas, where wooded hills give way to alluvial grasslands and tropical forests, the Manas sanctuary is home to a great variety of wildlife, including many endangered species such as the tiger, pygmy hog, red panda, Indian rhinoceros and Indian elephant. In April 1973, the sanctuary was established as the core of the Manas Tiger Reserve. UNESCO decided to include this site on the List of World Heritage in Danger in 1992, when it was invaded by militants of the Bodo tribe in Assam.

"India, being home to about 60% of the world's wild tiger population, is now the best hope for tiger survival."

The Sierra Club

Elephanta Caves (11)

The "City of Caves", located on Elephanta Island in the Sea of Oman, close to Bombay, contains a collection of rock art linked to the cult of Shiva. Here, Indian art has found one of its most perfect expressions, particularly the huge high reliefs in the main cave. These caves are thought to date back to the Silhara kings of the 9th through 12th centuries (810-1260).

"On the walls, all around, there are sculptured images of elephants, lions, tigers and many human images, some like Amazons, and in many other shapes well sculptured ..."

16th century Portuguese doctor and naturalist Garcia da Orta

Sun Temple, Konarak (12)

On the shores of the Bay of Bengal, bathed in the rays of the rising sun, the temple at Konarak is a monumental representation of the sun god Surya's chariot. Its 24 wheels are decorated with symbolic designs and the chariot is led by a team of six horses. Built in the 13th century, it is one of India's most famous Brahman sanctuaries.

"Even those who are difficult to please stand astonished at its sight."

Abdul Fazl, poet of the Mughal Dynasty, about the Sun Temple

Ajanta Caves (13)

The first Buddhist cave monuments at Ajanta date from the 2nd and 1st centuries BC. During the Gupta period (5th and 6th centuries AD), many more richly decorated caves were added to the original group. The paintings and sculptures of Ajanta, considered masterpieces of Buddhist religious art, have had considerable artistic influence.

Nanda Devi National Park (14)

Nanda Devi is one of the most spectacular wilderness areas in the Himalayas. It is dominated by the peak of Nanda Devi, which rises to over 7,800 m (25,590 feet). No humans live in the park, which has remained more or less intact due to its inaccessibility. It is the habitat of several endangered mammals, especially the snow leopard, Himalayan musk deer, and bharal.

"Today, on October 14, 2001, in front of our revered Nanda Devi, and drawing inspiration from Chipko's radiant history, we dedicate ourselves to the transformation of our region into a global centre for peace, prosperity and biodiversity conservation."

Extract of the Nanda Devi Biodiversity Conservation and Eco-tourism Declaration

Ellora Caves (15)

These 34 monasteries and temples, extending over more than 2 km (1.2 mile), were dug side by side in the wall of a high basalt cliff, not far from Aurangabad, in Maharashtra. Ellora, with its uninterrupted sequence of monuments dating from AD 600 to 1000, brings the civilization of ancient India to life.

Keoladeo National Park (16)

This former duck-hunting reserve of the Maharajas is one of the major wintering areas for large numbers of aquatic birds from Afghanistan, Turkmenistan, China and Siberia. It is a famous avifauna sanctuary that sees thousands of rare and highly endangered birds nest here during the winter season. Some 364 species of birds, including the rare Siberian crane, have been recorded in the park.

"With so many demands on water, maintenance of inflow during drought is often a major problem, even at Keoladeo National Park, one of the most actively protected wetlands in Asia.

BirdLife International

Humayun's Tomb, Delhi (17)

This tomb, built in 1570, is of particular cultural significance as it was the first garden-tomb on the Indian subcontinent. It inspired several major architectural innovations, culminating in the construction of the Taj Mahal. The tomb of Humayun was built by Haji Begham, Humayun's widow from around 1565.

"... it's got a power and strength behind it because it's playing with new ideas for the first time. It's innovative."

*Art historian
Shobita Punja,
about Humayun's Tomb*

Champaner - Pavagadh Archaeological Park   (18)

The park is a concentration of largely unexcavated archaeological, historic and living cultural heritage properties, cradled in an impressive landscape that includes prehistoric (chalcolithic) sites, the hill fortress of an early Hindu capital, and remains of the 16th century capital of the state of Gujarat. It also features other vestiges such as fortifications, palaces, religious buildings, residential precincts, agricultural structures and water installations from the 8th to the 14th century. The site is the only complete and unchanged Islamic pre-Mughal city.

Group of Monuments at Mahabalipuram   (19)

This group of sanctuaries, founded by the Pallava kings, was carved out of rock along the Coromandel coast in the 7th and 8th centuries. It is known especially for its rathas (temples in the form of chariots), mandapas (cave sanctuaries), giant open-air reliefs, and the temple of Rivage, with thousands of sculptures to the glory of Shiva.

Sundarbans National Park   (20)
(Site shared with Bangladesh)

Sundarbans covers 10,000 sq. km (2.5 million acres) of land and water (more than half of it in India, the rest in Bangladesh) in the Ganges delta. It contains the world's largest area of mangrove forests. A number of rare or endangered species live in the park, including tigers, aquatic mammals, birds and reptiles.

396

Buddhist Monuments at Sanchi (21)

On a hill overlooking the plain and about 40 km (25 miles) from Bhopal, the site of Sanchi comprises a group of Buddhist monuments (monolithic pillars, palaces, temples and monasteries), all in different states of conservation, most of which date back to the 2nd and 1st centuries BC. It is the oldest Buddhist sanctuary in existence and was a major Buddhist centre in India until the 12th century AD.

"Mangroves help protect coastlines from erosion, storm damage, and wave action. The stability mangroves provide is of immense importance."

Alfredo Quarto, director of the Mangrove Action Project

Chhatrapati Shivaji Terminus - formerly Victoria Terminus (22)

Finished in 1888, the Chhatrapati Shivaji Terminus, formerly known as Victoria Terminus in Mumbai, is an outstanding example of Victorian Gothic Revival architecture in India, blended with themes deriving from Indian traditional architecture. The building, designed by British architect F.W. Stevens, became the symbol of Bombay as the "Gothic City" and the major international mercantile port of India.

Group of Monuments at Hampi (23)

The austere, grandiose site of Hampi was the last capital of the last great Hindu Kingdom of Vijayanagar. Its fabulously rich princes built Dravidian temples and palaces which won the admiration of travellers between the 14th and 16th centuries. Conquered by the Deccan Muslim confederacy in 1565, the city was pillaged over a period of six months before being abandoned. The construction of two suspension bridges threatens the World Heritage site's integrity. As a result, it was inscribed on the List of World Heritage in Danger in 1999.

"If dreams were made out of stone, it would be Hampi."

Famous saying

Great Living Chola Temples (24)

The Great Living Chola Temples were built in the state of Tamil Nadu by kings of the Chola Empire. The site now includes the three great 11th- and 12th-century Chola Temples: the Brihadisvara Temple of Thanjavur, the Temple of Gangaikondacholisvaram, and the Airavatesvara Temple at Darasuram. The temples testify to the Cholas' brilliant achievements in architecture, sculpture, painting, and bronze casting.

Mahabodhi Temple Complex at Bodh Gaya (25)

The Mahabodhi Temple Complex is one of the four holy sites related to the life of the Lord Buddha, and particularly to the attainment of Enlightenment. The first temple was built by Emperor Asoka in the 3rd century BC, and the present temple dates from the 5th or 6th centuries. It is one of the earliest Buddhist temples built entirely in brick still standing in India from the late Gupta period.

"We are shaped by our thoughts; we become what we think. When the mind is pure, joy follows like a shadow that never leaves."

Buddha,
Indian philosopher & religious leader
(563 - 483 BC)

Rock Shelters of Bhimbetka (26)

Located in the foothills of the Vindhyan Mountains on the southern edge of the central Indian plateau, the Rock Shelters of Bhimbetka are the earliest known traces of human life in India. Within massive sandstone outcrops, above comparatively dense forest, are five clusters of natural rock shelters, displaying paintings that appear to date from the Mesolithic Period right through to the historical period.

Sri Lanka

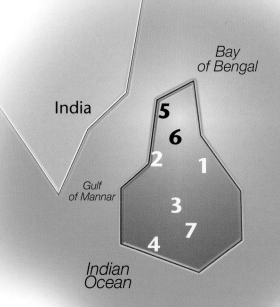

India

Bay of Bengal

Gulf of Mannar

Indian Ocean

5
6
2   1
3
7
4

Ancient City of Polonnaruwa (1)

The second most ancient of Sri Lanka's kingdoms, Polonnaruwa was first declared the capital city by King Vijayabahu I, who defeated the Chola invaders. It comprises the Brahmanic monuments built by the Cholas, as well as the monumental ruins of the fabulous garden-city created by Parakramabahu I in the 12th century. Polonnaruwa remains one of the best-planned archaeological relic sites in the country, standing testimony to the discipline and greatness of the Kingdom's first rulers.

Golden Temple of Dambulla (2)

A sacred pilgrimage site for 22 centuries, this cave monastery, with its five sanctuaries, is the largest and best-preserved cave-temple complex in Sri Lanka. The Buddhist mural paintings are of particular importance, as are the 157 statues.

Sacred City of Kandy (3)

Located in the centre of Sri Lanka, this sacred Buddhist site was the last capital of the Sinhala kings, whose patronage enabled the Dinahala culture to flourish for more than 2,500 years until the occupation of Sri Lanka by the British in 1815. It is also the site of the Temple of the Tooth Relic (the sacred tooth of the Buddha), which is a famous pilgrimage site.

In the Sinhala language, Kandy is referred as "mahanuwara", meaning the "great city".

Old Town of Galle and its Fortifications (4)

Founded in the 16th century by the Portuguese, the ancient port city of Galle reached the height of its development in the 18th century, before the arrival of the British. It is the best example of a fortified city built by Europeans in South and South-East Asia, showing the interaction between European architectural styles and South Asian traditions.

"The mountainous isle of Sri Lanka lies in the south of the ocean, and its Buddhist temples are sanctuaries of your gospel, where your miraculous-responsive power imbues and enlightens."

Extract of the great Chinese Admiral Zheng's Galle trilingual inscription, left in 1411

Sacred City of Anuradhapura (5)

Capital of the country continuously from the 5th century BC to AD 1017, this sacred city was established around a cutting from the "tree of enlightenment", the Buddha's fig tree, brought there in the 3rd century BC by Sanghamitta, the founder of an order of Buddhist nuns. Anuradhapura, a Ceylonese political and religious capital that flourished for 1,300 years, was abandoned after an invasion in 993. Hidden away in dense jungle for many years, the splendid site, with its palaces, monasteries and monuments, is now accessible once again.

"In Anuradhapura are many Buddhist laymen, elders and merchants of all trades, whose houses are stately and beautiful. The roads and byways are kept clean and in order."

Fa-Shien,
Chinese monk who visited
Lanka in AD 412

Ancient City of Sigiriya (6)

The ruins of the capital, built by the parricidal King Kassapa I (477–95), lie on the steep slopes and at the summit of a granite peak standing some 370 metres high (1,214 feet). This is the "Lion's Rock", which dominates the jungle from all sides. A series of galleries and staircases emerging from the mouth of a gigantic lion constructed of bricks and plaster provides access to the site.

"Oh Sigiri, my sanctuary in the sky."

Dying words of King Kasyapa,
AD 495

Sinharaja Forest Reserve (7)

The hilly virgin rainforest was saved from the worst of commercial logging by its inaccessibility, and was designated a World Biosphere Reserve in 1978. The reserve's name translates as Lion King. More than 60% of the trees are endemic and many of them are considered rare. There is also much endemic wildlife, especially birds.

"The forest and the people of Sinharaja derive their names from the word 'Sinha' (lion), and the race is the result of the union between a King's daughter and a mighty lion who lived in the forest."

Sri Lankan legend

Nepal

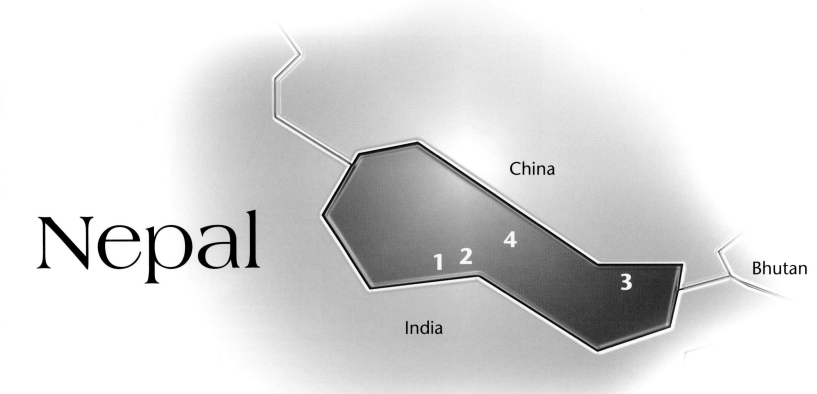

China

India

Bhutan

1 2 4

3

Lumbini, the Birthplace of the Lord Buddha (1)

Siddhartha Gautama, the Lord Buddha, was born in 623 BC in the famous gardens of Lumbini, which soon became a place of pilgrimage. Among the pilgrims was the Indian emperor Ashoka, who erected one of his commemorative pillars there. The site is now being developed as a Buddhist pilgrimage centre, where the archaeological remains associated with the birth of the Lord Buddha form a central feature.

"Oh, Maharaj!
Here the Blessed One was born."

Emperor Ashoka the Great
(294 – 232 BC)

Royal Chitwan National Park (2)

Established in 1973, Royal Chitwan is the oldest national park of Nepal. At the foot of the Himalayas, the park is one of the few remaining undisturbed vestiges of the Terai region, which formerly extended over the foothills of India and Nepal. It has a particularly rich flora and fauna. Indeed, one of the last populations of single-horned Asiatic rhinoceros lives in the park, which is also one of the last refuges of the Bengal tiger.

Sagarmatha National Park (3)

Dominated by Mount Everest, the highest peak in the world at 8,848 metres (29,028 feet), Sagarmatha is an exceptional area with dramatic mountains, glaciers and deep valleys. Several rare species, such as the snow leopard and the lesser panda, are found in the park. The presence of the Sherpas, with their unique culture, adds further interest to this site. Sagarmatha means "goddess of the sky" and is the Nepalese name for Mount Everest.

"For in my heart, I needed to go . . .
the pull of Everest was stronger for me
than any force on earth."

Nepalese Sherpa Tenzing Norgay,
first man to reach the Everest summit,
with New Zealander Sir Edmund Hillary,
May 1953

Kathmandu Valley (4)

At the crossroads of the great civilizations of Asia, seven groups of Hindu and Buddhist monuments, as well as the three residential and palace areas of the royal cities of Kathmandu, Patan and Bhaktapur, illustrate Nepalese art at its peak. Among the 130 monuments are pilgrimage centres, temples, shrines, bathing sites and gardens. Unfortunately, the exceptional architectural design of Kathmandu, Patan and Bhaktapur is gradually disappearing due to uncontrolled urban development, leading it to be inscribed on the List of World Heritage in Danger in 2003.

Bangladesh

**Ruins of the Buddhist Vihara
at Paharpur   (1)**

A testament to the rise of Mahayana Buddhism in Bengal from the 7th century onwards, Somapura Mahavira, or the Great Monastery, was a renowned intellectual centre until the 12th century. This monastery-city, with a layout perfectly adapted to its religious function, represents a unique artistic achievement. With its simple, harmonious lines and its profusion of carved decoration, it influenced Buddhist architecture as far away as Cambodia.

Historic Mosque City of Bagerhat   (2)

In the suburbs of Bagerhat, at the meeting-point of the Ganges and Brahmaputra rivers, this ancient city, formerly known as Khalifatabad, was founded by the Turkish general Ulugh Khan Jahan in the 15th century. The city's infrastructure reveals considerable technical skill, and an exceptional number of mosques and early Islamic monuments, many built of brick, can be seen there.

Malaysia

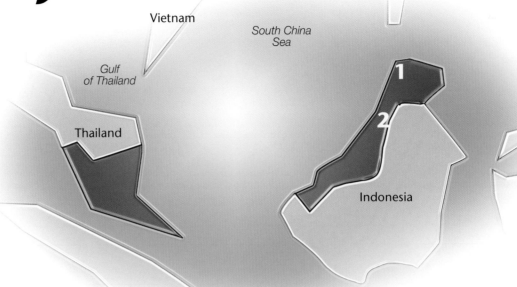

Vietnam

Gulf
of Thailand

South China
Sea

Thailand

1

2

Indonesia

Kinabalu Park (1)

Located in the State of Sabah on the northern end of the island of Borneo, Bagerhat Park is dominated by Mount Kinabalu. At 4,095 metres (13,435 feet), it stands as the highest mountain between the Himalayas and New Guinea. It has a very wide range of habitats, from rich tropical lowland and hill rainforest, to tropical mountain forest and sub-alpine forest.

"A Chinese Prince ascended the mountain to seek a huge pearl on the top of the mountain, which was guarded by a ferocious dragon. The Prince succeeded in slaying the dragon and stealing the pearl. He then married a Kadazan woman, but eventually abandoned her and returned to China. Heartbroken, she wandered to the mountain to mourn and then she turned into a stone."

Kadazan legend

Gunung Mulu National Park (2)

Important both for its high biodiversity and for its karst features, Gunung Mulu National Park, on the island of Borneo in the State of Sarawak, is the most studied tropical karst area in the world. The 52,864-ha (130,630-acre) park contains seventeen vegetation zones, exhibiting some 3,500 species of vascular plants. At least 295 km (183 miles) of explored caves provide a spectacular sight. The Sarawak Chamber is the largest known cave chamber in the world.

"To many in the caving community, Mulu is a holy grail, possessing some of the largest and most spectacular caves in the world."

Gunung Mulu National Park

Angkor (1)

Located amidst forests and farmland to the north of the Great Lake (Tonle Sap), Angkor is one of the most important archaeological sites in South-East Asia. Stretching over some 400 sq. km (98,842 acres), including forested area. Angkor Archaeological Park contains the magnificent remains of the different capitals of the Khmer Empire, which lasted from the 9th to the 15th century.

"It is grander than anything left us by Greece and Rome."

French naturalist Henri Mouhot, who rediscovered Angkor in 1860

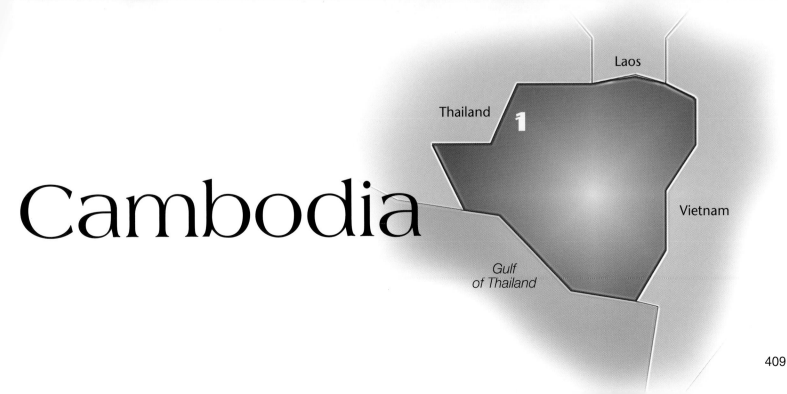

Cambodia

Laos

Thailand

1

Vietnam

Gulf of Thailand

Thailand

Myanmar (Burma)

Laos

2

3

4 **5** **1** Cambodia

Gulf of Thailand

Malaysia

Dong Phayayen - Khao Yai Forest Complex (1)

This forest complex spans 230 km (143 miles) between Ta Phraya National Park on the Cambodian border in the east, and Khao Yai National Park in the west. It is a rugged mountainous area ranging between 100 and 1,351 metres high (328 to 4,432 feet), with about 7,500 of its 615,500 hectares above 1,000 m. It is internationally important for the conservation of globally threatened and endangered mammal, bird and reptile species.

Ban Chiang Archaeological Site (2)

Located in the Udon Thani province, Ban Chiang is considered the most important prehistoric settlement so far discovered in South-East Asia. It marks an important stage in human cultural, social and technological evolution. The site presents the earliest evidence of farming in the region, and of the manufacture and use of metals.

"I stumbled over the root of a kapok tree and ended up spread-eagled in the dirt, and under my face was the rim of a pot."

Harvard student Stephen Young describing how he discovered the site in July 1966

Historic Town of Sukhotai and Associated Historic Towns (3)

Situated in the north of Thailand, Sukhothai was the capital of the first Kingdom of Siam in the 13th and 14th centuries. It has a number of fine monuments, illustrating the beginnings of Thai architecture. The great civilization that evolved in the Kingdom of Sukhothai absorbed numerous influences and ancient local traditions, and the rapid assimilation of all these elements forged what is known as the "Sukhothai style".

"This Muang Sukhothai is good. In the water there are fish, in the field there is rice. The ruler does not levy a tax on the people who travel along the road together, leading their oxen on the way to trade and riding their horses on the way to sell."

Extract of a famous stone inscription in Sukhotai

Thungyai - Huai Kha Khaeng Wildlife Sanctuaries (4)

Stretching over more than 600,000 ha (1.5 million acres) along the Myanmar border, the sanctuaries, which are relatively intact, contain examples of almost all the forest types of continental South-East Asia. They are home to a very diverse array of animals, including 77% of the large mammals (especially elephants and tigers), 50% of the large birds and 33% of the land vertebrates to be found in this region.

Historic City of Ayutthaya and Associated Historic Towns (5)

Founded in 1350 by King U-Thong (King Ramathibodi I), Ayutthaya became the second Siamese capital after Sukhothai. It was destroyed by the Burmese in the 18th century, but its remains, characterized by the prang (reliquary towers) and gigantic monasteries, give an idea of its past splendour.

My Son Sanctuary (1)

"My Son was once a veritable forest of towers, many of which were destroyed by the ravages of time and war."

The Global Heritage Fund

Between the 4th and 13th centuries, a unique culture which owed its spiritual origins to Indian Hinduism developed on the coast of contemporary Vietnam. This is graphically illustrated by the remains of a series of impressive tower-temples, located in a dramatic site that was the religious and political capital of the Champa Kingdom for most of its existence.

Vietnam

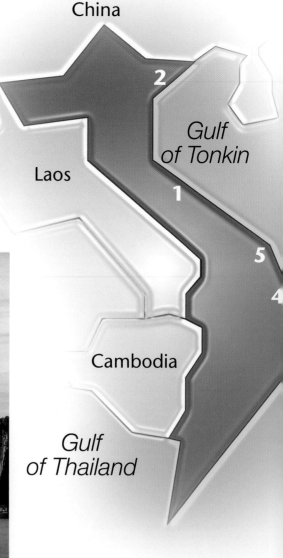

China

Laos

Gulf
of Tonkin

Cambodia

Gulf
of Thailand

Ha Long Bay (2)

Situated in the Gulf of Tonkin, Ha Long Bay includes some 1,600 islands and islets, forming a spectacular seascape of limestone pillars. Because of their precipitous nature, most of the islands are uninhabited and unaffected by a human presence. The site's outstanding scenic beauty is complemented by its great biological interest.

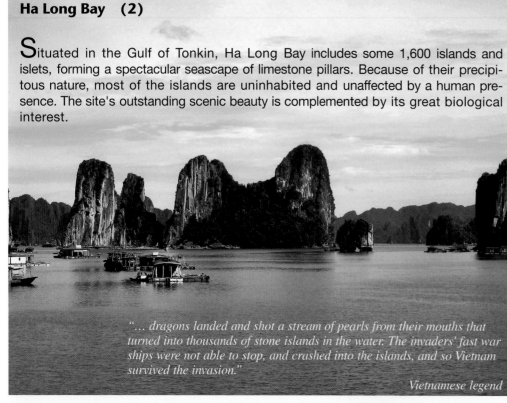

"... dragons landed and shot a stream of pearls from their mouths that turned into thousands of stone islands in the water. The invaders' fast war ships were not able to stop, and crashed into the islands, and so Vietnam survived the invasion."

Vietnamese legend

Phong Nha-Ke Bang National Park (3)

The karst formation of Phong Nha-Ke Bang National Park has evolved since the Palaeozoic, some 400 million years ago. It is now the oldest major karst area in Asia. Subject to massive tectonic changes, the park's karst landscape is extremely complex, with many geomorphic features of considerable significance. The vast area contains spectacular formations including 65 km (40 miles) of caves and underground rivers.

Ancient Town of Hoi An (4)

The coastal town of Hoi An is an exceptionally well-preserved example of a South-East Asian trading port dating from the 15th to the 19th century. Its buildings and its street plan reflect the influences, both indigenous and foreign, that have combined to produce this unique heritage site.

Complex of Hué Monuments (5)

Established as the capital of the unified country in 1802, Hué was not only the political, but also the cultural and religious centre under the Nguyen dynasty until 1945. The Perfume River winds its way through the Capital City, the Imperial City, the Forbidden Purple City and the Inner City, giving this unique feudal capital a setting of great natural beauty.

"Hué is a masterpiece of urban poetry."

Amadou-Mahtar M'Bow,
Director-General of UNESCO
from 1974 to 1987

Lao People's Democratic Republic

Town of Luang Prabang   (1)

Hidden in north central Laos, on the Mekong River about 425 km (264 miles) north of Vientiane, Luang Prabang is an outstanding example of the fusion of traditional architecture and Lao urban structures with those built by the European colonial authorities in the 19th and 20th centuries. Its unique, remarkably well-preserved townscape illustrates a key stage in the blending of these two distinct cultural traditions.

"Luang Prabang's appeal is its unsurpassed jungle setting, and the feeling that the people have lived here for ages, unaffected by time."

American journalist
Ron Gluckman

Vat Phou and Ancient Settlements of Champasak   (2)

Located in southern Laos, the Champasak cultural landscape, including the Vat Phou temple complex, is a remarkably well-preserved planned landscape, over 1,000 years old. It was shaped to express the Hindu vision of the relationship between nature and humanity, using an axis from mountain top to river bank to lay out a geometric pattern of temples, shrines and waterworks.

Uvs Nuur Basin (1)

Uvs Nuur is the northernmost of the enclosed basins of Central Asia. It takes its name from Uvs Nuur Lake, a large, shallow and very saline lake, important for migrating birds, waterfowl and seabirds. The site is made up of twelve protected areas representing the major biomes of eastern Eurasia. The steppe ecosystem supports a rich diversity of birds and the desert is home to a number of rare gerbils, jerboas and the marbled polecat. The mountains are an important refuge for the globally endangered snow leopard, mountain sheep and the Asiatic ibex.

Mongolia

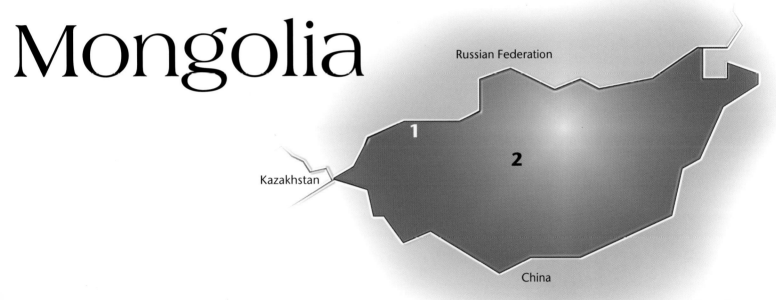

Russian Federation

Kazakhstan

1

2

China

Orkhon Valley Cultural Landscape (2)

The 121,967-ha (301,387-acre) valley encompasses an extensive area of pastureland on both banks of the Orkhon River and includes numerous archaeological remains dating back to the 6th century. The site also includes Kharkhorum, the 13th- and 14th-century capital of Chingis (Genghis) Khan's vast Empire. The grassland is still grazed by Mongolian nomadic pastoralists.

"... a great palace, situated next to the city walls, enclosed within a high wall like those which enclose monks' priories among us. There are many buildings as long as barns, in which are stored his provisions and his treasures."

Flemish Franciscan explorer
William of Rubruck,
describing Karakorum in 1254

China

Map of China showing numbered World Heritage site locations, with surrounding countries and seas labeled: Russian Federation, Sea of Japan, North Korea, South Korea, Kazakhstan, Mongolia, Yellow Sea, Kyrgyzstan, Tajikistan, Afghanistan, Pakistan, India, Nepal, Bhutan, Myanmar (Burma), Vietnam, Laos, Gulf of Tonkin, South China sea, Taiwan, Pacific Ocean.

Numbered locations: 7, 12, 8, 22, 30, 32, 25, 23, 17, 11, 6, 18, 19, 4, 26, 15, 5, 9, 24, 16, 21, 14, 29, 28, 1, 3, 27, 10, 2, 20, 33, 13, 31.

Dazu Rock Carvings (1)

The steep hillsides of the Dazu area contain an exceptional series of rock carvings dating from the 9th to the 13th century. They are remarkable for their aesthetic quality, their rich diversity of subject matter (both secular and religious), and the light that they shed on everyday life in China during this period. They provide outstanding evidence of the harmonious synthesis of Buddhism, Taoism and Confucianism.

Wulingyuan Scenic and Historic Interest Area (2)

A spectacular area stretching over more than 26,000 ha (64,247 acres) in China's Hunan Province, the site is dominated by more than 3,000 narrow sandstone pillars and peaks, many over 200 metres (656 feet) high. Between the peaks lie ravines and gorges with streams, pools and waterfalls, some 40 caves, and two large natural bridges.

Lushan National Park (3)

Mount Lushan, in Jiangxi, is one of the spiritual centres of Chinese civilization. Buddhist and Taoist temples, along with landmarks of Confucianism, where the most eminent masters taught, blend effortlessly into a strikingly beautiful landscape that has inspired countless artists who developed the aesthetic approach to nature found in Chinese culture.

Temple and Cemetery of Confucius and the Kong Family Mansion in Qufu (4)

The temple, cemetery and family mansion of Confucius, the great philosopher, politician and educator of the 6th–5th centuries BC, are located at Qufu, in Shandong Province. Built to commemorate him in 478 BC, the temple has been destroyed and reconstructed over the centuries. Today, it comprises more than 100 buildings. The cemetery contains Confucius' tomb and the remains of more than 100,000 of his descendants.

"By nature, men are nearly alike; by practice, they get to be wide apart."

Confucius
(551 - 479 BC)

Mausoleum
of the First Qin Emperor   (5)

Qin (260 - 210 BC), the first unifier of China, is buried, surrounded by the famous terracotta warriors, at the centre of a complex designed to mirror the urban plan of the capital, Xianyan. The small figures are all different. With their horses, chariots and weapons, they are masterpieces of realism, in addition to being of great historical interest. The site was discovered in March 1974 during the sinking of wells for farmland irrigation construction near Xi'an, Shaanxi province.

"Emperor Qin believed that the life under the ground was a continuation of it in the world; he ordered such a huge mausoleum to be constructed 2,200 years ago. At the same time, he left his highly developed civilization to people today."

Emperor Qin's Terra-cotta Museum

Sichuan Giant Panda Sanctuary (6)

Home to more than 30% of the world's highly endangered pandas, the sanctuary includes seven nature reserves and nine scenic parks in the Qionglai and Jiajin Mountains. They constitute the largest remaining contiguous habitat of the giant panda, a relict from the palaeotropical forests of the Tertiary Era. This is also the species' most important site for captive breeding.

"To protect an animal is not just putting it living in the zoo, but keeping it alive in its home."

Lu Zhi,
panda specialist at Peking University

Yungang Grottoes (7)

Near Datong City in Shanxi Province, the Yungang Grottoes, with their 252 caves and 51,000 statues, represent the outstanding achievement of Buddhist cave art in China in the 5th and 6th centuries. The five caves created by Tan Yao, with their strict unity of layout and design, constitute a classical masterpiece of the first peak of Chinese Buddhist art.

Mountain Resort and its Outlying Temples, Chengde (8)

Hidden in the northeast of Beijing, the Mountain Resort (the Qing dynasty's summer palace) in Hebei Province was built between 1703 and 1792. It is a vast complex of palaces and administrative and ceremonial buildings. Temples of various architectural styles and imperial gardens blend harmoniously into a landscape of lakes, pastureland and forests.

Longmen Grottoes (9)

In the south of modern Luoyang, in Henan province, the grottoes and niches of Longmen contain the largest and most impressive collection of Chinese art from the late Northern Wei and Tang Dynasties (316-907). These works, entirely devoted to the Buddhist religion, represent the high point of Chinese stone carving.

Mount Emei Scenic Area, including Leshan Giant Buddha Scenic Area (10)

The first Buddhist temple in China was built here in Sichuan Province in the 1st century AD, in the beautiful surroundings of the summit of Mount Emei. The addition of other temples turned the site into one of Buddhism's holiest. Over the centuries, the cultural treasures grew in number. The most remarkable is the Giant Buddha of Leshan, carved out of a hillside in the 8th century and looking down on the confluence of three rivers. At 71 metres (233 feet) high, it is the largest Buddha in the world.

Mogao Caves (11)

Situated at a strategic point along the Silk Route, at the crossroads of trade as well as religious, cultural and intellectual influences, the 492 cells and cave sanctuaries in Mogao are famous for their statues and wall paintings, spanning 1,000 years of Buddhist art.

The Great Wall   (12)

In c. 220 BC, under Qin Shi Huang, sections of earlier fortifications were joined together to form a united defence system against invasions from the north. Construction continued up to the Ming dynasty (1368–1644), when the Great Wall became the world's largest military structure. Its historic and strategic importance is matched only by its architectural significance.

"A young woman by the name of Ming Jiangnu came to the Great Wall looking for her husband. Hearing the sad news of the death of her beloved, she sat down at the foot of the Wall and started crying. She cried day and night, and her wailing made the wall fall. She finally saw her husband's bones under the wall."

Meng Jiangnu's Bitter Weeping Legend

Old Town of Lijiang   (13)

Located in northwestern Yunnan Province, the Old Town of Lijiang, which is perfectly adapted to the uneven topography of this key commercial and strategic site, has retained a historic townscape of high quality and authenticity. Its architecture is noteworthy for the blending of elements from several cultures that have come together over many centuries.

"The old town is a tiny Chinese Venice. The streets suddenly give way to rushing streams. Navigating the narrow cobbled streets and humpbacked bridges is all part of the fun."

Dee O'Connell, The Observer, August 17, 2003

Mount Huangshan   (14)

Located in the southern Anhui province in eastern China, Huangshan was acclaimed through art and literature during a good part of Chinese history. Known as "the loveliest mountain in China", today it holds the same fascination for visitors, poets, painters and photographers who come on pilgrimage to the site, which is renowned for its magnificent scenery made up of many granite peaks and rocks emerging out of a sea of clouds.

"The day broke through the rolling clouds and the sky was red for 10,000 miles."

Chinese President Ji_ng Zémín (1993 – 2003), describing his visit to Mount Huangshan

Jiuzhaigou Valley Scenic and Historic Interest Area   (15)

Stretching over 72,000 ha (177,915 acres) in the northern part of Sichuan Province, the jagged Jiuzhaigou valley reaches a height of more than 4,800 m (15,750 feet), thus comprising a series of diverse forest ecosystems. Its superb landscapes are particularly interesting for their series of narrow conic karst land forms and spectacular waterfalls. Some 140 bird species also inhabit the valley, as well as a number of endangered plant and animal species, including the giant panda and the Sichuan takin.

Ancient Building Complex in the Wudang Mountains   (16)

The palaces and temples that form the nucleus of this group of secular and religious buildings exemplify the architectural and artistic achievements of China's Yuan, Ming and Qing dynasties. Situated in the scenic valleys and on the slopes of the Wudang Mountains in Hubei Province, the site contains Taoist buildings from as early as the 7th century.

Temple of Heaven: an Imperial Sacrificial Altar in Beijing (17)

Founded in the first half of the 15th century, the Temple of Heaven is a dignified complex of fine cult buildings set in gardens and surrounded by historic pine woods. In its overall layout and that of its individual buildings, it symbolizes the relationship between heaven and earth – the human world and God's world – which stands at the heart of Chinese cosmogony. It also evokes the special role played by the emperors within that relationship.

Ancient City of Ping Yao (18)

During the Qing dynasty, Pingyao was the financial centre of China. Founded in the 14th century in central Shanxi Province, it is an exceptionally well-preserved example of a traditional Han Chinese city. Its urban fabric shows the evolution of architectural styles and town planning in Imperial China over five centuries. It is also renowned for its well-preserved ancient city wall.

Mount Taishan   (19)

Located in Shandong Province, the sacred Mount Taishan was the object of an imperial cult for nearly 2,000 years, and the artistic masterpieces found there are in perfect harmony with the natural landscape. It has always been a source of inspiration for Chinese artists and scholars and symbolizes ancient Chinese civilizations and beliefs.

"When Pangu, the ancestor of all things, died, his head turned into Mount Tai ... Mount Tai thus has become the head of all mountains, symbol of China's national spirit."

Ancient Chinese mythology

Historic Ensemble of the Potala Palace, Lhasa   (20)

Winter palace of the Dalai Lama since the 7th century, the Potala Palace symbolizes Tibetan Buddhism and its central role in the traditional administration of Tibet. The complex, comprising the White and Red Palaces with their ancillary buildings, is built on Red Mountain in the centre of Lhasa Valley, at an altitude of 3,700 m (12,139 feet). Also founded in the 7th century, the Jokhang Temple Monastery is an exceptional Buddhist religious complex. Norbulingka, the Dalai Lama's former summer palace, constructed in the 18th century, is a masterpiece of Tibetan art.

"The majestic, brilliant, magnificent and uninhibited Potala Palace has a strong artistic appeal and is an architectural art treasure that can be shown off to the world."

Ministry of Culture of the People's Republic of China

Classical Gardens of Suzhou   (21)

On the shores of lake Taihu in the province of Jiangsu, the Classical Chinese garden design, which seeks to recreate natural landscapes in miniature, is nowhere better illustrated than in the nine gardens in the historic city of Suzhou. Dating from the 11th-19th centuries, the gardens are generally acknowledged to be masterpieces of the genre.

"A very great and noble city ... It has 1,600 stone bridges under which a galley may pass."

Venetian explorer Marco Polo
(1254 – 1324)

Imperial Palaces of the Ming and Qing Dynasties in Beijing and Shenyang   (22)

Known as The Forbidden City and located at the exact centre of the ancient City of Beijing, The Imperial Palace of the Qing Dynasty, in Shenyang, consists of 114 buildings, constructed between 1625 and 1783. It contains an important library and testifies to the foundation of the last dynasty that ruled China, before it expanded its power to the centre of the country and moved the capital to Beijing. The palaces are the largest collection of preserved ancient wooden structures in the world.

"Without seeing the magnificence of the royal palace, one can never sense the dignity of the Emperor."

Line from a Tang Dynasty poem

Peking Man Site at Zhoukoudian   (23)

Scientific work at the site, which lies 42 km (26 miles) south-west of Beijing, is still underway. So far, it has led to the discovery of the remains of Sinanthropus pekinensis, who lived in the Middle Pleistocene, along with various objects, and remains of Homo sapiens dating as far back as 18,000 -11,000 BC. The site is not only an exceptional reminder of the prehistoric human societies of the Asian continent, but also illustrates the process of evolution.

Huanglong Scenic and Historic Interest Area   (24)

Situated in the north-west of Sichaun Province, the Huanglong valley is made up of snow-capped peaks and the easternmost of all Chinese glaciers. In addition to its mountain landscape, diverse forest ecosystems can be found, as well as spectacular limestone formations, waterfalls and hot springs. The area also has a population of endangered animals, including the giant panda and the Sichuan golden snub-nosed monkey.

"We wanted an animal that is beautiful, endangered, and loved by many people in the world for its appealing qualities."

Sir Peter Scott, one of the founders of the WWF, about the logo of the organization

Summer Palace, an Imperial Garden in Beijing   (25)

First built in 1750, largely destroyed in the war of 1860 and restored on its original foundations in 1886, the Summer Palace in Beijing is a masterpiece of Chinese landscape garden design. The natural scenery of hills and open water is combined with artificial features such as pavilions, halls, palaces, temples and bridges to form a harmonious ensemble of outstanding aesthetic value.

"The Garden of Health and Harmony (Yi He Yuan)."

Empress Dowager Cixi, renaming the Palace in 1888

Yinxu (26)

Famous for the discovery of oracle bones and their inscriptions, which are thought to be the beginnings of Chinese characters and writing, Yinxu was the capital city of the Shang Dynasty (1600 - 1100 BC). Fifty large buildings within the palace areas of Yinxu have been excavated in the imperial tomb area. In addition, the site includes tombs of the noble as well as the poor, and the ruins of stone and jade manufacturing workshops.

"Yinxu occupies an indisputable status in Chinese culture and history. What we have to do now is improve our work on its protection and display."

Xiao Jiye,
Vice-Mayor of Anyang
Central China's Henan Province

Mount Wuyi (27)

Located on the northern border of Fujian province, Mount Wuyi is the most outstanding area for biodiversity conservation in south-east China, as well as a refuge for a large number of ancient, relict species, many of them endemic to China. The serene beauty of the dramatic gorges of the Nine Bend River, with its numerous temples and monasteries, many now in ruins, provided the setting for the development and spread of neo-Confucianism, which has been influential in the cultures of East Asia since the 11th century.

"A clear and shallow water runs through the mountain, and on its way downhill it makes nine bends."

Li Gang (1083-1140),
an official of the Northern Song Dynasty

Mount Qingcheng and the Dujiangyan Irrigation System (28)

Construction of the Dujiangyan irrigation system began in the 3rd century BC. This system still controls the waters of the Minjiang River and distributes it to the fertile farmland of the Chengdu plains. Mount Qingcheng was the birthplace of Taoism, which is celebrated in a series of ancient temples.

"Stupidity leads to force."

One of Tao Te Ching's principles,
by Lao Zi, founder of Taoism

Ancient Villages in Southern Anhui - Xidi and Hongcun (29)

The two traditional villages of Xidi and Hongcun preserve to a remarkable extent the appearance of non-urban settlements of a type that largely disappeared or was transformed during the last century. Their street plan, architecture and decoration, as well as the integration of houses with comprehensive water systems, are unique surviving examples.

429

Imperial Tombs of the Ming and Qing Dynasties (30)

The Ming and Qing tombs are dazzling illustrations of the beliefs, world view, and geomantic theories of Fengshui, prevalent in feudal China. They have served as burial edifices for illustrious people and as the theatre for major events that have marked the history of China.

"Dignitaries, officials and other persons arriving here must dismount from their horses."

Historical inscriptions on two tablets of the Ming Tombs' Great Red Gate

Historic Centre of Macao (31)

This historic city is located on the southern coast of China, a few miles southwest of Hong Kong. Macao, a lucrative port of strategic importance in the development of international trade, was under Portuguese administration from the mid 16th century until 1999, when it came under Chinese sovereignty. With its historic streets and its series of residential, religious and public Portuguese and Chinese buildings, this sector of Macao provides a unique testimony to the meeting of aesthetic, cultural, architectural and technological influences from East and West.

Capital Cities and Tombs of the Ancient Koguryo Kingdom (32)

This site includes archaeological remains of three cities – Wunu Mountain City, Guonei City and Wandu Mountain City – and 40 tombs, 14 of which are imperial and 26 noble. All belong to the Koguryo culture, named after the dynasty that ruled over parts of northern China and the northern half of the Korean Peninsula from 37 BC to AD 668.

"Having gotten to know that what I face everyday is something significant in human history, I agree to get relocated. I think it is worthwhile sacrificing a little for the benefit of children of future generations."

Jiang Yuhua,
a 53-year-old farmer, who lived some
100 metres from the Tombs

Three Parallel Rivers of Yunnan Protected Areas (33)

Consisting of eight geographical clusters of protected areas within the boundaries of the Three Parallel Rivers National Park, in the mountainous north-west of Yunnan Province, this 1.7-million-hectare site features sections of the upper reaches of three of the great rivers of Asia: the Yangtze (Jinsha), Mekong and Salween. The site is an epicentre of Chinese biodiversity, and one of the world's richest temperate regions in terms of biodiversity.

"Because of its high elevation and the deep gorges of the three rivers, the ecosystem in this region is extremely fragile, and once damaged, is almost impossible to restore."

The World Wildlife Funds (WWF)

Republic of Korea

China

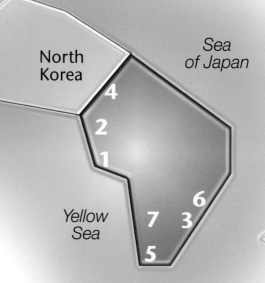

North Korea

Sea of Japan

Yellow Sea

Hwaseong Fortress (1)

When the Choson Emperor Chongjo moved his father's tomb to Suwon at the end of the 18th century, he surrounded it with strong defensive works, laid out according to the precepts of an influential military architect of the period, who brought together the latest developments in the field from both East and West. Hwaseong, meaning "Brilliant Fortress", is an outstanding example of early modern military architecture.

"I will then be able to fulfill my greatest wishes. I will retire to Hwaseong with Your Ladyship…"

King Jeongjo, founder of Hwaseong, to his mother Lady Hyegyeong

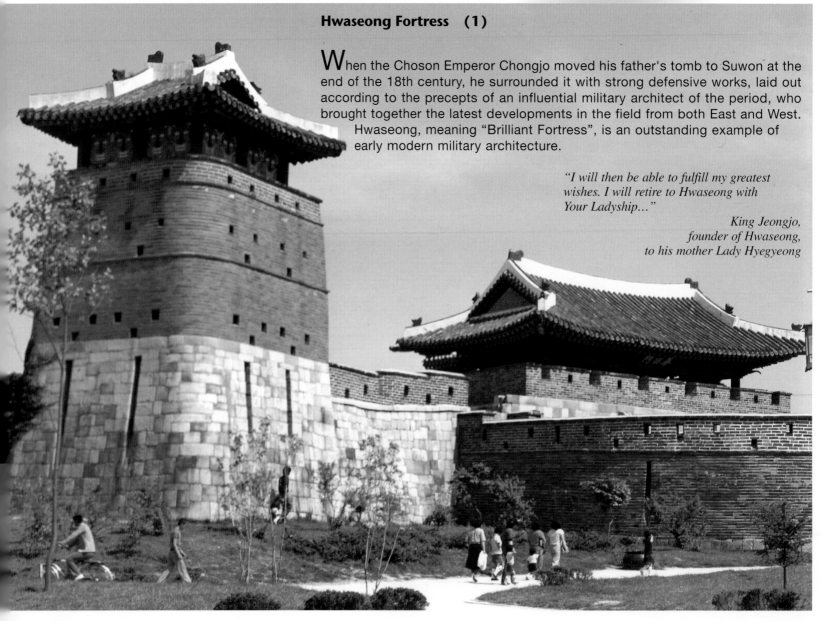

Jongmyo Shrine   (2)

Jongmyo is the oldest and most authentic of the Confucian royal shrines to have been preserved. Dedicated to the forefathers of the Choson dynasty (1392–1910), the shrine has existed in its present form since the 16th century and houses tablets bearing the teachings of members of the former royal family. Ritual ceremonies linking music, song and dance still take place there, perpetuating a tradition that goes back to the 14th century.

"Jongmyo is ... where kings prayed for national security and peace before the altars for the gods governing national territory and major farm products."

LEE, Hwan Ey,
President of The Society
for the Preservation of Jongmyo Jerye,
2004

Seokguram Grotto and Bulguksa Temple   (3)

Established in the 8th century on the slopes of Mount T'oham, the Seokguram Grotto contains a monumental statue of the Buddha looking at the sea in the bhumisparsha mudra position. With the surrounding portrayals of gods, Bodhisattvas and disciples, all realistically and delicately sculpted in high and low relief, it is considered a masterpiece of Buddhist art in the Far East.

"... Dae-seong was moved by the heavenly grace. He built the beautiful Bulguksa in memory of his parents of the present life and the wonderful cave temple of Seokguram for his parents of the previous life."

The Korean legend of a filial son

Changdeokgung Palace   (4)

Located in Seoul, the Changdokkung Palace complex is an outstanding example of Far Eastern palace architecture and garden design, exceptional for the way in which the buildings are integrated into and harmonized with the natural setting, adapting to the topography and retaining indigenous tree cover.

Gochang, Hwasun, and Ganghwa Dolmen Sites   (5)

The prehistoric cemeteries at Gochang, Hwasun and Ganghwa contain many hundreds of examples of dolmens - tombs from the 1st millennium BC constructed of large stone slabs. They form part of the Megalithic culture, found in many parts of the world, but nowhere in such a concentrated form.

Gyeongju Historic Areas   (6)

Located in North Gyeongsang Province, Gyeongju contains a remarkable concentration of outstanding examples of Korean Buddhist art, in the form of sculptures, reliefs, pagodas, and the remains of temples and palaces from the flowering period of this form of unique artistic expression, in particular between the 7th and 10th centuries.

Haeinsa Temple Janggyeong Panjeon   (7)

The Temple of Haeinsa, on Mount Kaya, is home to the Tripitaka Koreana, the most complete collection of Buddhist texts, engraved on 80,000 woodblocks between 1237 and 1248. The buildings of Janggyeong Pangeon, which date from the 15th century, were constructed to house the woodblocks, which are also revered as exceptional works of art.

Democratic People's Republic of Korea

China

Sea of Japan

1

Yellow Sea

South Korea

Complex of Koguryo Tombs　(1)

The site includes several groups and individual tombs, totalling about 30 individual graves, from the later period of the Koguryo Kingdom, one of the strongest kingdoms in northeast China and half of the Korean peninsula between the 3rd century BC and 7th century AD. The tombs, many with beautiful wall paintings, are almost the only remains of this culture. These paintings offer a unique testimony to daily life of this period.

"Mural paintings dating back to the period of Koguryo are a precious cultural heritage which the Korean nation boasts before the world."

History Faculty,
Kim Il Sung University

Japan

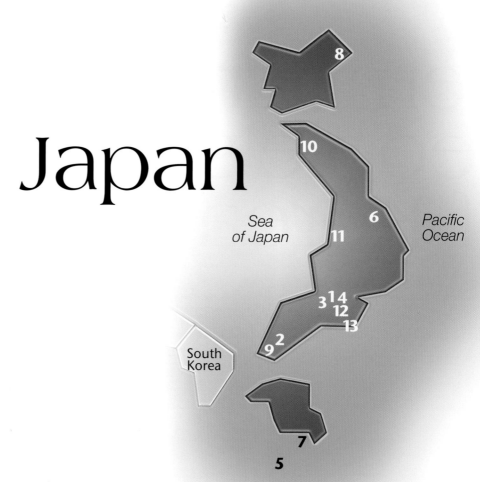

Sea of Japan

Pacific Ocean

South Korea

Historic Monuments of Ancient Kyoto (1)

Built in AD 794 on the model of the capitals of ancient China, Kyoto was the imperial capital of Japan from its foundation until the middle of the 19th century. As the centre of Japanese culture for more than 1,000 years, Kyoto illustrates the development of Japanese wooden architecture, particularly religious architecture, and the art of Japanese gardens.

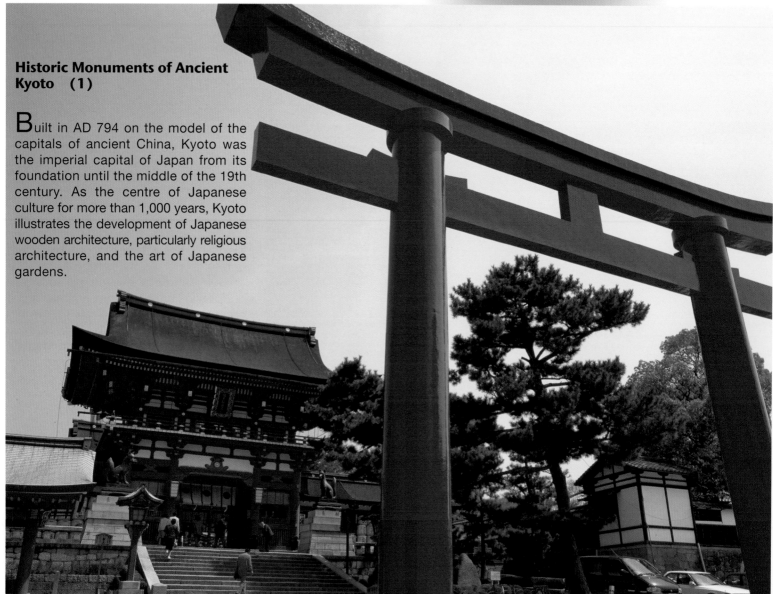

Hiroshima Peace Memorial
- Genbaku Dome   (2)

The August 6, 1945 atomic explosion was almost directly above the Hiroshima Prefectural Commercial Exhibition building, and it was the closest structure to withstand the explosion. The building has been preserved in the same state as immediately after the bombing. Not only is it a stark and powerful symbol of the most destructive force ever created by humankind, it also expresses the hope for world peace and the ultimate elimination of all nuclear weapons.

"This horrible weapon brought about a "Revolution of Thought", which has convinced us of the necessity and the value of lasting peace."

First line of the first Peace Declaration read by Hiroshima Mayor Shinzo Hamai on August 6, 1947

Himeji-jo   (3)

Located in Hyogo Prefecture, Himeji-jo is the finest surviving example of early 17th-century Japanese castle architecture, comprising 83 buildings with highly developed systems of defence and ingenious protection devices dating from the beginning of the Shogun period.

Historic Monuments of Ancient Nara (4)

Near Kyoto in the Kansai region, Nara was the capital of Japan from 710 to 784. During this period, the framework of national government was consolidated and Nara enjoyed great prosperity, emerging as the fountainhead of Japanese culture. The city's historic monuments provide a vivid picture of life in the Japanese capital in the 8th century, a period of profound political and cultural change.

"When the Sun Goddess dispatched her grandson to Earth, he landed on the island of Kyushu, and was enthroned as the first ruler of Yamato (present-day Nara)."

Nara's origins according to Japanese mythology

Gusuku Sites and Related Properties of the Kingdom of Ryukyu (5)

Five hundred years of Ryukyuan history (12th-17th century) are represented by this group of sites and monuments. The ruins of the castles, on imposing elevated sites, are evidence of the social structure prevalent over much of that period, while the sacred sites provide testimony to the rare survival of an ancient form of religion into the modern age.

Shrines and Temples of Nikko (6)

The shrines and temples of Nikko, together with their natural surroundings, have for centuries been a sacred site known for its architectural and decorative masterpieces. They are closely associated with the history of the Tokugawa Shoguns.

"You cannot say 'Kekko' (meaning magnificent) until you have seen Nikko."

Japanese saying

Yakushima (7)

Nestled in the interior of Yaku Island, at the meeting point of the palaearctic and oriental biotic regions, Yakushima exhibits a rich flora, with some 1,900 species and subspecies, including ancient specimens of the sugi (Japanese cedar). It also contains a remnant of a warm-temperate ancient forest that is unique in this region.

"Japan's most ancient example of Yakusugi is estimated to be 7,200 years old."

Japan National Tourist Organization

Shiretoko (8)

Shiretoko Peninsula is located in the north-east of Hokkaido, the northernmost island of Japan. It provides an outstanding example of the interaction of marine and terrestrial ecosystems, as well as extraordinary ecosystem productivity largely influenced by the formation of seasonal sea ice at the lowest latitude in the northern hemisphere.

Itsukushima Shinto Shrine   (9)

The island of Itsukushima, in the Seto inland sea, has been a holy place of Shintoism since the earliest times. The first shrine buildings here were probably erected in the 6th century. The present shrine dates from the 13th century and the harmoniously arranged buildings reveal great artistic and technical skill.

"Love of nature: nature is sacred; to be in contact with nature is to be close to the gods. Natural objects are worshipped as sacred spirits."

One of the Four Affirmations in Shinto

Shirakami-Sanchi   (10)

This trackless site in the northern Honshu includes the last virgin remains of the cool-temperate forest of Siebold's beech trees that once covered the hills and mountain slopes of northern Japan. The black bear, the serow and 87 species of birds can be found in this forest.

Historic Villages of Shirakawa-go and Gokayama　(11)

Hidden in a mountainous region that was cut off from the rest of the world for a long period of time, these villages, with their Gassho-style houses, subsisted on the cultivation of mulberry trees and the rearing of silkworms. The large houses, with their steeply pitched thatched roofs, are the only examples of their kind left in Japan.

Buddhist Monuments in the Horyy-ji Area　(12)

Horyu-ji, meaning Temple of the Flourishing Law, is a Buddhist temple in Ikaruga, Nara Prefecture. Several of the 48 Buddhist monuments date from the late 7th or early 8th century, making them some of the oldest surviving wooden buildings in the world. These masterpieces of wooden architecture are important for the history of art and religion.

"Empress Suiko and Crown Prince Shotoku fulfilled Emperor Yomei's deathbed wish by building, in 607, a temple and a statue of a Buddha, to which the temple was dedicated."

Historical writings engraved on the Yakusi Nyorai Buddha statue in the Horyy-ji area.

Sacred Sites and Pilgrimage Routes in the Kii Mountain Range (13)

Set in the dense forests of the Kii Mountains, overlooking the Pacific Ocean, three sacred sites – Yoshino & Omine, Kumano Sanzan, and Koyasan – linked by pilgrimage routes to the ancient capital cities of Nara and Kyoto, reflect the fusion of Shinto, rooted in the ancient tradition of nature worship in Japan, and Buddhism, which was introduced to Japan from China and the Korean peninsula.

Indonesia

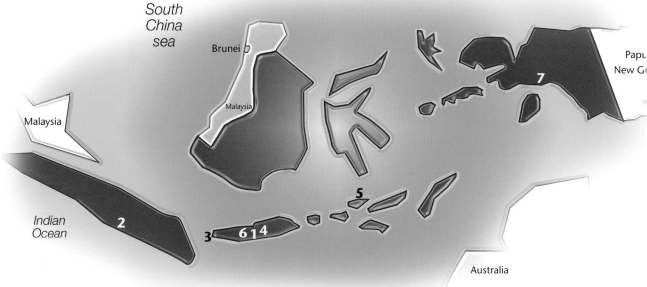

South
China
sea

Pacific
Ocean

Brunei

Malaysia

Malaysia

Papu
New G

7

Indian
Ocean

2

3 6 1 4

5

Australia

Prambanan Temple Compounds   (1)

Built in the 10th century in central Java, this is the largest temple compound dedicated to Shiva in Indonesia. Rising above the centre of the last of these concentric squares are three temples decorated with reliefs illustrating the epic of the Ramayana, dedicated to the three great Hindu divinities (Shiva, Vishnu and Brahma), and three temples dedicated to the animals who serve them.

"Roro Jonggrang, daughter of King Boko, was cursed by Prince Bandung into the last and most beautiful of the temple's statues, which was built for her."

Legend of Princess Roro Jonggrang

Tropical Rainforest Heritage of Sumatra (2)

The 2.5-million-hectare (6.2-million-acre) site called Tropical Rainforest Heritage of Sumatra comprises three national parks: Gunung Leuser, Kerinci Seblat and Bukit Barisan Selatan. The site holds the greatest potential for long-term conservation of the distinctive and diverse biota of Sumatra, including many endangered species. The protected area is home to an estimated 10,000 plant species, including 17 endemic genera; more than 200 mammal species; and some 580 bird species, of which 465 are resident and 21 are endemic. Of the mammal species, 22 are Asian, not found elsewhere in the archipelago, and 15 are confined to the Indonesian region, including the endemic Sumatran orangutan. It also provides biogeographic evidence of the island's evolution.

Ujung Kulon National Park (3)

Located in the extreme south-western tip of Java on the Sunda shelf, this national park includes the Ujung Kulon peninsula and several offshore islands, as well as the natural reserve of Krakatoa. In addition to its natural beauty and geological interest, it contains the largest remaining area of lowland rainforests in the Java plain.

Sangiran Early Man Site (4)

Excavations on this site in the island of Java, from 1936 to 1941, led to the discovery of a hominid fossil. Later, 50 fossils of Meganthropus palaeo and Pithecanthropus erectus/Homo erectus were found – half of all the world's known hominid fossils. Inhabited for the past one and a half million years, Sangiran is one of the key sites for the understanding of human evolution.

Komodo National Park (5)

These volcanic islands are inhabited by a population of around 5,700 giant lizards, whose appearance and aggressive behaviour have led to them being called "Komodo dragons". They exist nowhere else in the world and are of great interest to scientists studying the theory of evolution.

"Now listening to the short hissing that came like a gust of evil wind, and observing the action of that darting, snake-like tongue, that seemed to sense the very fear that held me, I was affected in a manner not easy to relate."

William Douglas Burden,
director of the Zoological Museum and Botanical Gardens
at Bogor, Java (1927)

Borobudur Temple Compounds (6)

This famous Buddhist temple, dating from the 8th and 9th centuries, is located in central Java. It was built in three tiers: a pyramidal base with five concentric square terraces, the trunk of a cone with three circular platforms and, at the top, a monumental stupa. The monument was restored with UNESCO's help in the 1970s.

"There is a mountain south of Borobudur that when viewed from the monument looks very much like the profile of a man. The story goes that the ridge depicts Gunadharma, the architect of Borobudur, who is believed to keep watch over his creation through the ages."

Jan Fontein,
Asian art historian

Lorentz National Park (7)

This site, located in the province of Papua, is the largest protected area in Southeast Asia with 2.35 million ha (5.8 million acres). It is also the only protected area in the world which incorporates a continuous, intact transect from snow cap to tropical marine environment, including extensive lowland wetlands.

Philippines

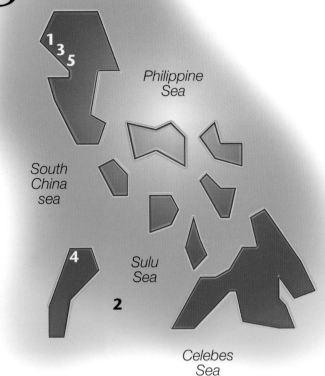

Historic Town of Vigan   (1)

This city on the western coast of the large island of Luzon was established in the 16th century. Vigan is the best-preserved example of a planned Spanish colonial town in Asia. Its architecture reflects the coming together of cultural elements from elsewhere in the Philippines, as well as from China and Europe, resulting in a culture and townscape that have no parallel anywhere in East or South-East Asia.

"It seemed best to send Captain Juan de Salcedo with 70 or 80 soldiers to people the coast of Los Ilocano, on the shores of the river called Bigan."

*Letters of Governor General
Guido de Lavezares to King Philip II of Spain,
in 1572, which led to the birth of Vigan*

Tubbataha Reef Marine Park   (2)

Tubbataha Reef covers 33,200 ha (82,038 acres), including the north and south reefs. It is a unique example of an atoll reef with a very high density of marine species. The North Islet serves as a nesting area for birds and marine turtles. The pristine coral reef with also features a spectacular 100-m (328-foot) perpendicular wall, extensive lagoons and two coral islands.

"Tubbataha Reef Marine Park in the Philippines is home to a diversity of marine life that matches or exceeds any other diving location in the world."

World Wildlife Fund (WWF)

Baroque Churches
of the Philippines   (3)

These four churches, the first of which was built by the Spanish in the late 16th century, are located in Manila, Santa Maria, Paoay and Miag-ao. Their unique architectural style is a reinterpretation of European Baroque by Chinese and Philippine craftsmen.

Puerto-Princesa Subterranean River National Park (4)

This park features a spectacular limestone karst landscape with an underground river. One of the river's distinguishing features is that it emerges directly into the sea, and its lower portion is subject to tidal influences. The area also represents a significant habitat for biodiversity conservation.

Rice Terraces of the Philippine Cordilleras (5)

For 2,000 years, the high rice fields of the Ifugao have followed the contours of the mountains. They bear the fruit of knowledge handed down from one generation to the next, and the expression of sacred traditions and a delicate social balance. They have also helped create a landscape of great beauty that expresses the harmony between humankind and the environment. About 25-30% of the terraces are now abandoned, which has led to some of the walls being damaged because parts of the irrigation system have been neglected. The site is inscribed on the World Heritage List in Danger.

Oceania

Many have referred to it as the end of the world. Indeed, Oceania can be seen as quite remote, but most of its visitors would gladly settle there after witnessing the richness of the culture and the beauty of the land.

The fauna and flora are extremely abundant here, mainly because of the variety of ecosystems in Australia (although most of this country is semi-arid or desert). Most of the animals and flowers are endemic, but unfortunately, many of them are threatened by human activity and by plant and animal species that were introduced after colonization.

Oceania is also home to New Zealand's unforgettable scenery, the Land of the Long White Cloud. Because of its historic isolation from the rest of the world and its island biogeography, this country has preserved an extraordinary array of flora and fauna, with roughly 80% of the flora exclusive to New Zealand.

These two countries, and the magnificent surrounding islands of the Pacific Ocean, are the keepers of a fragile natural heritage. Despite this continent's remoteness, every person in the world should be mindful of its collective wonders.

Australia

Tasmanian Wilderness   (1)

In a region that has been subjected to severe glaciation, these parks and reserves, with their steep gorges, covering an area of over 1 million ha (xxx acres), constitute one of the last expanses of temperate rainforest in the world. Remains found in limestone caves attest to human occupation of the area for more than 20,000 years.

"In the afternoon, about 4 o'clock, we saw land, which we had east by north from us by our estimate ten miles distant. It was very high land."

First words of Dutch explorer Abel Tasman when he discovered the island on November 24, 1642

Shark Bay, Western Australia (2)

At the most westerly point of the Australian continent, Shark Bay, with its islands and the land surrounding it, has three exceptional natural features: its vast sea-grass beds, which are the largest and richest in the world; its dugong population; and its stromatolites.

"The sea fish that we saw here are chiefly sharks. There is an abundance of them in this particular sound, and I therefore give it the name of Shark's Bay."

English explorer William Dampier,
the first European to visit the bay,
in July 1699

Uluru-Kata Tjuta National Park (3)

This park, formerly called Uluru Uluru or Ayers Rock, features spectacular geological formations that dominate the vast red sandy plain of central Australia. Uluru, an immense monolith, and Kata Tjuta, the rock domes located west of Uluru, form part of the traditional belief system of one of the oldest human societies in the world. The traditional owners of Uluru-Kata Tjuta are the Anangu Aboriginal people.

"Uluru is both sacred site and physical wonder. A giant red rock rising from the floor of the vast inland Australian desert, glowing in the face of the sun."

Peter Garrett,
Australian politician and lead singer
of the band Midnight Oil

453

Lord Howe Island Group (4)

Isolated in the Pacific Ocean 600 km (375 miles) east of Australia, the site is a remarkable example of remote oceanic islands, born of volcanic activity more than 2,000 m (xxx feet) under the sea. These islands boast a spectacular topography and are home to numerous endemic species, especially birds.

"One of the safest places on earth for a bird to nest is Lord Howe Island, a remote, predator-free dot off Australia.

English environment and wildlife journalist Gareth Huw Davies

Central Eastern Rainforest Reserves (5)

This site, which includes several protected areas, is situated predominantly along the Great Escarpment on Australia's east coast. The outstanding geological features displayed around shield volcanic craters, as well as the high number of rare and threatened rainforest species, are of international significance for science and conservation.

Australian Fossil Mammal Sites - Riversleigh/Naracote (6)

Riversleigh and Naracoorte, situated in the north and south respectively of eastern Australia, are among the world's 10 greatest fossil sites. They are a superb illustration of the key stages of evolution of Australia's unique fauna.

"Only in one or two places on the surface of our planet, in the course of the last three thousand million years, have conditions been just right to preserve anything like a representative sample of the species living at any particular time ... Riversleigh is one of them."

Anthropologist and BBC presenter
Sir David Attenborough

Great Barrier Reef (7)

Located on the north-east coast of Australia, the Great Barrier Reef is a site of remarkable variety and beauty. It contains the world's largest collection of coral reefs, with 400 types of coral, 1,500 species of fish and 4,000 types of mollusc. It also holds great scientific interest as the habitat of species such as the dugong and the large green turtle, which are threatened with extinction.

"We were called up with the alarming news of the ship being fast ashore upon a rock, which she in a few moments convinced us of by beating very violently against the rocks."

Discovery of the Great Barrier – excerpt from English naturalist and botanist Joseph Banks' journal, when the ship Endeavour ran aground the Great Barrier on June 11, 1770

Fraser Island (8)

Lying just off the east coast of Australia, Fraser Island, at 122 km (76 miles) long, is the largest sand island in the world. Majestic remnants of tall rainforest growing on sand and half the world's perched freshwater dune lakes are found inland from the beach. The combination of shifting sand dunes, tropical rainforests, and lakes makes it an exceptional site. The freshwater lakes on Fraser Island are some of the cleanest in the world.

Greater Blue Mountains Area   (9)

Roughly 100 kilometres (62 miles) west of Sydney, the Greater Blue Mountains Area consists of 1.03 million ha (2.55 million acres) of sandstone plateaux, escarpments and gorges dominated by temperate eucalypt forest. The site, comprised of eight protected areas, is noted for its representation of the evolutionary adaptation and diversification of the eucalypts in post-Gondwana isolation on the Australian continent. Ninety-one eucalypt taxa occur within the Greater Blue Mountains. Koalas live almost entirely on eucalyptus leaves.

Royal Exhibition Building and Carlton Gardens   (10)

The Royal Exhibition Building and its surrounding Carlton Gardens were designed for the great international exhibitions of 1880 and 1888 in Melbourne. The building and grounds were designed by Joseph Reed. The building is constructed of brick and timber, steel and slate. It combines elements from the Byzantine, Romanes-que, Lombardic and Italian Renaissance styles. The property is typical of the international exhibition movement, which saw over 50 exhibitions staged between 1851 and 1915 in venues including Paris, New York, Vienna, Calcutta, Kingston (Jamaica) and Santiago (Chile).

Kakadu National Park   (11)

This unique archaeological and ethnological reserve, located in the Northern Territory, 171 km (106 miles) east of Darwin, has been inhabited continuously for more than 40,000 years. The cave paintings, rock carvings and archaeological sites record the skills and way of life of the region's inhabitants, from the hunter-gatherers of prehistoric times to the Aboriginal people still living there.

"Some Creation Ancestors put themselves on rock walls as paintings and became djang (dreaming places). Some of these paintings are andjamun (sacred and dangerous) and can be seen only by senior men or women; others can be seen by all people."

Warradjan Aboriginal Cultural Centre

Purnululu National Park   (12)

Purnululu National Park is located in the state of Western Australia. It contains the deeply dissected Bungle Bungle Range, composed of Devonian-age quartz sandstone eroded over a period of 20 million years into a series of beehive-shaped towers or cones, whose steeply sloping surfaces are distinctly marked by regular horizontal bands of dark-grey cyanobacterial crust.

"You can't see what's holding them together. I don't know how to describe it. It is like a place not from this earth."

Canyon expert Richard D. Fisher, about the Bungle Bungles of Purnululu

Willandra Lakes Region   (13)

The fossil remains of a series of lakes and sand formations that date from the Pleistocene can be found in south-western New South Wales, together with archaeological evidence of human occupation dating from 45-60,000 years ago. It is a unique landmark in the study of human evolution on the Australian continent.

Heard and McDonald Islands (14)

These two islands are approximately 1,700 km (1,056 miles) from the Antarctic continent and 4,100 km (2,548 miles) south-west of Perth. As the only volcanically active subantarctic islands, they "open a window into the earth", thus providing the opportunity to observe ongoing geomorphic processes and glacial dynamics. The distinctive conservation value of Heard and McDonald lies in the complete absence of alien plants and animals, as well as human impact.

"The Australian territory of Heard Island and McDonald Islands, 53° 05' S, 73° 30' E, is one of the world's wildest, most remote and breathtakingly beautiful places."

Australian Antarctic Division, Department of the Environment and Heritage

Wet Tropics of Queensland (15)

This area, which stretches along the north-east coast of Australia for some 450 km (280 miles), is made up largely of tropical rainforests. This biotope offers a particularly extensive and varied array of plants, as well as marsupials and singing birds, along with other rare and endangered animals and plant species.

Macquarie Island (16)

About halfway between Australia and Antarctica in the Southern Ocean, Macquarie Island is the exposed crest of the undersea Macquarie Ridge, raised to its present position where the Indo-Australian tectonic plate meets the Pacific plate. It is a site of major geoconservation significance, being the only place on the planet where rocks from the earth's mantle (6 km below the ocean floor) are being actively exposed above sea level.

Solomon Islands

East Rennell   (1)

East Rennell makes up the southern third of Rennell Island, the southernmost island in the Solomon Island group in the western Pacific. At 86 km long by 15 km wide (53 by 9 miles), Rennell is the largest raised coral atoll in the world. The site includes approximately 37,000 ha (91,428 acres) and a marine area extending 3 nautical miles to sea. A major feature of the island is Lake Tegano, which was the former lagoon on the atoll. This brackish lake, the largest in the insular Pacific, contains many rugged limestone islands and endemic species.

New Zealand

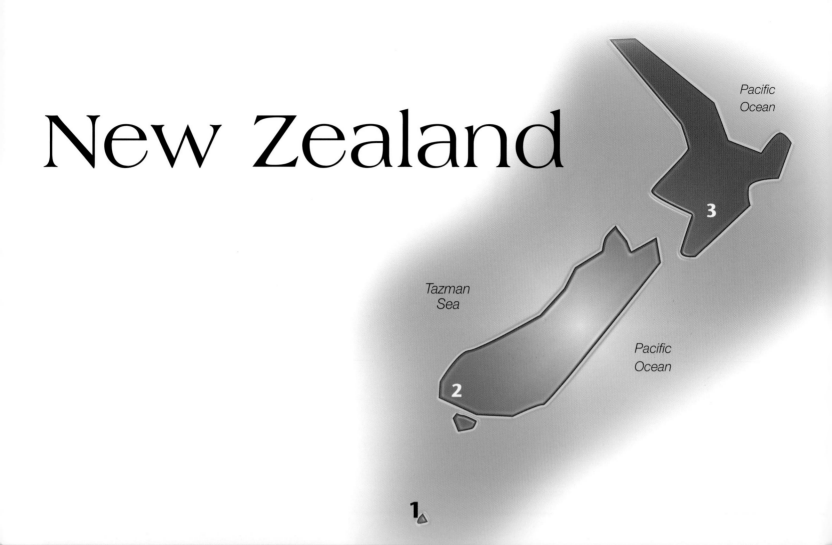

Pacific
Ocean

3

Tazman
Sea

Pacific
Ocean

2

1

New Zealand Sub-Antarctic Islands   (1)

This site consist of five island groups (the Snares, Bounty Islands, Antipodes Islands, Auckland Islands and Campbell Island) in the Southern Ocean, south-east of New Zealand. The islands, lying between the Antarctic and Subtropical Convergences and the seas, have a high level of productivity, biodiversity, wildlife population densities and endemism among birds, plants and invertebrates. A total of 126 bird species nest in the region, including 40 seabirds, of which five breed nowhere else in the world.

Te Wahipounamu
- Southwest New Zealand (2)

The landscape in Te Wahipounamu (the place of greenstone), situated in southwest New Zealand, has been shaped by successive glaciations into fjords, rocky coasts, towering cliffs, lakes and waterfalls. Two-thirds of the park is covered with southern beech and podocarps, some of which are over 800 years old. The kea, the only alpine parrot in the world, lives in the park, as does the rare and endangered takahe, a large flightless bird.

Tongariro National Park (3)

The mountains at the heart of the park have cultural and religious significance for the Maori people and symbolize the spiritual links between this community and its environment. Located in the central North Island of New Zealand, the park has active and extinct volcanoes, a diverse range of ecosystems and some spectacular landscapes. Tongariro volcano is also known as "Mount Doom" in the "Lord of the Rings" movie.

"It is a place of extremes and surprises,
a place to explore and remember.
From herb fields to forests, from tranquil lakes
to desert-like plateaus and active volcanoes,
Tongariro has them all."

Tongariro National Park

Photo Credits

Aachen Cathedral	Andreas Herrmann
Aapravasi Ghat	Aapravasi Ghat Trust Fund
Abu Mena	Irène Quilichini
Acre	Israel Government Tourist Office
Acropolis, Athens	Sandra vom Stein/istockphoto.com
Aflaj Irrigation Systems	Robert & Hootoksi Tyabji
Agave Landscape of Tequila	Carlos Sanchez Pereyra/ bigstockphoto.com
Aggtelek	Gulyas Laszlo/UNESCO
Agra Fort	Michael L. Kaufman
Agrigento	Robert Moser/bigstockphoto.com
Air and Ténéré	Tristan Clements
Ajanta Caves	Ryszard Laskowski/ dreamstime.com
Aksum	Niamh Burke/UNESCO
Al Qal'a of Beni Hammad	M. Bouchenaki/UNESCO
Alberobello	Alessandro Giacobazzi/ bigstockphoto.com
Alcalá de Henares	Daniel Diaz/sxc.hu
Alcobaça	Portuguese Trade and Tourism Office
Aldabra Atoll	Paul Cowan/istockphoto.com
Alejandro de Humboldt	George Hinopoulos
Aleppo	Simon Gurney/dreamstime.com
Altai	Igor Harlamov/dreamstime.com
Altamira Cave	Museum of Altamira
Alto Douro	Charles Humpries/istockphoto.com
Ambohimanga	www.barbara-and-stu.com
Amiens Cathedral	Bernard Maison, Ville d'Amiens
Angra do Heroismo	Portuguese Trade and Tourism Office
Anjar	Joerg Muehlbacher
Antigua Guatemala	Simon Gurney/bigstockphoto.com
Antoni Gaudí	Rafael Laguillo/bigstockphoto.com
Anuradhapura	David White/bigstockphoto.com
Aquileia	Pedro Prats
Arabian Oryx Sanctuary	Office of the adviser for Cultural Affairs
Aranjuez	Ramón Durán
Arequipa	Promperu
Arles	Eva Madrazo/dreamstime.com
Asante Traditional Buildings	Christina Koukkos
Ashur	Giovanni Boccardi/UNESCO
Askia	Stéphane Aubut
Assisi	Iain Frazer/bigstockphoto.com
Atapuerca	Locutus Borg
Atlantic Forest South-East Reserves	Octavio Campos/istockphoto.com
Auschwitz	State Museum of Auschwitz – Birkenau
Australian Fossil Mammal Sites	UNESCO
Avignon	Jean-Pierre Campomar, Ville d'Avignon
Ávila	Anthony Hathaway/ dreamstime.com
Ayutthaya	Tourism Authority of Thailand
Baalbek	Thomas Olsson/istockphoto.com
Bagerhat	Tito Dupret/ www.world-heritage-tour.org
Bagrati Cathedral and Gelati Monastery	UNESCO
Bahla Fort	Office of the adviser for Cultural Affairs
Baku	Rashad I. Gasimov
Bam	Mounir Bouchenaki/UNESCO
Bamberg	Dainis Derics/istockphoto.com
Bamiyan Valley	Tito Dupret/ www.world-heritage-tour.org
Ban Chiang	Tourism Authority of Thailand
Banc d'Arguin	Jolanda Koning
Bandiagara (Land of the Dogons)	Oumar Konaré/UNESCO
Banská stiavnica	Andreas van Greunen
Barcelona	Jorge Felix Costa/dreamstime.com
Bardejov	Jacopo Siracusa
Baroque Churches of the Philippines	Tito Dupret/ www.world-heritage-tour.org
Bassae	Sergio Bertino/dreamstime.com
Bat, Al-Khutm and Al-Ayn	Office of the adviser for Cultural Affairs
Batalha	Portuguese Trade and Tourism Office
Bath	British Tourist Authority
Bauhaus	City of Dessau/Kleber
Belfries	Courtesy of Belgian Tourist Office NYC/USA
Belize Barrier Reef	Dennis Sabo/istockphoto.com
Bellinzone	City of Bellinzone
Belovezhskaya Pushcha	Heinz Effner/bigstockphoto.com
Bend of the Boyne	Tourism Ireland
Berne	City of Berne
Biblical Tels	Evgene Gitlits/dreamstime.com
Birka and Hovgården	Swedish Heritage National Board
Bisotun	Mohammadreza Ghandforoush-Sattari
Blaenavon	Malcolm Romain/istockphoto.com
Blenheim Palace	British Tourist Authority
Bom Jesus do Congonhas	Eduardo Mota/sxc.hu
Borobudur	Dan Cooper/istockphoto.com
Bosra	Mira Pavlakovic/sxc.hu
Bourges Cathedral	Maison de la France Montreal
Boyana Church	Georgi Genchev/www.seebg.net
Brasilia	Brasil2/istockphoto.com
Bremen	Stadt Bremen
Bridge of Mostar	City of Mostar
Brimstone Hill Fortress	Brimstone Hill Fortress National Park Society
Brugge	Philippe Hemono
Brühl	Verwaltung Schloss Brühl
Bryggen	Bergen Tourist Board
Budapest	Franc Podgoraiek/ bigstockphoto.com
Bukhara	J. Sutter von d. Burg/UNESCO
Burgos Cathedral	George Krauss
Butrint	Ed Dicks
Bwindi	wikipedia
Byblos	Olga Kolos/dreamstime.com
Cáceres	Ivan Ribas/istockphoto.com
Cahokia Mounds	Cahokia Mounds State Historic Site
Calakmul	Rebecca Bria
Campeche	Carlos Sanchez/Visit Mexico Press
Canadian Rocky Mountains	Till Von Rennenhampff/ istockphoto.com
Canaima	Victor Ignatov/UNESCO
Canal du Midi	Luc Gillet/istockphoto.com
Canterbury Cathedral	British Tourist Authority
Cape Floral	South African Tourism
Cape Girolata, Cape Porto	Jean Schweitzer/istockphoto.com
Cappadocia	Geoff Hartman/sxc.hu
Carcassonne	Catherine Bibolet/Maison de la France Montreal
Carlsbad Caverns	Henry Lucenius/istockphoto.com
Cartagena	Alvaro Sanchez/istockphoto.com
Carthage	Alessandro Bolis/dreamstime.com
Caserta	Emiliano Maria Maniaci/ istockphoto.com
Castel del Monte	Els Slots/www.worldheritagesite.org
Centennial Hall in Wroclaw	Stephanie Mielcarek
Central Amazon	Izonemedia/istockphoto.com
Central Eastern Rainforest (Australia)	Australian Tourism Commission
Central Suriname Nature Reserve	Stevegeer/istockphoto.com
Cerrado Protected Areas	Amelia Abra/sxc.hu
Cesky Krumlov	Czech Tourist Authority
Chaco Culture	David Lloyd/dreamstime.com
Champaner-Pavagadh	Tito Dupret/ www.world-heritage-tour.org
Chan Chan	Promperu
Changdeokgung	Korea National Tourism Organization
Chartres Cathedral	Gautier Willaume/dreamstime.com
Chavin	Promperu
Chengde	Ministry of Culture, P.R.China
Chhatrapati Shivaji Terminus	Rad dcr/sxc.hu
Chichen-Itza	Kinetic Imagery/bigstockphoto.com
Chiloé	Consejo de Monumentos Nacionales de Chile
Choirokoitia	Cyprus Tourist Organization
Chongoni Rock Art	Dave Midgley/Project African Wilderness
Church Village of Gammelstad	Swedish Heritage National Board
Churches of Moldavia	Romanian National Tourist Office
Cienfuegos	Gianluca Biondi/istockphoto.com
Cilento and Vallo di Diano	Laura Frenkel/dreamstime.com
Ciudad Universitaria de Caracas	Paolo Gasparini, Fundación Villanueva Archive
Classical Gardens of Suzhou	Tomasz Resiak/istockphoto.com
Classical Weimar	Tourist-Information Weimar
Côa Valley	Rui Fernandes
Cocos Island	Avi Klapper
Coiba	Asociación Nacional para la Conservación de la Naturaleza
Cologne Cathedral	Stadt Koln
Colonia del Sacramento	Leaf O'Donnell/istockphoto.com
Comoé	Kwest19/dreamstime.com
Convent of Christ in Tomar	Portuguese Trade and Tourism Office
Convent of St Gall	Stadt St.Gallen
Copan	Julio Antillon/www.hondurastravel mall.com
Cordoba	Alexandre Fagundes/ dreamstime.com
Córdoba	Mercedes Soledad Manrique/ dreamstime.com
Cornwall and West Devon	saint4757/istockphoto.com
Coro	Instituto del Patrimonio Cultural de Venezuela
Costiera Amalfitana	Marco van Belleghem/ bigstockphoto.com
Crac des Chevaliers	Iorganda Florin/dreamstime.com
Cracow	Polish National Tourist Office
Crespi d'Adda	Marco Pedroncelli/ www.villagiocrespi.it
Cuenca	Ryan Fox/dreamstime.com
Cueva de las Manos	Jose Fuente/dreamstime.com
Curonian Spit	Greenpeace Russia
Cuzco	Promperu/ Jorge Sarmiento & Carlos Sala
Cyrene	Thierry Jolly/UNESCO
Dacian Fortresses	Romanian National Tourist Office
Damascus	Simon Gurney/istockphoto.com
Dambulla	Suzanne Bickerdike/ dreamstime.com
Danube Delta	Romanian National Tourist Office
Daphni, Hossios Luckas and Nea Moni	Dean Christakos/ www.christakos.com
Darien	Ryszard Laskowski/ dreamstime.com
Dazu Rock Carvings	Ministry of Culture, P.R.China
Decani Monastery	Serbian Orthodox Church
Defence Line of Amsterdam	René G.A. Ros/ englis-amsterdam.orgh.stelling
Delos	David H. Lewis/istockphoto.com
Delphi	Motordigital/istockphoto.com
Derbent	Alex Gavriloff
Derwent Valley Mills	British Tourist Authority
Desembarco del Granma	Michael Runkel/ www.michaelrunkel.com
Dessau-Wörlitz	Bernd Helbig, Stadtardriv, Dessau
Diamantina	Marcelo Terraza/sxc.hu
Dinosaur Provincial Park	Karl Naundorf/dreamstime.com
Discovery Coast Atlantic Forest	UNESCO
Divrigi	Marie-Aude Serra
Dja	Martina Berg/dreamstime.com
Djémila	Fabian Charaffi/UNESCO
Djenné	Bytesttrolch/istockphoto.com
Djoudj	Stijm Lombaerts/ bigstockphoto.com
Doñana	Valterza/UNESCO
Dong Phayayen-Khao Yai	Naisa Élyse Bujold
Dorset and East Devon Coast	British Tourist Authority
Dougga/Thugga	Lise Tremblay/istockphoto.com
Dresden Elbe Valley	Tomasz Resiak/istockphoto.com
Droogmakerij de Beemster	RDMZ/UNESCO
Dubrovnik	Damir Fabijanic/Croatian National Tourist Office New York
Durham	British Tourist Authority
Durmitor	Vladimir P
East Rennell	Dennis Sabo/dreamstime.com
Edinburgh	Stephen Finn/dreamstime.com
Eisleben and Wittenberg	Peter Kuhn/Wittenberg-Information
El Jem	Tomasz Resiak/istockphoto.com
El Tajin	Guillermo Aldana/Visit Mexico Press
Elephanta Caves	Tito Dupret/ www.world-heritage-tour.org
Ellora Caves	Tito Dupret/ www.world-heritage-tour.org
Engelsberg Ironworks	Swedish Heritage National Board
Epidaurus	Roman Miller/dreamstime.com
Escurial, Madrid	Sergei Shimorin/dreamstime.com
Essaouira	dreamstime.com
Everglades	William Mahnken/ bigstockphoto.com
Évora	Portuguese Trade and Tourism Office
Falun	Swedish Heritage National Board
Fasil Ghebbi	LongShots/istockphoto.com
Fatehpur Sikri	Nitya Jacob/istockphoto.com
Fernando de Noronha	Luiz Baltar/sxc.hu
Ferrapontov Monastery	Grigory Gusev
Ferrara	Sandro Cuozzo/istockphoto.com
Fertö / Neusiedlersee	Neusiedler See Tourismus GmbH
Fez	Moroccan National Tourist Office
First Coffee Plantations of Cuba	Ali Woodcraft
Flemish Béguinages	Courtesy of Belgian Tourist Office NYC/USA
Florence	John Mckinlay/bigstockphoto.com
Fontainebleau	Patrick Bonneville
Fontenay	Carla Magnani-de Laat
Fortress of Suomenlinna	Marko Kivelä
Fraser Island	Australian Tourism Commission
Fuerte de Samaipata	Pieter de Raad/samaipata.info
Galápagos Islands	Rebecca Picard/istockphoto.com
Galle	Tito Dupret/ www.world-heritage-tour.org
Garajonay	Anthony Lacoudre/UNESCO
Garamba	Niels Van gijn/dreamstime.com
Gebel Barkal	Shaun Embury
Geghard and the Upper Azat Valley	Anna Chelnokova/istockphoto.com
Genoa	Rocco D. Minasi
Ghadamès	W. Tochtermann/UNESCO
Giant's Causeway	British Tourist Authority
Gjirokastra	Victoria/onanalphabet.com
Goa	Sunil Lal/sxc.hu
Gochang, Hwasun, Ganghwa Dolmen	Korea National Tourism Organization
Goiás	Jose Assenco/sxc.hu
Gough and Inaccessible Islands	Marie-Helene Burle
Granada	dreamstime.com
Grand Canyon	Jeff Logan/istockphoto.com
Graz	Christian Bauer, sxc.hu
Great Barrier Reef	KJA/istockphoto.com
Great Living Chola Temples	V.Harihara Subramanian
Great Smoky Mountains	Kateleigh/dreamstime.com
Great Zimbabwe	Hans Joachin Dohle/UNESCO
Greater Blue Mountains	Australian Tourism Commission
Greater St Lucia Wetland	South African Tourism
Gros Morne	Newfoundland and Labrador Department of Tourism
Guanacaste	Alvaro Pantoja/istockphoto.com
Guanajuato and Adjacent Mines	Pablo de Aguinaco/Visit Mexico Press
Guimarães	Portuguese Trade and Tourism Office
Gulf of California	Michael Wood/dreamstime.com
Gunung Mulu	Calvin Ng/istockphoto.com
Gwynedd	British Tourist Authority
Gyeongju Historic Areas	Korea National Tourism Organization
Ha Long Bay	Mark Tasker/bigstockphoto.com
Hadrian Wall	British Tourist Authority
Haeinsa Temple Janggyeong Panjeon	Korea National Tourism Organization
Haghpat and Sanahin	Nick Fraser
Hal Saflieni Hypogeum	Malta Tourism Authority
Hallstatt-Dachstein Salzkammergut	Stroie Mihai Razvan/ dreamstime.com

Prambanan Temple Compounds	Dan Cooper/istockphoto.com
Provins	Office du Tourisme de Provins
Puebla	Jose Luis Tamez/sxc.hu
Pueblo de Taos	National Park Service
Puerto-Princesa	Emman
Purnululu	Australian Tourism Commission
Pyramid Fields from Giza to Dahshur	Michael Hoefner/istockphoto.com
Pyrénées - Mont Perdu	Mike Morley/istockphoto.com
Pythagoreion and Heraion of Samos	John Sfondilias/istockphoto.com
Qal'at al-Bahrain	Kingdom of Bahrain, Ministry of Culture and National Heritage
Québec	Park Canada
Quebrada de Humahuaca	Michael Runkel/ www.michaelrunkel.com
Quedlinburg	Wolfgang Fisher, Quedlinburg-Tourismus-Marketing GmbH
Querétaro	Guillermo Aldana/Visit Mexico Press
Querétaro	BL Photo/istockphoto.com
Qufu	Ministry of Culture, P.R.China
Quirigua	Randy R. Johnson
Quito	Ryan Fox, bigstockphoto.com
Quseir Amra	S. Zeghidour/UNESCO
Qutb Minar and its Monuments, Delhi	J Tan/istockphoto.com
Rammelsberg and Goslar	Reinhard Roseneck Der Rammelsberg
Rapa Nui	Consejo de Monumentos Nacionales de Chile
Ravenna	Alessandro Contadini/ istockphoto.com
Redwood National Park	Yovonne Autrey-Schell/ istockphoto.com
Regensburg	Sitha Suppalertpisit/ dreamstime.com
Reims	Molly Tomlinson
Rhine Valley	Koblenz-Touristik
Rhodes	Aaron Brand/dreamstime.com
Rice Terraces of the Philippine	Andrew Caballero-Reynolds/ istockphoto.com
Rietveld Schröderhuis	Central Museum/Jannes Linders
Riga	Marc Johnson/dreamstime.com
Rila Monastery	José Warletta/sxc.hu
Rio Abiseo	Promperu
Río Plátano	Sandra Dunlap/istockphoto.com
Robben Island	South African Tourism
Rock Art of the Mediterranean Basin	Daniel Cohen
Rock Carvings in Tanum	Swedish Heritage National Board
Rock Drawings of Alta	Alta Museum
Rock Paintings Sierra de San Francisco	Guillermo Aldana/Visit Mexico Press
Rock Shelters of Bhimbetka	Marc Shandro
Rock-Art Sites of Tadrart Acacus	Miles Hunter
Rock-Hewn Churches of Ivanovo	Paloma Llieva/UNESCO
Rock-Hewn Churches, Lalibela	Klass Lingbeek van Kranen/ istockphoto.com
Rohtas Fort	Tito Dupret/ www.world-heritage-tour.org
Rome	Bryce Newell/bigstockphoto.com
Røros	Ståle Edstrom/dreamstime.com
Roskilde Cathedral	Jakob Mikkelsen/istockphoto.com
Routes of Santiago de Compostela	Guillaume Dubé/istockphotoc.om
Royal Botanic Gardens, Kew	British Tourist Authority
Royal Chitwan	Jez Gunnell/istockphoto.com
Royal Domain of Drottningholm	Swedish Heritage National Board
Royal Exhibition Building	Ben Ryan/istockphoto.com
Royal House of Savoy	Gina Parsons
Royal Palaces of Abomey	B. Mondichao/UNESCO
Royal Saltworks of Arc-et-Senans	Georges Fessy, Photothèque Institut C-N Ledoux
Rwenzori Mountains	Maarten Dankers
Ryukyu	Japan National Tourist Organization
Sabratha	Michel Claude/UNESCO
Sacri Monti	Mauro Del Romano
Safranbolu	Simon Gurney/scx.hu
Sagarmatha	Wang Sanjun/dreamstime.com
Saint Catherine Area	Vladimir Pomortsev/ istockphoto.com
Saint Petersburg	Dreamstime.com
Saint-Savin sur Gartempe	Dominique Roger/UNESCO
Salamanca	JL Gutierrez/istockphoto.com
Salonga	Mike Carlson/dreamstime.com
Saltaire	British Tourist Authority
Salvador de Bahia	Celso Pupo/istockphoto.com
Salzburg	City of Salzburg
Samarkand	Frank Hespe
Sammallahdenmäki	UNESCO
San Agustín Archeological Park	UNESCO
San Cristóbal de La Laguna	Jean-Paul Choisne
San Gimignano	Lesia Hickey/bigstockphoto.com
San Millán Yuso and Suso	UNESCO
Sana'a	Anne Thaysen/istockphoto.com
Sanchi	Nitya Jacob/istockphoto.com
Sangay	Jessie Walker/bigstockphoto.com
Sangiran Early Man	Armand Billard/Xavier Kroetz/ www.cousinsmigrateurs.com
Sans Souci, Ramiers	G. Hyvert/UNESCO
Santa Ana de los Ríos de Cuenca	Carlo Ricchiardi/istockphoto.com
Santa Cruz de Mompox	Alfonso Mogollon/sxc.hu
Santa María de Guadalupe	Rogier Boogaard
Santa Maria delle Grazie	Jess Dixon/sxc.hu
Santiago de Compostela	Alexandre Fagundes/ dreamstime.com
Santiago de Cuba	Bjorn Hotting/istockphoto.com
Santo Domingo	Al Fernandes/istockphoto.com
São Luís	Preston Grant/ www.prestongrant.com
Schokland	Anthony Lacoudre/UNESCO
Schönbrunn	David Monniaux
Segovia	elrphoto/istockphoto.com

Selous Game Reserve	Tanzania High Commission
Semmering Railway	Tourismusbüro Semmering
Senegambia	pastry9607
Seokguram Grotto	Korea National Tourism Organization
Serengeti	Tanzania High Commission
Sergiev Posad	Guitinov Ali/UNESCO
Serra da Capivara	Julien Barbière/UNESCO
Seville	Thomas Snaaijer/dreamstime.com
Sewell Mining Town	Mark Feldman
SGaang Gwaii	Gwaii Haanas National Park Reserve and Haida Heritage Site
Shakhrisyabz	Tito Dupret/ www.world-heritage-tour.org
Shark Bay	Michael Efford/istockphoto.com
Shibam	Toni Delgado
Shirakami-Sanchi	Japan National Tourist Organization
Shirakawa-go	Hikari Mimura
Shiretoko	Yukiko Yamamoto/Veroyama
Sian Ka'an	Carlos Sanchez/Visit Mexico Press
Sibenik	Damir Fabijanic/Croatian National Tourist Office New York
Sichuan	Mike Hollman/dreamstime.com
Siena	Dreamstime.com
Sighisoara	Romanian National Tourist Office
Sigiriya	Emma Holmwood/istockphoto.com
Sikhote-Alin	Cindy Haggerty/bigstockphoto.com
Simien	Steffen Foerster/istockphoto.com
Sinharaja	Tito Dupret/ www.world-heritage-tour.org
Sintra	Portuguese Trade and Tourism Office
Skellig Michael	Tourism Ireland
Skocjan Caves	Skocjan Caves Regional Park
Skogskyrkogården	Swedish Heritage National Board
Solovetsky Islands	Vladimir Georgievsky/ dreamstime.com
Soltaniyeh	Tito Dupret/ www.world-heritage-tour.org
Sousse	Nikolajs Strigins/dreamstime.com
Southern Anhui	Zhang Xiao Qiu/istockphoto.com
Southern Öland	Swedish Heritage National Board
Speyer Cathedral	Stadt Speyer
Spissky Hrad	UNESCO
Split	Damir Fabijanic/Croatian National Tourist Office New York
Srebarna	André Karwath
St George, Bermuda	Dennis Morris/istockphoto.com
St Kilda	Alan Crawford/istockphoto.com
Stari Ras and Sopocani	Sasa Z. Cvetkovic/UNESCO
Statue of Liberty	National Park Service
Sterkfontein	South African Tourism
Stonehenge	British Tourist Authority
Stralsund and Wismar	Tourismus Zentrale Stralsund
Strasbourg	Thomas Hirsch
Struve Geodetic Arc	wikipedia
Studenica Monastery	Serbian Orthodox Church
Studley Royal Park	The National Trust
Su Nuraxi di Barumini	Andrea Pastore/dreamstime.com
Sucre	Seimens
Sukhotai	Tourism Authority of Thailand
Sukur	Nicholas David
Sumatra	Moodville/istockphoto.com
Summer Palace, Beijing	Ministry of Culture, P.R.China
Sundarbans	Daniel Gustavsson/ bigstockphoto.com
Svaneti	UNESCO
Sveshtari	Rick Beck
Syracuse	Els Slots/www.worldheritagesite.org
Taï National Park	Mairead Neal/dreamstime.com
Taj Mahal	Dario Diament/dreamstime.com
Takht-e Soleyman	Tito Dupret/ www.world-heritage-tour.org
Takht-i-Bahi	Tito Dupret/ www.world-heritage-tour.org
Talamanca Range-La Amistad	Steffen Foerster/istockphoto.com
Tallinn	Ivars Zolnerovics/ bigstockphoto.com
Tamgaly	Davis-Kimball/Center for the Study of Eurasian Nomads
Tarquinia	Ed Cormany
Tárraco	Luke Robinson
Tasmanian Wilderness	Australian Tourism Commission
Tassili n'Ajjer	Bousquet/UNESCO
Taxila	Tito Dupret/ www.world-heritage-tour.org
Tchogha Zanbil	Tito Dupret/ www.world-heritage-tour.org
Te Wahipounamu	Eldad Yitzhak/bigstockphoto.com
Tel-Aviv	Israel Government Tourist Office
Telc	Czech Tourist Authority
Temple of Heaven, Beijing	Kwok Chan/istockphoto.com
Teotihuacan	Celso Diniz/istockphoto.com
Tétouan	Peter Thornton
Thatta	Tito Dupret/ www.world-heritage-tour.org
The Great Wall	Ministry of Culture, P.R.China
Thebes	bigstockphoto.com
Thingvellir	Timothy Ball/istockphoto.com
Three Parallel Rivers of Yunnan	Tomasz Resiak/istockphoto.com
Thungyai-Huai Kha Khaeng	Jack Schiffer/dreamstime.com
Tierradentro	J.C. Segura/UNESCO
Tikal	George Bailey/istockphoto.com
Timbuktu	Bytesttrolch/istockphoto.com
Timgad	Majid Hatna
Tipasa	Fabian Charaffi/UNESCO
Tiwanaku	Mark Van Overmeire
Tiya	D. Michols/UNESCO
Tlacotalpan	Guillermo Aldana/Visit Mexico Press
Tokaj	Adam Molnar
Toledo	Jorge Felix/bigstockphoto.com
Tongariro	Amra Pacis/bigstockphoto.com
Torun	Daniel Zollinge IV
Tower of Belém	Fernando Dinis/bigstockphoto.com
Tower of London	British Tourist Authority
Transylvania	Romanian National Tourist Office

Trebíc	Czech Tourist Authority
Trier	Presseant Trier
Trinidad	Arjan Schreven/istockphoto.com
Trogir	Milan Babic/Croatian National Tourist Office New York
Troodos	Cyprus Tourist Organization
Troy	Luke Daniek/istockphoto.com
Tsingy de Bemaraha	Rhett Butler/ www.wildmadagascar.org
Tsodilo	Nxamaseri Island Lodge
Tubbataha Reef	Daniel Gustavsson/dreamstime.com
Tugendhat Villa in Brno	Czech Tourist Authority
Tunis	Tomasz Resiak/istockphoto.com
Tyre	Javarman/dreamstime.com
Úbeda and Baeza	Paco Gómez
Ujung Kulon	Tito Dupret/ www.world-heritage-tour.org
uKhahlamba / Drakensberg	Kate Els/dreamstime.com
Uluru-Kata Tjuta	Timothy Ball/istockphoto.com
Um er-Rasas	Rick Beck
Urbino	Stephano Raffini/istockphoto.com
Urnes Stave Church	Gian/sxc.hu
Uvs Nuur Basin	Steffen Foerster/istockphotos
Uxmal	Matej Michelizza/istockphoto.com
Val di Noto	Sandy di Noto/bigstockphoto.com
Val d'Orcia	Moreno Bettini/bigstockphoto.com
Valcamonica	Gyrus 2006/dreamflesh.com
Vall de Boí	Ismael Montero/dreamstime.com
Vallée de Mai	Sebastian Ruchti/istockphoto.com
Valletta	Malta Tourism Authority
Valparaíso	Consejo de Monumentos Nacionales de Chile
Varberg Radio Station	Swedish Heritage National Board
Vat Phou	Tito Dupret/ www.world-heritage-tour.org
Vatican City	Marc C. Johnson/istockphoto.com
Vegaøyan	Bjarne Kvaale/istockphoto.com
Venice	John Rattle/bigstockphoto.com
Vergina	Peter Nelson
Verla	UNESCO
Verona	Ryan Fox/bigstockphoto.com
Versailles	Kenneth C. Zirkel/istockphoto.com
Vézelay	Yves Grau/istockphoto.com
Vézère Valley	CMN – Les Eyzies
Vicenza	Vincent Mosch/istockphoto.com
Victor Horta (Brussels)	Courtesy of Belgian Tourist Office NYC/USA
Vienna	Martin Hennig/dreamstime.com
Vigan	Tito Dupret/ www.world-heritage-tour.org
Villa Adriana (Tivoli)	Luigi Pulcini/dreamstime.com
Villa d'Este, Tivoli	Thomas Anthony/Schuman Junior Houston
Villa Romana del Casale	Els Slots/www.worldheritagesite.org
Vilnius	Vilnius City
Viñales Valley	Andreas Ligtvoet/sxc.hu
Virgin Komi Forests	Sergey Anatolievich Pristyazhnyuk/ dreamstime.com
Virunga	Yves Grau/istockphoto.com
Visby	Swedish Heritage National Board
Vizcaya Bridge	Xosé Castro
Vladimir and Suzdal (1992)	UNESCO
Vlkolínec	UNESCO
Völklingen Ironworks	Völklinger Hütte
Volta, Greater Accra	Peeter Viisimaa/istockphoto.com
Volubilis	Mira Pavlakovic/sxc.hu
Vredefort Dome	Mike Gaylard
W National Park	Stefan Ekernas/dreamstime.com
Wachau	Walter Hochauer
Wadi Al-Hitan (Whale Valley)	Benjamin Romberg
Warsaw	Zbigniew Panow/Warsaw Tourist Office
Wartburg Castle	Wartburg-Stiftung Eisenach
Waterton	Mike Norton/dreamstime.com
West Norwegian Fjords	Ashok Rodrigues/istockphoto.com
Western Caucasus	Oleg Kozlov/dreamstime.com
Westminster Palace	British Tourist Authority
Wet Tropics of Queensland	Australian Tourism Commission
Whale Sanctuary of El Vizcaino	Holger Wulschaeger/ istockphoto.com
Wieliczka Salt Mine	Cracow Saltworks Museum
Wies	Tourismus Verland Pfaffenwinkel
Willandra	Iris Millikan/istockhpoto.com
Willemstad	Juana Van burg/dreamstime.com
Wood Buffalo	Daniel Hyans/istockphoto.com
Wrangel Island	Anthony Hathaway/ dreamstime.com
Wudang Mountains	Ministry of Culture, P.R.China
Wulingyuan	Ministry of Culture, P.R.China
Würzburg	Congress Tourismus Würzburg
Xanthos-Letoon	Simon Gurney/sxc.hu
Xochicalco	Dennis Poulette
Yakushima	Japan National Tourist Organization
Yaroslavl	Wisky Studio/istockphoto.com
Yellowstone	National Park Service
Yin Xu	Judy Zhu
Yosemite	Eli Mordechai/istockphoto.com
Yungang Grottoes	Ministry of Culture, P.R.China
Zabid	P. Bonnenfant/UNESCO
Zacatecas	Carlos Sanchez/Visit Mexico Press
Zamosc	Polish National Tourist Office
Zanzibar	Lance Bellers/dreamstime.com
Zelená Hora	Czech Tourist Authority
Zollverein	Entwicklungsgesellschaft «Zollverein»
Zvartnots	Hayk